BLOOD SEASON

BLOOD SEASON

PHIL BERGER

Macdonald
Queen Anne Press

The author wishes to thank *The New York Times* and *Playboy* magazine for permission to excerpt from articles of his that originally appeared in those publications.
Copyright © 1985, 1986, 1987, 1988 by The New York Times Company. Reprinted by permission.
Lyrics from 'Don't Believe the Hype' are reprinted by permission. Copyright © 1988 by Def Jam Music, Inc.

A QUEEN ANNE PRESS BOOK

© 1989 by Phil Berger

First published in the United States of America in 1989 by William Morrow and Company, Inc.
First published in Great Britain in 1990 by
Queen Anne Press, a division of
Macdonald & Co (Publishers) Ltd
Orbit House
1 New Fetter Lane
London EC4A 1AR

A member of Maxwell Macmillan Pergamon Publishing Corporation

Jacket photograph: All-Sport

Jacket design: Deborah Holmes

British Library Cataloguing in Publication data
Berger, Phil
  Blood season: Tyson and the world of boxing.
  1. Boxing, Tyson, Mike, 1966
  I. Title
  796.83092

ISBN 0-356 19051 X

Printed and bound in Great Britain by Butler & Tanner Limited, Frome

To my father, Jack Berger

Acknowledgments

On November 15, 1985, Mike Tyson was living in Catskill, New York. That was when I visited him for the first time. In the years since, I interviewed Tyson in limousines, restaurants, TV studios, his East 40th Street apartment in New York, casinos, at press conferences and at the office of his managers, and over long-distance telephone wires. While talking to the press has never been Tyson's idea of R&R, he was almost always professional and, when in the mood, could be quite revealing.

This book was also aided by the cooperation of those closely involved with the business of boxing: Tyson's managers, Bill Cayton and the late Jim Jacobs; his trainer, Kevin Rooney; his cut man, Matt Baranski; his aide-de-camp, Steve Lott; his "adopted" mother, Camille Ewald; his ex-wife, Robin Givens; his ex–mother-in-law, Ruth Roper (and her associate Olga Rosario); his friends Rory Holloway and Jay Bright; promoters Don King (and his director of boxing, Al Braverman), Butch Lewis (and his spokesman, Rock Newman), Dan Duva, Bob Arum, Cedric Kushner, Lucien Chen, Sam Glass, Loren Cassina, Stan Hoffman, and Jeff Levine; managers Dennis Rappaport, Mike Jones, Lou Duva, Shelly Finkel, Alan Kornberg, Carl King,

Robert Tucker, Dave Wolf, Mickey Duff, and Smokin' Joe Frazier; trainers Eddie Futch, Richie Giachetti, George Benton, Angelo Dundee, Teddy Atlas, and Victor Valle; attorneys Milt Chwasky, Marc Risman, Dennis Richard, Cary Medill, Neil Gerst, Don Kerr, Jim Binns, Richard Emery, Greg Reed, Irving Gruber, David Wood, Mike Perlman, Raoul Felder, Michael Winston, Thomas Puccio, Howard Weitzman, and Peter Parcher; and casino executives Donald Trump, Bob Halloran, Mark Etess, Gary Selesner, Rich Rose, and John Giovenco.

Thanks to colleagues in the boxing press, with special gratitude to Wally Matthews of *Newsday*, Colin Hart of the *Sun*, Mike Katz of the New York *Daily News*, and Bert Sugar of *Boxing Illustrated*, who went out of their way to help; to publicists Irving Rudd, Murray Goodman, Sy Roseman, the late Mike Cohen, Tony Fox, Bryan Harris, John Totaro, Kathy Duva, Patti Dreifuss, Karen Hirschberg Tuso, Dan Klores, Doug Kelly, Debbie Munch, Pam Sinderbrand, and Jim Hunter; to boxing officials José Torres, Marvin Kohn, José Sulaiman, Steve Crosson, Bob Lee, Chuck Minker, Duane Ford, and Flip Homansky; and TV's Seth Abraham, Ross Greenburg, Bob Greenway, Larry Merchant, Jay Larkin, Mort Sharnik, Kevin Monaghan, Bob Yalen, and Alex Wallau.

Recognition for help, advice, and kind attention is extended to Joe Vecchione, sports editor of the *New York Times;* to the editors of this book, Stacy Schiff and Liza Dawson; to my agent, Henry Dunow; and especially to my wife, Leslie, and our brand-new daughter, Julia.

Finally, a heartfelt acknowledgment to a special breed, the fighters: besides Tyson, Muhammad Ali, Leon and Michael Spinks, Gerry Cooney, Mitch Green, Marvis Frazier, Quick Tillis, Trevor Berbick, Bonecrusher Smith, Tim Witherspoon, Tony Tubbs, Larry Holmes, Pinklon Thomas, Tony Tucker, and Tyrell Biggs, all of whom gave time, beyond the call of duty, to a nosy inquisitor.

Introduction

The idea was to prowl the boxing scene for whatever time span seemed to constitute a "season" and then come back and write it, showing as best as one could a world often as beguiling as it is repellent, never more so than when some of its contradictions—violence as art, innocent dreams poised against sleazoid schemes—are stood up to light.

But in late 1985, when that boxing odyssey began, it was hard to say just how any such opus would take shape. For there was no pulsing story line to the sport; at that moment the fight game was in a quiet phase.

Then it changed—by God, did it change. For along came broad-beamed Tyson—Mike Tyson, a two-bit prepubescent hood who took up his reformation in the ring, and found glory, a few dollars, and that dizzying celebrity that offers up millionaire's mansions right along with *National Enquirer* headlines.

Tyson became the lightning rod along which all the grand themes—ambition, love, greed, sex, and money—would be played out over a season that by now has become an era. This is the story of that Tyson era and those fighters, writers, sharpies, and showmen who constitute the best and worst of boxing.

While the book tracks the ups and downs of some others in the heavyweight division (Michael Spinks, Gerry Cooney, Larry Holmes) and many of the backstage players, the dominant figure is Tyson.

Blood Season follows Tyson's passage from prelim fighter through the tumults of an ascent that led to a ninety-one-second fight against Spinks that earned him $20 million and turned out to be a prelude to real-life antics that make St. Vitus' dance look like the minuet.

But enough. As Mills Lane, a Nevada prosecutor who is one of boxing's top referees, tells fighters just before sending them out to do battle: "Let's get it on."

1

In 1978 the heavyweight champion of the world was thought to be a dufus.

His name was Leon Spinks, Jr., and on a February night in Las Vegas, he beat up Muhammad Ali and won boxing's most prestigious title.

As it would turn out, Spinks won more than he bargained for. In the brief time he held the title—Ali licked him seven months later in the rematch—Spinks never quite did get the hang of his newly attained celebrity.

Practically from the moment his hand was raised in victory, Spinks was hip-deep in problems. Sued by a motel for unpaid bills. Sued by his landlord in Philadelphia for back rent. Arrested—and then photographed in handcuffs—for driving the wrong way down a one-way street without a license.

A look-alike of the new champion even turned up in Philadelphia. In Leon's word, the dead ringer was "imposturing" him—signing autographs in public and encouraging local merchants to shower him with complimentary goods. For a couple of weeks, the man sampled the high times, then he prudently faded away.

The look-alike may have known something. For by then, the pleasure of being Leon Spinks, Jr., was paling.

The media's response to Leon was somewhat cautious. In the new champion, it appeared they had a hero-naïf, a character who, at his best, might end up being the sort of unlettered but quotable source that Yogi Berra had been.

But with his first missteps, the view shifted, and a collective hunch arose that in time parody might be the proper key to strike with Spinks. Spinks made an easy enough target. With his gap-toothed warrior's mug and raspy-throated diction that practically required subtitles, he was the brother from another planet.

There was no rush to judgment, though. The fact that Spinks was a black man out of St. Louis's worst ghetto briefly won him a reprieve from ridicule, most newsmen being wary of charges of racial insensitivity. But as one incident followed the next after he had won the title, Spinks became fair game.

Among the hired hands on Spinks patrol at the time was a free-lance writer. Most of the prose that he cranked on his favored 1920s typewriters—he loved the clacking of those ancient keys—had been on sports, though little prior to Spinks had concerned boxing. That was not out of the kind of reflex distaste that many civilians have for boxing, with its perceived barbarity, but was the result of the chance commerce that rules modern lives.

In truth, the free-lance man was a born fan of boxing. Friday nights in the early 1950s with his old man he would catch whatever fight the NBC network beamed from the old Madison Square Garden, on Eighth Avenue between 49th and 50th streets, his heart quickening at the first words of the sponsor's snappy jingle: *Look sharp. /Feel Sharp. /Be sharp. /Use Gillette Blue Blades . . . with the sharpest edges ever honed.*

At the same time, his interest was encouraged by the success of a crowd-pleasing welterweight named Chico Vejar, whom TV executives decided had sales potential. Long before the television industry had its Q index, its executives knew how to recognize and nurture a talent with populist appeal. That was how Vejar became a regular on the snowy Philco screen, one of the first boxers the networks consciously cultivated. It was not long before Vejar was showing up on the home screen as regularly as Señor Wences.

In 1951, when his boxing career was getting legs, Vejar was a freshman at NYU, studying business administration and theater arts. That didn't hurt him any in a business which then as now was partial to a novel story line—in this case that of a kid who was, so to speak, fighting his way through college.

Vejar had more going for him than his baccalaureate program. He was a fine-looking young man, with neatly barbered jet-black hair, an olive complexion, and a face that a café singer could have lived in. And Chico was clean-cut and earnest in the way sports heroes back then were.

Not only that: he was well-spoken. In Vejar, a network had a boxer it could separate out from the rough trade. If the idea was to create a warm feeling among viewers for the sponsor's razor blades, then Chico—nice as a Norman Rockwell cover—was more likely to do it than any bent-nosed dese-and-dem type.

Of course, in the 1950s when our free-lance man was a boy, those connections went unmade. But because Vejar was from his hometown, Stamford, Connecticut, the boy was attentive to the elements at play in bringing the fighter into the arena. Years later, he would begin to connect the dots, but in those early days of TV he was indiscriminately loading up his impressionable mind with raw data.

On occasion Vejar conducted his workouts in Stamford facilities that were open to the public. It got the boy up close to fighters who sweated, who bled, who—unthinkable—spat as casually as other men blinked, prompting their small-fry admirers, once out on the street, to mimic what they had seen.

The sounds of boxing were unique when heard in person. There was the mechanical report of the speed bag rattling against its wooden overhang as the fighter turned hand over hand to create that snappy percussion; the hollow thud of the heavy bag being assaulted by one man's pile-driving blows; the scuff of high-top shoes against canvas as a shadow-boxing fighter pivoted on the balls of his feet, a move as natural as steel rolling along ball bearings.

As striking as these training procedures were for the poker-faced efficiency with which the fighters executed them, the real show was the sparring. When the fighters tore at each other, the boy marveled at their capacity for enduring the indignity of being rapped in the face. But he recognized that there was more involved than dumb-animal irreverence toward being struck a blow.

He realized, if only in a kid's limited way, that the feints and footwork of the fighter—part of what sportswriters referred to as "ring generalship"—counted too. But more than that he hadn't a clue. Those who did fathom what went on in the ring were the adult males—trainers and managers—who stood against the ring ropes with a fiercely proprietary air and stared hard at their charges, nodding almost imperceptibly at some fine-line technical moment from time to time, the meaning of which usually eluded the boy. He saw only the bop-bop of punches landed and little else, but was crazy to know what?—what?—what? had those perspicacious old bastards seen.

In the years that followed, he made a passing effort to find out. He kept up with boxing, and later, very occasionally, he wrote about the sport.

"Occasionally" because he was nudged in another direction by the small waves he made with a book that recounted one season of a pro basketball team, a championship season as it turned out. The team was the 1969–70 New York Knickerbockers, the Knickerbockers of Reed, Frazier, DeBusschere, Bradley, and Barnett. The book entertained a bit of notoriety. It's author, nicknamed Sly by the players for his tippytoe ubiquity, was barred from the team's dressing room the following season, presumably for lapses in reportorial discretion. Whatever. One man's sharp-eyed observer is another's blabbering scumsucker.

Several years (and a book or two) later Sly began to write about boxing—the occasional profile that was the result of a long day's visit to the fighter's camp. The articles were professionally correct—that proper balance of quotes, scene, and character; in the end they offered up a reasonable likeness of the subject, whoever he happened to be. But Sly was never really pleased with the result, recognizing that boxing was too complex to be absorbed in a single day's outing. The hitch was time, the time to inhabit a special world and become an accepted addition, gaining trust and momentum that, with any luck, got a man closer to how things really were.

Sly's chance to explore the fighter's world at a more leisurely pace came in November 1977 with Leon Spinks. The

year before, Spinks had won a gold medal at the Olympics.
Now he was training for a fight against his first ranked opponent, Alfio Righetti of Italy. At the time, Spinks was undefeated—a record of five wins, all knockouts, and a draw against
Scott LeDoux. Sly flew to Las Vegas to watch Spinks train.

If Spinks beat Righetti he would fight Ali for the title—a
rather accelerated opportunity after only eleven months as a
pro. Typically, it took a fighter several years to acquire the expertise and experience expected of a title contender. But then,
nothing much about the career of Leon Spinks, Jr., would turn
out to be typical.

Remember the childhood game in which a message is whispered through a Dixie cup to the next in a line of listeners until
by final utterance the words are mangled beyond recognition?
Well, that spirit of misinformation and confusion was in the
air the day that Sly parked himself ringside at a Leon Spinks
workout.

The first visible sign of a troubled camp was the way in
which the advice of Sam Solomon, Spinks's trainer, was treated.
Solomon was sixty-two years old, a short, rotund man who had
boxed in tent shows and had been a catcher in Negro baseball.
As Spinks's trainer, he was supposed to give advice to his man
between rounds of sparring. This he did, but the message did
not go directly to the fighter, as is the custom. Instead, Solomon
would advance his thoughts to Spinks's younger brother, Michael, a '76 Olympic gold medalist too, who would then whisper
into Leon's ear.

It got even more curious. On a folding chair not far from the
ring, a compactly built coffee-brown man in a short-brimmed cap
watched with an implacable expression. He was George Benton, a
former middleweight contender. Benton now trained fighters for
past-heavyweight champion Smokin' Joe Frazier, who owned a
gym in North Philadelphia.

As a fighter, Benton had been a clever operative, with a
knack for avoiding punches. A classic stylist. In routine circumstances, it would have gone without notice for a man like him to
fine-tune Spinks, as Benton did that afternoon. Heavyweight
title shot or not, Spinks was a newcomer to the pro game.

That day Benton would show Spinks how to handle an opponent trying to flee from him. The term was "cutting the ring"
in boxing parlance, and it referred to the angles of pursuit a

fighter used to block an opponent's escape route. A tutorial like the ten or fifteen minutes Benton took with him was not only helpful but necessary.

In this instance, though, there was a complication. Sam Solomon clearly resented Benton's horning in. Not that Solomon said so. His was the eloquence of a body's abruptly rearranged angles and torque—that complex circuitry that turns a frumpy little man into a stiff-necked sentry.

Within an hour, Sly could feel the emanations. Between a fighter who took his advice in relays and a pair of rival trainers who dispensed it, L. Spinks's was plainly a training camp experiencing technical difficulties.

For a fighter who only needed to get past Righetti to have a title shot at the great Ali, that seemed inexcusable. Sly had had the ingenuous notion that at this exalted level of the boxing business it would be smooth going.

Happily, he was wrong. For what would make Spinks's story of such keen interest to Sly was the chaotic and often illogical world it revealed. Here was a world occupied by citizens who were cut to dimensions grander than their fellow travelers. The extent of formal education varied, but the best of them had the bluster of their conviction—and the raw energy to make *me-first* a career. More than anything, they reminded Sly of those rapacious yet charming rogues of Dickens—the ruling elite of lawyers and bosses who had the fervor of privilege and the nonstop hooey to justify it.

The protocol that shaped other institutions—politics, business, even sports—did not exist here. What rules there were in boxing, Sly would discover, were routinely bent or ignored, as suited the operatives who for the moment held the power.

In the case of Spinks, the hustle to control the fighter was as intricate as a Swiss watch and fascinating to see. Since Sly was new to boxing, he assumed that the backstage maneuvers with Spinks were as elaborate as a man would ever observe.

In fact, they were mickeymouse compared to the machinations he would track a decade later while a frontline witness to another heavyweight champion's chaos.

But that was later. In 1977, it was Leon Spinks's trick journey on which Sly embarked.

When a fighter steps into the ring, he may have aides who wipe his sweat, stem his cuts, and offer advice and encouragement, but the reality is that once the bell rings a boxer is as alone as any athlete can be.

Yet it is the nature of this complex freewheeling business that the lone warrior must rely on others—typically a manager, who plots his career, and a promoter, who stages the bouts—to get ahead.

Gold medal or not, like any other fighter Leon Spinks depended on the kindness of strangers. He could not have taken his first step toward a pro career, for instance, without a white man named Millard Barnes.

"Mitt" Barnes, like Spinks, was from St. Louis. He was a slow-walking, plain-talking man, a Teamster organizer who on the side ran a hotel with a basement gym that Spinks had wandered into years before. When Leon spoke of fighting in the Olympics someday and demonstrated the ability to get there, Barnes made sure he had the funds to reach his goal. Barnes paid travel expenses and gave Leon spending money. Spinks vowed that Mitt would be his manager if and when Leon Spinks turned professional.

A day after he won the gold medal at the 1976 Montreal Olympics, true to his word Spinks signed with Barnes for a three-year period, entitling his manager to a cut of 30 percent of his purses—just under the typical 33 1/3 percent that managers draw. With a contract in his pocket, Barnes began to negotiate Leon's future.

It led him to boxing promoter Bob Arum and his company, Top Rank, Inc. Arum once had been *the* promoter in the boxing business, by virtue of his position as Ali's promoter. That changed when a flamboyant ex-convict, Don King, persuaded Ali's manager, Herbert Muhammad, that a black man could do exactly what a Jew had already done: make money for Ali. King ended up promoting a series of Ali's fights in the early 1970s, effectively short-circuiting Arum's power.

By 1976, when Spinks and Barnes first approached Top Rank, Bob Arum was on the rise again, an ascent that even he had not expected. "Because," said Arum, "I said the hell with it, I ain't going to spend my life chasing Ali."

And he didn't. Ronald (Butch) Lewis did, taking Top Rank with him.

The collaboration of Arum and Lewis was a curious association.

Arum, out of the Crown Heights section of Brooklyn, had been a Talmudic student as a youth; he was a 1956 *cum laude* graduate of Harvard Law School, and had worked in the Kennedy Justice Department. He and Don King had dominated boxing promotions through the 1970s—the both of them secure as the Hertz and Avis of their business.

Arum was a back-room operative. He had no desire to be involved in the daily lives and problems of the sweathogs under contract to him. King tended to insinuate himself with his fighters—the better to control them, some said.

There were times, though, when a promoter like Arum needed a liaison to keep a capricious fighter from self-destructing, blowing Arum's stake in a boxing future. Lewis, it turned out, became Arum's go-between with Leon Spinks, displacing Mitt Barnes—sitting out there in the Missouri heartlands—as the active force in the fighter's career.

In 1977, Lewis was a thirty-year-old with a winning smile, a flair for clothes (at fights, he turned out in white suits and walking canes), and the sort of patter that made him, in Don King's term, an "interface," a black operative who was sharp enough to talk to white men and soulful enough to handle his own.

While Lewis's involvement with Spinks would cause him many headaches, it would educate him to his business, preparing him to play a major role a decade later in the most lucrative boxing promotion to that moment in boxing history. And that time the other Spinks, Michael, would be the fighter Butch Lewis would control.

But well before Lewis was calling the shots for Leon, or Michael, he first had to overcome a fight establishment not eager to let him belong.

The route that Lewis took into the boxing business would have strained a novelist's capacity for invention. Yet in its wild improbability Lewis shared with others doing business in boxing, the Arums and Kings, the same very random impetus to try. Neither Arum nor King, who had been a power in the Cleveland numbers racket until he was sentenced to four years in the Marion (Ohio) Correctional Institution for manslaughter, had planned to make their fortunes in the fight game. They more or less stumbled into boxing and, like Lewis, found their natures were suited to its hustle.

Lewis was accustomed to living by his wits. From a middle-class background—his father, John L., ran a thriving used-car business in Ridley Township, Pennsylvania—Butch was in spite of his advantages attracted to the bustle of the streets. Not long after he was graduated from high school, he set himself up on Market Street in Philadelphia with a cache of rings that he had the gumption to tell prospective customers were worth $400 to $500 apiece and were, he insisted, absolutely a steal at his $50 asking price.

If customers expressed skepticism, Lewis urged them to have the ring appraised at jewelry shops along Market Street. The nearest such establishment had a collaborator of Lewis's inside. The man would put the jeweler's eyeglass on and, after a painstaking examination, would proclaim the ring to be worth $1,500. With that encouragement, the customer would fairly fly to Lewis to drop $50 with him for a ring worth a buck and a quarter.

Lewis's father eventually put an end to his son's flimflam, dragooning him into his used-car business. Lewis worked his way up from a factotum to a salesman who, by age twenty-one, was earning $50,000 to $60,000 a year. It was on the used-car lot that he also made an important connection when he met a heavyweight contender from Philadelphia named Smokin' Joe Frazier.

"My father," said Lewis, "was one of the original Cloverlay stockholders, the syndicate that sponsored Joe's career at the beginning. And this helped to jell the relationship Joe and I had. We were both around the same age, and Joe liked the way I dressed and the way I talked. We got along great. Like brothers. Anytime Joe traveled, I'd be with him. I'd be in on the meetings with him and Ali and the promoters, I got to see how the wheels turned in the fight business. And the more I saw, the more I liked it.

"Now after having traveled with Joe—and I mean all around the world—people would always see me at fights, and a group from Germany took it for granted when we were in Zaire, Africa, for the Foreman-Ali fight that I was a promoter. This group wanted to bring an Ali fight to Germany, and when they mentioned the possibility to me, I played along, as if I *was* a promoter. After meeting me in Zaire, we met again in Malaysia when Ali fought Joe Bugner. And in between there was a correspondence between myself and the German group."

Departing from Malaysia, Lewis began a nearly year-long odyssey in which he quit the used-car business and spent his savings in his quest to promote an Ali title fight. He followed Ali and Herbert Muhammad around the country.

"Flying around like crazy—Chicago, Florida," said Lewis. "And Herbert Muhammad's telling me, 'What? Are you nuts? I mean, you never promoted a fight in your *life*.'"

In what seemed an impossible mission, Lewis found a friend in Ali himself, who had met Lewis through Frazier. Ali liked Lewis enough to slip him Herbert Muhammad's ever-changing home phone number.

"And every single morning," said Lewis, "Monday through Sunday, every day, every day, I don't care where I was, I called Herbert. I had telephone bills of like seventeen hundred, two thousand dollars a month. He would wake up to my voice and Herbert would say, 'If you ever call me again, I'll this and that. Don't ever call me again.' And every single morning I'd call him. He'd change his number, and I'd call him. He didn't know how I got his number. And Ali would say, 'You just keep calling him until maybe he'll weaken.'"

In the meantime, Lewis had contacted Arum, who agreed to provide the technical expertise that Lewis would need if he ever put together an Ali title match. Eventually Lewis made enough progress to be invited to Chicago, where Herbert Muhammad had his offices. The deal that Lewis thought he was on the verge of closing abruptly collapsed when King flew to Chicago and dissuaded Herbert from committing to the newcomer.

With no encouragement from family and friends, who viewed his objective as a fool's errand (Frazier told him, "Forget it—you know they ain't gonna give it to you"), Lewis persisted. After eleven months of persevering he finally made the Ali–Richard Dunn match of May 1976 in Munich, and as his reward, Arum made him a vice-president at Top Rank.

Lewis's tenacity would serve him well when Spinks signed a contract with Top Rank in 1976.

In the ring Spinks competed with such maniacal energy that an outsider could be forgiven if he assumed the man was dedicated to his work. In fact, Spinks felt put upon by the slavish commitment to training required of fighters, and was happily diverted from it by a social life he waged with pretty near the same intensity he did his bouts. Problems occurred when a scheduled fight got in the way of a good time.

Sly, being the first journalist to spend serious time on Spinks patrol, was put wise to this tendency of Spinks's early on and was privy to the low-grade seismic rattlings that followed whenever Spinks bolted camp. Which he did routinely. Leon had a name for his AWOL habit: he called it "swooping." By any name it made him a problem for Arum, who held promotional paper on him.

Arum, however, was not inclined to become entangled in the sticky convolutions of his fighters' lives. He was a dealmaker. If he remained the party of the first part and they the party of the second part, that was perfectly all right. No problem at all. In deciding to accelerate Spinks's race for the heavyweight title, Arum was showing good business sense—getting his money's worth out of his fighter before that value went permanently AWOL.

Lewis was more the party animal than the boss. He liked being around fighters and having hands-on contact. It was action that put him stage center, a location from which he has never shied. But as vice-president in charge of finding and furthering Leon Spinks, he became the custodian of a man born in the spirit of the wind—who could say which way he would blow, or when?

From very early on, Lewis was his fighter's keeper. It was why he and his wife, Savannah, boarded a commercial airline flight bound for Des Moines, Iowa, on New Year's Eve 1976. With Spinks's pro debut scheduled for January 15 and Leon gone, without permission, from training camp, Lewis had no choice but to follow his trail.

In Des Moines, Lewis and his wife rented a car and headed for the black section of town. There in the wee hours of the morning he found a youngster who knew where Spinks was staying.

But when he rang the bell, there was no answer. The Lewises waited, and waited. At noon on the first day of 1977, Leon arrived. He was drinking and laughing and in no mood for the fun to cease.

The conversation went like this:

SPINKS:	Butch, what are you doing here?
LEWIS:	What am I doing here?! Hey, you're fighting in fourteen days! Your pro debut!
SPINKS:	Oh man. I'm coming back tomorrow.
LEWIS:	No. Today.
SPINKS:	No I ain't.
LEWIS:	Get packing.

So it went for the fugitive Spinks and the bring-'em-back-alive Mr. Lewis. That New Year's Day 1977 would establish the pattern of their often noisy and tumultuous relationship. As willing as Spinks was once inside the ropes, he never really did embrace the idea of seriously training for those afternoons and evenings that constituted his livelihood.

When Spinks arrived in Monticello, New York, to train for his title shot against Ali, Lewis discouraged any thought of "swooping" by pitching his rollaway bed at the front door of the big house in which Spinks and his camp were lodged.

With such vigilance *and* a back door that did not open, Lewis figured he had boxing's rambling man outflanked. Wrong. On a wintry morning, with the snow piled knee-deep, Lewis was roused from sleep to learn the big guy was gone. Spinks had stepped out the window of his bedroom and onto the roof over the porch; he had jumped from there to the snow-cushioned earth. As it turned out, he had not fled for the high life. When Lewis found him, Spinks was standing around a local pool hall, watching a game of eight ball. He had, he told Lewis, wearied of being "cooped up."

If Spinks was an Excedrin headache for Lewis, for Sly he was, in the parlance, great copy, a source of unexpected twists and turns, of unending tensions that give any narrative jet-fueled propulsion.

But being on Spinks patrol was never a guarantee that the boyo himself would appear as scheduled. In late March 1978, Sly went to Detroit for *Playboy* magazine, to hang out with the new champion. Three days later, in Suite 840 of Detroit's Buhl Building, where Spinks's law firm had its office, he was still waiting for Leon.

Sly was not one of life's patient men. As a workaholic and a compulsive, he was not amused by this no-show. At first he experienced the nerve-twitching that excessive waiting induced. But then, as it dawned on him that the very absence of Spinks might be a richer experience than Spinks's presence, he relaxed and did the necessary: watched, listened, and made notes.

Spinks's attorneys, Edward Bell and Lester Hudson, waited with him, hoping that the former Detroit police officer that they had dispatched to St. Louis could find the heavyweight champion. They wanted to get negotiations rolling for his rematch that September against Ali.

Bell and Hudson were not the only people who wanted Spinks in Detroit. Richard J. Smit did, too. Smit was a car salesman who had driven up from the Johnny Kool Oldsmobile Agency, in Indianapolis, Indiana, in a 1977 custom-built white Lincoln Continental limousine that he meant to sell to Spinks for $35,000—$5,000 down, a ten-month lease, and a final "balloon" cash payout.

The vehicle went with the new "star" image that Bell and Hudson were insisting would soon fit their client as snugly as the three size-42 tailor-made suits that had been hand-delivered from across the border in Windsor, Ontario.

While grand plans for fiscal responsibility and speech lessons were being formulated in Detroit, Spinks was doing what came naturally: living hard and fast and secretly in the present tense.

As Sly tracked it, Leon was all over St. Louis with a woman friend. But the social whirl turned a bit more complicated when the fighter's wife, Nova, suddenly flew in. Leon solved the problem by putting Nova in the hotel suite he had occupied and moving the other woman two flights up. Then Leon went "swooping" on his Mrs.

Soon after, Nova got a lead on Spinks's whereabouts; she went with the champion's bodyguard to find him. When the bodyguard saw Leon's silver Chrysler New Yorker, he told Nova that he'd retrieve Leon. Instead, he told Spinks, "Your wife is here, man," which gave Spinks and his St. Louis woman the chance to drive away.

At the time this was occurring, Smit was emerging from Bell and Hudson's office in Detroit to say, "They're contacting a guy with the St. Louis police who knows Spinks. To see if they can dig him up. The word is, be discreet."

A smile flickered across Smit's lips. Each screwy twist of

waiting-for-Leon was as perverse an entertainment for him as it was for Sly. But that was about to end. Smit left Detroit that afternoon, regretting he hadn't had the chance to try his pitch on the heavyweight champion.

"'Cause I know Spinks is a buyer," Smit said. "All I got to do is stick his ass in the seat. Boom! Thirty-five gees. Cashier's check, if you please. All I need is five minutes."

Three days after arriving in Detroit, Sly left on an evening flight to New York.

Naturally, Spinks flew back on his own to Detroit the next day. He hadn't much to say, except about the limousine. Richard Smit had read his customer right. Spinks saw the white Lincoln Continental limousine with the gold striping, the AM/FM stereo cassette player, the small-screen color TV, the digital clock, the bar, the sunroof, the phones for in-car communications, and the two back rows of facing seats in crushed velour. He saw all that and knew what he knew.

As Leon put it: "That my motherfucking car. I'm buying."

Where Ali was open, accessible, Spinks was mistrusting of the inkstained wretches, and just not smart enough to know how to play them.

The kind of elusive cat he was made him a difficult subject for deadline journalists, who moved from one topic to another, hardly drawing a breath. The daily press hadn't the time, as Sly did, to go on Spinks patrol. As a result, the press for the most part saw Spinks filtered through his most extreme incidents. The easy take on him was that he was a kind of bozo, a distortion only by a little.

With a chance to earn a lifetime's financial security for a dutiful passage in the prize ring, Spinks, it seemed, was intent on ambushing the future. In fact, he appeared to take a mad pleasure in the warped gesture, the attraction to which brought unanticipated twists: Spinks would experience seizures of laughter in the midst of a sober account of one of his St. Louis driving busts or while he analyzed his impromptu disappearances. They were great gurgling sounds—laughter shot through with an unhinged quality.

At those times, the phrase "inappropriate response" flashed in Sly's mind like the TILT light on a pinball machine, the laughter suggesting a self-destructive impulse. Yet the plea-

sure of Spinks's company was in just this sort of unpredict-
ability. While Spinks was never eager to have the press around,
when he did materialize it was as unadulterated, unexpurgated
Leon.

At the airport in Miami, hours after a news conference in
New Orleans for the rematch with Ali, a TV sportscaster asked
Spinks to describe how it felt to whip Ali. Leon smiled and,
without blinking an eye, did a softshoe routine, at the finish of
which he extended his hands and said, "Like that."

Late that day in April, with the sun sinking toward the
horizon, Spinks, a welterweight named Roger Stafford, and Sly
stood by a low stone wall at the end of Lincoln Road, watching
the ocean break against the shore just below. Spinks wore a
form-fitting maroon shirt and cream-colored slacks. He and
Stafford were drinking pink California champagne. A gentle
breeze blew.

"It gonna be good to hit some motherfucker again," said
Spinks, putting his glass on the wall and inhaling a cigarette.

"Yeahhhh, I know," said Stafford, setting his drink down
too.

Spinks struck a fighting pose, bent at the knees, and let his
hands go.

"Whap! Whap!" Stafford said, as he watched. Then
Stafford was moving punches through the air, emitting small
grunting sounds as he did. "That's the way I did it to that
dude," he said, referring to a preliminary bout he had fought
that weekend on national TV. "All over the motherfucker."

"Yeahhhh," said Spinks.

"I whupped that dude good—"

"Hey. My man," Spinks interrupted, addressing Sly. "Hey,
you ain't gonna put in the ar-ti-cle that I smoke, is you?"

"Heyyyy," Sly said, with an elaborate shrug that was not
quite an answer.

"'Count of my image," Spinks said.

Spinks thought about it and then forgot about it and began
to move sinuously, reducing his shadow punches to a stoned
dance.

"Women," said Stafford. "Got to get women."

"Women," answered Spinks.

"Got to."

"Sweet nothings?" Sly prodded.

"No. Lies," said Stafford. "Tell 'em lies."

"Liiiees," crooned Spinks, his body rocking as he grinned. "Tell 'em liieees."

They doubled over in laughter, Spinks making plashing sounds with his mouth.

"Liieees."

"Tell 'em liiees,"

For that moment at least, life with Leon seemed to be blissfully free of complexities. But if there was any lesson that an observer took from hanging around the camp of Leon Spinks it was how infernally susceptible to change things were in boxing. With all the players that could be involved at any one moment in a fighter's career—those who were part of his camp and those who were not—and with their objectives so often and so sharply in conflict, there was always pressure to jog the status quo.

That pressure led to abrupt shifts in power that made the characters in the Spinks episode resemble the fauna in a frenzied feeding chain. To keep abreast of the shifting hierarchy was like tracking a Dow Jones whose control had been overthrown by an anarchist on the order of, say, Spike Jones. Spinks himself reflected the changes.

Toward noon on a day in April, not quite two months after he won the title, Spinks was standing in Penthouse 1, his posh lodgings at the Hotel DiLido in Miami Beach, idling for a moment before he would plunge into another day. The sun was streaming through a space in the drapes. His step had a loose, easy swing. Then suddenly he was holding up the index finger of each hand and, with a rhumbalike motion of his hips, he was moving while in a comically falsetto voice he chanted, "Penthouse number one, Penthouse number one." The style was Carmen Miranda's, but the pleasure was all Spinks's. Penthouse number 1: top of the world, Momma.

Then the phone rang—a call from Lewis, whose Svengali's grip he had slipped by giving the Detroit attorneys control of his daily business. The grin on Spinks's face turned down at its corners and his expression became abruptly subdued. As a vice-president of Top Rank, which was promoting Spinks-Ali #2, Lewis always had a pretext for contacting Spinks. Minutes later, as Spinks hung up, he was muttering, "One thing after another. Shit. Shit. Shit."

That struck the right note for the Spinks High Times and Soul Aplenty Caravan. There was a continuing sense of the whole works' being slightly out of whack, bent in a way no orderly vision could possibly straighten.

Shitshitshit: no end to it as the players jockeyed for position around Spinks, urging, entreating, wheedling as the camp swung from Hilton Head, South Carolina, to Kutsher's in the Catskills, to Hammonton, New Jersey, and finally to New Orleans, where the Spinks-Ali rematch would take place. Barnes consulted attorneys about his diminished role as manager while Lewis, the man who had usurped him, sought to regain control of Spinks from Bell and Hudson, who were insulating the champion from Lewis as best they could.

Leon's brother Michael, a partisan of Lewis, pushed for Leon to divest Bell and Hudson of their power and return it to Butch, and when he heard Leon say that family and business don't mix, Michael decided he was listening to a man who had been brainwashed. So Michael kept at Leon, trying to tell him the way things were or should be.

By now, the *Playboy* article was in, the check was cashed, but Sly was nonetheless following events. Like a soap-opera junkie, he was curious about what would happen next. So by phone he tracked the latest developments, the swooping, the partying, the shitshitshit. Through various sources, he kept posted:

"So Butch say to Leon, says, 'Lee-on, you got my back against the waa-ll,' and Leon said, 'Keep it there.'"

"Always keeping Leon upset, always arguing about something and screaming. And you know . . . he never did that with the Ali camp. He never ran to Ali's room. . . ."

"One bar in Chester, Pennsylvania. A crummy little joint. The type of place he likes to frequent. A place where they have a jukebox and a bunch of niggers. No credit cards. Anyway. There was one guy who was beckoning Spinks: 'Come on, you motherfucker. I'll beat your ass. You can't fight.' And Spinks: 'That's on you. Put up the money and I'll fight you . . .'"

"The few times that I see Leon—early-morning hours and night in New Orleans—he appears to me to be intoxicated. . . ."

"Nobody talks to Leon. Everybody manipulates. I mean,

everybody in everything they say to him. Everybody has an ax to grind. Get him to do this, get him to do that, calm him down, be nice to him. Do this, do that. Give him the idea that it's his idea and get him to do it."

"They're kissing his ass. 'Whatcha want to do today, Champ?' 'I wanna run.' 'What time ya going to run, Champ?' 'Call me at eight.' They call him at eight. 'You're not going to run right now, Champ?' 'No, I'll run about twelve.' 'Okay, Champ. You run at twelve.' Five o'clock comes. He's not going to run today. Tell the press. . . ."

Amid all the intrigue, the sad part was the opportunity, and talent, that Leon would waste. While he had been an Olympic gold medalist and heavyweight champion, he had taken his hour in the arena for granted. Soon enough, the flame would flicker and go dark, leaving Leon, as the years rolled by, to think about could-have and should-have, as fuck-ups always do.

What it left Sly was a healthy skepticism for boxing's life at the top, an attitude useful a decade later when the vagaries of another heavyweight champion's life would preoccupy civilized society. In both instances, problems grew out of factional disputes for control of the fighter.

Most troubling to Leon was the quarreling and the infighting occasioned between him and his brother, Michael, who continued to insist Leon had erred in leaving Lewis.

A week or so before Spinks's rematch with Ali, as Leon skipped rope during a training session, his feelings spilled over. As the rope turned, tears fell down his cheeks.

The chaos around him was typified by a scene that occurred on the night of the rematch. When Spinks's very large entourage arrived at its corner that night, it was discovered that Leon had forgotten his protective cup.

The cry went up. "Did you bring the cup?" "No." "Did you bring the cup?" "No." "Did you bring the cup?" Finally: "Go get the cup." "Go get the cup." One of the many camp aides was dispatched to the dressing room to retrieve the cup. He raced up the aisle to the back of the arena, and when he returned, it was with a cup . . . of water!

2

Covering Spinks had had the immediacy that any journalist looks for—a complexity of events and characters with enough laughs along the way to keep the body fluids in perfect harmony. While in many respects Spinks encouraged the potential for convolutions that boxing held, what Sly could sense of the sport's normalcy was still two rings more than most workday circuses could boast.

In the years that followed he trundled off to one place or another from time to time to work up a few thousand words about this or that fight personage. While he would have liked to have spent more time writing boxing, that was not really in the cards; the reasons involved not only the dollars and cents of the free lance's life but the way in which boxing is perceived.

Boxing has always had a more amorphous following than have team competitions. Pro baseball, football, and basketball are grounded in the patterned particulars of preseason rites, in-season schedules, and athletes who, by and large, swear allegiance to the same team year after year. All that familiarity makes for fans who tend to feel loyal to the franchise.

Boxing is not so dutiful a spectacle. It is more like show

biz—offering up ever-changing excitements, established heroes in collision with rising challengers, reputations made or shattered with violent abruptness. What that meant was that boxing's constituency was bound to be a fickle one, more responsive to the latest name up on the marquee. When a compelling figure, such as Ali, was doing business, then many who regarded boxing as *déclassé* would override their so-called better instincts and begin following the sport. What activated that marginal fan was nothing less than what keeps readers of popular fiction turning pages—an urgency to know what happens next.

The editor of a mass-market magazine is an awful lot like the average fan—a little better, maybe, at Scrabble. For such a man boxing is only worth bothering with when it stirs up a fuss among people who normally have the good taste to ignore it. For a while, Sly lived at the whim of such editors. The moment a fighter emerged who, like a chic new restaurant or a hot-ticket Broadway show, prompted conversation among the editor's acquaintances was the moment when Sly would be put to work.

As a part-timer Sly would mingle with boxing's stars, for invariably it was those hotshots whom he was asked to cover. With each assignment, he was expanding his sphere of acquaintances and his awareness of the business, an education that would help when, unexpectedly, he became more deeply entrenched in the fight game than he had ever anticipated.

But that was still a ways off. In the late 1970s and early 1980s, when he was a for-hire word-cranking man, the assignments might be few and far between. Yet on occasion they were with fighters who would reappear in his life later on, when he began following boxing more dutifully.

Early in 1979, he reported on a welterweight prospect:

> The moon is dimming in the early-morning sky in Landover, Maryland, as two men appear at the top of a hilly street called Belle Haven.
>
> One wears a rust-colored knit mask that covers his face except for slits where the eye and mouth are supposed to be. The other has on a blue watch cap that is pulled back on his head, revealing a high-cheekboned dolorous face.
>
> At the bottom of the hill is George Palmer Highway.

On the corner is a shoestore designated as the place where they are to meet a pair of strangers—one with a notepad, the other with a camera—whom they find sitting on the hood of a rented car. "Who are you waiting for?" the one in the knit mask asks.

Told it's Sugar Ray they want, he rolls the mask up his face and smiles, an agreeable 100-kilowatt smile that has become as much Ray Leonard's trademark as the deft footwork and blurring combinations of punches that constitute his wage-earning skills.

At that time, Leonard was eight months and seven fights away from a shot at a world title. The flash he had then—right down to the prefight kisses he threw the crowd—reflected a showman's deep pleasure. As a fighter, he appeared to be in his element and enjoying it to the hilt. The moment he was away from the ring, the strut was gone and he was more detached. While not exactly moody, he seemed to be on guard somehow, to be cutting out a space for himself. "I consider myself," he said, "a loner. I have a couple of friends. But in my mind, I am a loner."

The following year, Sly was off to Atlantic City, where a rising heavyweight was hours away from his first televised main event.

. . . [Boxing manager] Dennis Rappaport has the prefight jitters.

He's pacing the lobby of the Boardwalk Regency . . . chain-smoking Newports, a few hours before his fighter, Gerry Cooney, climbs into the ring against Jimmy Young.

Young is the heavyweight who was slick enough to beat ex-champion George Foreman and win everything but the decision from Muhammad Ali in a title match. In recent times, Young has tended to put on weight, enough so that on occasion the only difference between Jimmy and Kate Smith was an octave. That and a few losses have tarnished his once-lustrous image.

For the Cooney bout, Young has slimmed down and is looking fit, evidently aware that the big money stops here if he loses. The thought of a possibly revitalized Young does not—contrary to Rappaport's worst fear—have Gerry Cooney on edge. He lies relaxed in his bed in Suite 500,

with a religious tract on his chest and a Tarzan movie on the
TV screen.

After a while, Cooney looks up to see the bind that
Johnny Weissmuller, as Tarzan, is in. Locked up in a cage
on circus grounds, Tarzan fears that Boy has been kid-
napped and knows that to rescue him he must escape. "The
elephants," says Cooney. "He'll get the elephants to help
him out." And sure enough, there goes Tarzan exhorting
the pachyderms to get him out of his fix. They do so, bend-
ing the bars of the cage so that he can flee. As Johnny
Weissmuller swings, the plot comes to its neat resolution.
Cooney gathers up religious mementos and telegrams from
friends and fans and stashes them in a bag with his fight
gear.

Now trainer Victor Valle, who is 62 years old and has
silver-gray hair, begins pumping his fighter up: "You got
people that love you. You gotta make sure that they love you
even more after this fight. . . . You gotta get through this
guy to get to the champion. He needs room to fight. Don't
give him room. Alive. Alive. Be alive all the time. Okay, let's
go down and do our job."

In those days, Cooney was that species of amiable lug
that covets attention and affection. The first time Sly met him
was at Cooney's training camp in Kiamesha Lake, New York.
Cooney had just stepped from the hallway into Valle's room.
After being introduced to Sly, he walked across the room
with his head tilted down and to the side—the body language
of an eager pup—a big smile on his face, his right hand out
to shake. With the other hand, he gave the visitor a Gerry
Cooney T-shirt. The T-shirt was yellow and had Cooney's
name in green letters, just beneath the fighter's likeness.
"How ya doin'?" Cooney asked. He seemed a very obliging
fellow.

That certain distance that Ray Leonard put between himself and an interviewer was not Cooney's way at all. He
wanted things on a personal basis. So it was probably no accident that while Valle would address him in the ring with stern
authority, out of it he would joke with and fuss over his
fighter. There was even a song the trainer had composed, to
the melody of Al Jolson's "Sonny Boy." Without much coaxing, he would sing:

Come along with me, Gerry Boy.
Come along with me, Gerry Boy.
You were sent from Heaven.
You were sent from Heaven.
For me, Gerry Boy.
While there's those gym days,
I don't mind the hard work.
For you are my son, Gerry Boy.

At the time Sly happened along, Leonard and Cooney were both on the cusp of big-time celebrity—just at that point where life can get crazy with pressure and complications, a good time for a reporter to be around. A man or woman left in the public spotlight long enough becomes cagey at media chat and able to convey a self that satisfies an interviewer without tapping deeply into his or her emotional reserves. Neither Leonard nor Cooney was yet at that point.

Cooney's in particular was an open camp. One afternoon at his training facility, weeks before he fought Young, Cooney was in the front seat of the shuttle van taking him to the gym. Suddenly, he put his index finger to the driver's head, as if it were a gun, and screamed, "Keep moving! Keep moving!" His eyes were wide, his body tense. Abruptly, he relaxed, turned around, and grinned to see how his prank was going over.

It was a small moment but just the kind that lends a piece of writing peephole immediacy. The trouble was, as fighters became more famous the viewing lines got restricted. Where, early in a fighter's career, a dressing room was an atmospheric and spontaneous setting, later on it would be off limits and one of the fighter's many functionoids would be standing in front of it barring entry.

For a writer who cared about boxing, it was a little strange. One moment Sly would be in Dressing Room 8 at the Atlantic City Convention Hall, just before Cooney was to fight Young, watching the fighter comically moon a TV camera being set up. Then two years would pass and Cooney would be fighting Larry Holmes for the world title while Sly, in the midst of a fire-breathing closed-circuit audience, viewed the bout on the big screen.

Keeping up with the twists and turns of a boxing season was full-time work, the sort of steady pull that just didn't exist for a free-lance writer. What did exist was another sort of pressure, that of the open market, a challenge that was obscured by the impression that many civilians had of Sly's line of work.

It was his experience that when a stranger heard the words "free-lance writer" he was inclined to conjure up a life poised somewhere between that of a Malibu lifeguard's and what the scion of a Texas oil fortune might enjoy. There was, apparently, something in the concept of an unstructured job that played to this fantasist's notion.

In truth, being a free lance was a slightly grayer day. Remember the sort of act that Ed Sullivan used to be partial to—a brisk-gaited boyo and his lady spinning plates, one after the other, at the end of long-stemmed poles, the cumulative effect like that of Salvador Dalí's cupboard?

Well, Sly thought of that image often. When the *New York Times* offered him the chance to cover boxing full time in October 1985, he closed the cupboard door and took the job. But his pleasure at landing a beat to which he was attracted did not obscure for him the timing of the move. Like any member of the working press, Sly was partial to a subject with the potential for surprise and excitations. The Ali years had had that kind of volatility.

Those had been convulsive times in America's history, and Ali existed as a part of—and not apart from—them. The racial schism, the polarization of the country through a Southeast Asian war—Ali was caught up in these events and was transformed by them. He leapfrogged from the sports section onto page one, taking with him the working stiffs of the boxing press and the auxiliary of prose-cranking stars—the Mailers and Sheeds and Plimptons who signified that for a flickering moment at least boxing had a star in residence.

Abruptly cast on a new beat, Sly could hardly help but take an envious glance backward. The Ali years had had the passion, the clamor, the technicolor grandeur that jump-start a writer's clogged circuits. Before Ali a heavyweight champion was supposed to be as rough as a mob enforcer in the ring and as upright and foursquare as a Methodist minister outside it. Ali had trashed that noble-warrior prototype and created his own glorious eccentric.

After the prime merriment and the hard news that Ali made, the heavyweight division of calendar year 1985 was a big letdown. Since the retirement of Ali in 1980, and with the exception of Larry Holmes, the heavyweight division had been the domain of mediocre titleholders whose reigns lasted about as long as the fragrance of the cheapest perfumes.

A baffling phenomenon. One after another heavyweight would win the title and then lose it in the blink of an eye. Had this been caused by the superiority of each claimant to the title, then the public might have been roused. But the constant transition was nothing but a seriocomic study in surrender, and the champions who succeeded one another had as much appeal as the late-night Veg-o-Matic pitchman.

A fighter—call him Tubbs or Page or Dokes or Coetzee— would win a version of the heavyweight title, and the next time he was seen his relatively firm body would have gone to fat: he would look like a candidate for the Maidenform Bra campaign. Or the fierce intent he had shown in winning the title would be subsumed by some queer creature impulse of indifference— and the next time out he would fight as though he were on tranquilizers.

While all these godawfuls were practicing their trade, Holmes traveled on a markedly different course, beating up whatever body was stood before him. In June 1978, he licked Ken Norton to become World Boxing Council champion. But by December 1983, as his relationship with Don King deteriorated, Holmes resigned his title rather than continue to fight for King. When he next boxed—he beat Bonecrusher Smith in November 1984—it was for the heavyweight title of the International Boxing Federation, the newest of the sport's governing bodies. It was as IBF champion that in September 1985 Holmes lost the first bout of his career—to Michael Spinks.

Spinks, at the time, was the undisputed light heavyweight champion; he had undergone a rigorous and scientific program to take on the added poundage of a heavyweight—real men's weight and not the hog flesh to which his peers were given. Bulked up from the 175-pound limit of a light heavyweight to 200 pounds, Spinks won a decision over Holmes, but with hardly the show of force that the public has come to expect from heavyweights.

Spinks was smaller but shrewder. His knack was for disrupting rhythm. Like that sort of pitcher who, lacking the overpowering fastball, mixes his junkball throws to confuse the batter, Spinks never let Holmes get comfortable. At times he would rush at Holmes and throw a barrage of punches, then suddenly sashay away, leaving the other man peering through his narrowed eyes like a wounded bear trying to make sense of a particularly feisty dog. Time and again Holmes failed to fire his explosive right hand when the opportunity seemed to be there. Spinks kept him off stride.

It was an intriguing performance. But for devotees of big-punch heavyweights, Spinks's victory was seen as flimflam—the result of Holmes's old age and suspect conditioning more than any virtue Spinks might possess. With a heavyweight division that had purists tapping out SOS on their telegrapher's keys, a rookie newsman like Sly could not be faulted for feeling out of luck.

The boxing business at this hour was humdrum. The best fighter, the shaven-headed middleweight champion Marvin Hagler, was reportedly thirty-one—some said he was older—and raising the prospect of his retirement. And it was unclear who out there had the talent and that intangible extra dimension to mobilize mass interest in the sport should Hagler quit. Certainly Sly could not see from where would come the chosen thrills and chills God meant the working press to have.

But late in 1985, semiseismic rumblings began occurring along several fronts that would rouse the sport and bring more twinkle than a laser-light reflection off the smooth scalp of M. Hagler.

And these emanations were occurring in that previously dim precinct, the heavyweight division, which, like the Frankenstein monster, was about to stir to life.

3

Don King worked a sentence like a man hunched over a pinball machine.

For him, words were not discrete links that eventually coalesced into sentences and thoughts.

With King, the mother tongue was a hoop-de-doo of polysyllabics that went crashing and caroming against one another, *sprockety boing* and lights flashing, all in the service of his latest (and greatest) deal.

Like that player poised over the pinball game, King had a way of humping the great Anglo language machine, of imparting a little spin here, a little emphasis there. He was a unique listening experience.

A word like "assiduous," for instance, would loll on his tongue . . . *as-sidddd-u-usss* . . . as if it were the last peppermint patty in these continental United States. Other words went rocketing off like tin cans shooting down a treacherous rapids.

The effect of this veritable—or as King himself might put it, this verrrr-i-ta-blllle cascade and pro-fuuuuu-sion of words—was to keep a listener transfixed.

King himself liked the sound of these mildly mutated

words he sent out. He took a delight in filling the air with them; occasionally his pleasure was such that a grin would break across his face and his body would shake from the top of his Dr. Zorba head to his size-12 shoes with that deep rumble *heh-heh-heh* that was his laugh.

Heh-heh-heh, oh God! he would say, the exclamation in a near falsetto, as though he were as damn near overcome as his listeners by the audacious concatenation of sound.

Through the summer of '85 and into the autumn, King was marshaling that splendid rhetorical arsenal of his on behalf of a fight he wanted to sell. The fight was Pinklon Thomas vs. Trevor Berbick. Thomas was the WBC heavyweight champion; Berbick was a Jamaican who, when not boxing, was given to evangelical works, a calling that had led King to introduce him from various daises as the Fighting Preacher.

As big fights go, Thomas vs. Berbick was not. But as the best match that King could offer to Home Box Office, he doggedly advanced it as a worthy attraction, intent on landing some of the prime-time money that HBO paid. But HBO was not buying. As persistent as King was in proposing Thomas-Berbick—and Lord, the man did not cease trying—so was Seth G. Abraham in turning it down.

Seth Abraham was HBO's senior vice-president of program operations and sports—less formally he was the "boxing guy" for Time Inc.'s pay cable service. His was the opinion that counted.

There had been a time—and not so long before—when what Abraham thought had virtually no impact on boxing. In fact, the first time that Abraham phoned King up in 1979 to inquire about a doubleheader of King's that the three networks had turned down, King heard Abraham's name and said, "Who?"

King could be excused for failing to recognize the name. In 1978, when Abraham had first gone to work for HBO, the company had only slightly more than two million subscribers and an ill-defined sports identity.

It wasn't that HBO paid no heed to sports. Its monthly calendar was full up with amateur boxing, college basketball, weekly baseball highlights—140 sports shows a year. But somehow the effect of all that on viewer consciousness was not the bang for the buck that Abraham believed it should be.

To his mind, there was a tendency toward the slaphappy indiscriminate at HBO Sports that had found its ultimate expression in one programming idea, conceived and approved by predecessors—that of team shark-tagging: two squads of professional divers scoured shark-infested water for sharks they could tag, the most tags won.

Abraham wanted to streamline, and by the time he had his first conversation with King, HBO was already moving in that direction. Abraham and his boss, Michael Fuchs, were looking for a focus to their sports programming, and boxing had begun to be their idea of a possible leader.

In the end, Abraham would pay King a modest $125,000 for a card featuring Larry Holmes vs. Mike Weaver and Roberto Duran vs. Carlos Palomino, programming that the networks had shot down. The networks' hesitation was attributed to doubts about Weaver, a fighter whose sculpted body had prompted sportswriters to call him Hercules.

Here and there Weaver had victories over credible foes like Bernardo Mercado (KO 5, October 22, 1978) and Stan Ward (TKO 9, January 18, 1979). But in a career that dated back to 1972, Weaver had lost eight times, on occasion to fighters who were not exactly pillars of the heavyweight community.

But it was HBO's good fortune that Weaver was a late-bloomer, with a punch that could make grown men goggle-eyed. That night, he staggered Holmes and hurt him repeatedly until Holmes rallied to stop Weaver in the twelfth round of a stirring fight that was part of an extended card.

In his column the next day, Red Smith would write: "It was Home Box Office's finest hour—finest three hours to be exact. The big brains of television's major networks turned down Friday night's big show in Madison Square Garden. . . ."

And so on.

"When the people at Time Inc. read that the next day," said Abraham, "they said we were geniuses for being able to pull it off and for Red Smith giving us the stamp of approval. It accelerated my decision to take HBO into boxing in a big way."

Ordinarily, King might have expected that, flush with success, HBO would cut new and better deals with him. But Abraham's attention had just been caught by Marvin Hagler. Marvelous Marvin had recently fought a disputed draw with the middleweight champion, Vito Antuofermo. Hagler's bravado, as conveyed by the quotes in an article he read, got Abraham to thinking: might this be a fighter who could build a pay cable service's boxing image?

Abraham contacted Hagler's promoter, Arum, who was King's archrival, and after Hagler won the title from Alan Minter in September 1980, a three-fight deal worth $1.1 million was struck. As Hagler became the dominant fighter over the first half of the 1980s, HBO kept renewing its interest with more generous checks: $17 million in all it would sink into Hagler while televising all his championship defenses save for Hagler-Hearns (for which it had delayed rights) and for what it perceived (correctly, it turned out) as a mismatch against one William (Caveman) Lee. On March 7, 1982, Lee fell in an abrupt heap onto the canvas some sixty-seven seconds after hostilities commenced and never troubled to get himself erect.

HBO and Hagler prospered. HBO's subscriber figures soared from slightly more than 2 million in 1978 to 8.5 million by the end of 1981 and 14.6 million by the end of 1985. But in the period HBO was having success with Hagler, it was buying other fights as well. So while King was not making the kind of posh deals Arum was through Hagler, he was not out in the cold either. He and Abraham had continuity; they had survived the probing and the testing that high-powered players assay where big stakes are involved.

King, for instance, had the workaholic's disregard for the nine-to-five. To get a deal on track, King would go anywhere, anytime, and work the deal for however long was necessary. He was an action guy, with a clock that was out of whack with most civilians'. But King had a way of using that idiosyncrasy to his advantage: at brutally early or late hours, he might suddenly phone Abraham and see what he could do about nudging a deal closer to the terms that Don King wanted.

Abraham recognized what the promoter was up to, and in his own way let him know. He would make it a point to phone at even less convenient hours, a tactic that very quickly restored a touch of normalcy to the hours when business between the two men was conducted.

In the course of making deals, this sort of parrying went on all the time, each man using whatever advantage he felt he could to tilt a business discussion his way.

One obvious edge that King had was his size: he stood six-foot-four and had Falstaff's own girth. Abraham is five-foot-ten and of average build. In 1981, when King and he were negotiating the Larry Holmes–Trevor Berbick heavyweight title match, they were at an impasse on how much the fight was worth.

"Don was stuck on eight hundred and fifty thousand dollars and I on about four hundred thousand," said Abraham. "For some reason, one of the negotiating sessions ended up at King's lawyer's office. I was still pretty new in my relationship with King. We'd had about a half-dozen deals. Well, at this day in his lawyer's office, at one point Don jumped out of his chair, like he'd been launched by a grenade launcher, and began screaming. The substance of what he was screaming was that this is Larry Holmes, the heavyweight champion of the world, how dumb can you be. I realized that what he was doing was trying to physically intimidate me. He meant me no harm. He was using his size to physically intimidate me to give him his price. I got up and said, 'Either sit down or I'm leaving. We've got no deal.' We had a staring contest for about fifteen seconds. That's a long time, if you think about it. Then he sat down. And from that point, King never tried to intimidate me with his size. We were able to strike a deal for five hundred and fifty thousand dollars, which was a fair price."

They were a curious pair. King, a big sprawling man who stepped into rooms with the assurance of a conquistador, was often heard before he was seen. He had that booming voice with which he might croon one after the other the names of familiar figures from boxing, punctuating his litany with the resonating har-de-har laugh: *Phil Berger, heh heh heh. My man. Dave Anderson, heh heh.*

Abraham was personable but not in that animated *tummler*'s fashion. He was merely conversational. That conversation could run far afield—he liked the theater and books—but the cumulative effect resembled normal dialogue. In a conversation with King, a listener always felt like a paid admission.

Against the big-bear expansiveness of King, Abraham was more measured and precise—neat office, crisp syntactical English, sartorial certitude. Where Don King in a coat and tie, however expensive, tended to look frayed in a hurry, Abraham had a *GQ* ease in his finery, which often included suspenders, a kind of trademark of his.

That sort of meticulous air usually translated into a play-safe style of doing business, but the lure of corporate security had not quashed an instinct for the imaginative in Abraham. He was willing to roll the dice—for the right idea.

Take it as a given—heavyweights had become a bore. In their respective worlds, of the WBA, the WBC, and the IBF, the champions held titles that, like those of bankrupt aristocracy, were the big pretend.

It was not just that the fighters lacked passion for and pride in their work, but with the constant succession of one sluggard by another, the heavyweight title—historically the most prestigious in the sport—was being cheapened.

To break the cycle, Abraham now proposed that King consider an idea: a series of fights that would lead, ultimately, to an undisputed heavyweight champion. An HBO heavyweight unification series.

In 1985, Don King had promotional contracts with two of the three heavyweight champions, Thomas and Tony Tubbs, and with most of the leading contenders. He was the power broker of boxing's most important division. In more than a few instances, his stepson, Carl, was the manager of the same fighters that King promoted, a parlay that was well within the rules of the sport, but surely had the potential for exploitation.

To ask a man in King's position how he felt about a series in which $16 million or so would be put on the table was, as objecting attorneys like to say, a leading question. King didn't need a Ouija board to recognize what a grand chance Abraham's series was for him.

But clear as he was on its potential for aggrandizing him, King knew that without the consent and cooperation of Ronald "Butch" Lewis, who promoted the other heavyweight champion, Michael Spinks, there was no HBO series.

Back in the limelight with another Spinks, the steady, self-reliant Michael, Lewis could relish the irony of being a veto away from making Don King unhappy. In the period after his 1978 dismissal from Top Rank—Arum had even accused him of fiscal improprieties—King had been among those who had impeded his progress.

In 1979, on his own as a promoter, Lewis was running fight cards in several cities where, without the cushion of network TV money, he occasionally had to reach into his own pocket to cover expenses the gate receipts wouldn't.

As once he had dogged Herbert Muhammad, now he pursued the networks. "I'd make the circuit—walk in without a meeting," he said. "They'd tell me: 'You gotta make an appointment.' I'd say, 'Bullshit. You guys are making fights. Let's do one with Butch Lewis.'"

Eventually, through Spinks, he worked his way back onto the network screen. Spinks was one of several fighters Lewis took on, including the heavyweight Greg Page, with whom he soon had problems. One day Page defected to King for reasons that Lewis thought were litigable. He sued Don King for inducing Page to breach his contract and, in settlement, got $250,000.

While that unpleasantry was not forgotten, business was business. The question for him was whether the HBO series was the best deal money could buy.

For King it was. It gave him the chance, for premium prices, to recycle the same gray heavyweights he had been abusing the public with for the better part of the 1980s.

Lewis was in a different position. There was another fight out there for Spinks that had big-money potential. In beating Holmes, Spinks had become an option for a heavyweight who had lost to Holmes and developed an obsession about fighting him again, a chance Holmes would never give him. Well, if Holmes was out of the picture, it turned out Spinks would do as well for the anguished pugilist, Gerald Anthony Paul Cooney.

On a wintry morning in Lancaster, Pennsylvania, Cooney ran along Lincoln Highway East. Traffic whooshed by, as the fighter, in a dark blue training suit and fingerless gloves, strode past Pizza Hut and Hardee's, on by Murray's Men's Wear and the House of Shanghai.

He took a right onto Oak View Road, a residential street of small houses with tidy front lawns, and pounded on, by Rutt's Antiques and the First Deaf Mennonite Church. Soon Cooney was moving past cows grazing in a field and a billboard for Dutch Wonderland Family Fun Park.

A typical boxing tableau, it seemed. A fighter doing road-work. But on this brisk morning in December 1985, the sight of Cooney reminded Sly of those riddlelike illustrations that as a grade-schooler he was given to solve: What's wrong with this picture?

Well, in this instance the answer was that, like an abruptly riderless racehorse still intent on the finish line, Cooney, for all his huffing and puffing, was a lot of waste motion. For each day rumors grew that Lewis was edging closer to signing Spinks into the HBO series rather than matching him against Cooney.

If that was the case, it would leave Cooney once again groping for a handle on his career.

Ever since he had lost to Holmes, his only defeat in twenty-eight bouts, Cooney had had more false starts than a jittery sprinter as he had tried to remobilize his career. If it wasn't the psychological effect of the defeat that kept him away from the prize ring, then there were injuries and postponed fights and eventually, after a short-lived two-bout comeback in late 1984, a retirement.

In returning to boxing after Spinks beat Holmes, Cooney was viewed by some as a blight on the sport. The mere thought of his getting a title shot against Spinks without having to fight real contenders to earn the chance galled his detractors, who saw his reemergence as opportunism that made capital of his being a white man in a predominantly black sport.

For the boxing press, Cooney was a choice target, treated with such persistent contempt that had he raised a white flag, it would have been splattered with ink in seconds.

This steady barrage of damning prose was curious. Was the savaging of Cooney a case of monkey-see, monkey-do jour-nalism, or was there in Cooney himself an incitement to write wild and crazy?

It was late on the day of Cooney's wintry morning run.

In the games arcade of the Americana Host Farm Resort, the bleeps and burbles of Pac-Man and pinball machines were silenced as the room was converted to a gym. A heavy bag was hung on a short length of chain in the low-ceilinged, fluores-cent-lit room, and a speed bag was brought out.

Cooney appeared.

"I dreamt I swallowed a thirty-pound marshmallow," he said. A few beats, then: "When I woke up, my pillow was gone."

He looked over his shoulder and, with an impish smile, engaged a visitor's gaze until he got the smile he wanted.

That charmer's insistent eye held a clue to the character of Cooney, who more than most fighters required smiles and the affirmation of others.

Through a career in which he had earned a reported $12 million in purses, Cooney had made a point of kibitzing with fans and signing autographs for them until writer's cramp set in. He did it not as a reflex of celebrity but as a part of an apparently deeply felt need to make contact. "I'm a real person," Cooney said. "I have real feelings. I have real thoughts. It's a quality people like about me. They can reach out and touch me. I wouldn't give it up for anything."

In his eagerness to please, Cooney, twenty-nine years old at the time, had occasionally gone to extremes. Earlier in his career, after scoring two straight one-round knockouts on HBO telecasts, Cooney apologized on the air for the condensed entertainment; later he apologized again to an executive of the pay-cable service for spoiling the show.

That was typical of Cooney, whose temperament was, like a hothouse flower, sensitive to an extreme. When *Newsday*, a newspaper aimed at readers in Long Island, where Cooney lived, made a change in boxing writers that brought with it unaccustomed harsh words about him, Cooney was so aggrieved that he took the extraordinary measure of phoning the sports editor of the paper, Richard Sandler, to complain. For at least fifteen minutes Cooney tried mightily to promote more benign coverage of his career.

The loss to Holmes in '82 sent Cooney into a deep depression, and he stopped boxing. The loss, and the reasons behind it, led to a version of the event—hereafter The Story—that Cooney told then and had not stopped telling since. The Story was by now a set piece, the same words and rhythms appearing, and in his incessant recounting, Cooney revealed just how deeply, despite denials, that night still cut him.

The Story: "If I lost and he was a better man, I could have dealt with it. But I was buffaloed about going the distance. I didn't fight my fight. The distance. The distance. They put that in my head, the press."

While The Story might explain, at least to his satisfaction, the loss, it could not and did not prepare him for days and nights beyond boxing.

Those newspapers that had treated him kindly began to malign him for his inactivity. Acquaintances to whom he had lent money—he earned about $9 million for fighting Holmes—chose not to make good on the payback, leaving Cooney feeling betrayed. He was booed when introduced at fights. Even the comedians in the Long Island clubs in which he hung out made jokes at his expense.

Anger, not usually a part of Cooney's makeup, began to surface, particularly when he'd had a little to drink. He developed a strange habit, while hanging around the clubs of Long Island, of casually backhanding comedians below the belt as he talked to them, a perverse response, it seemed, to the criticism he had received in the press for punches that had landed low on Holmes.

"I swear," said John Mulrooney, a comedian, "I almost threw up when he hit me. I walked to the men's room hunched over, like I'd dropped a contact lens. Came back. He's still laughing. Told him, 'You fucking idiot.'"

Some nights, Cooney would get up from his seat in a club and, wresting the microphone from a comedian, tell a few jokes before lapsing into The Story, which invariably became an apology—and a sometimes maudlin one—for his loss to Holmes.

The pain over the loss was exacerbated as it became clear that Holmes was not about to give Cooney a rematch.

They were not happy times, even at home. Cooney's brothers found themselves constantly assailed by friends and strangers with questions about GerryGerryGerry. They felt their own identities slipping away.

His home life became more difficult when one of the brothers developed a heroin addiction that required hospitalization and Cooney's constant attention. The fighter said it ate away at him and added to his own difficulties in reviving his boxing career, enough to make him consult a psychologist. "It takes a strong person to admit he's got problems," he said. "Things are bugging you, you've got to get it out. Life is supposed to be peaches and cream, but it doesn't turn out that way. I sometimes found things confusing and sometimes didn't understand how things could be so difficult."

Among the sensitive subjects discussed was his difficult relationship with his father. Cooney was frequently depicted as a young man who fought to please his father rather than himself, and probably there was a kernel of truth to that. When Cooney took up boxing as a gawky teenager, it was his father who prodded him. Tony Cooney monitored his son's roadwork, often rising at 6:00 A.M. and running with him to make sure the mileage was covered. Evenings, he insisted on early curfew, a stricture Cooney would circumvent by waiting until his father was asleep and then leaving the house.

"A lot of times," said Cooney, "he made it difficult. My mother was there, and she had so much love that it made up for it. I took the good from my father, and threw away the bad. I'd like to leave it vague. I don't want to hurt my mom—she loved my dad."

The veiled criticism of his father, who had died of lung cancer in 1976, was a shift in how Cooney had depicted that relationship back in 1980, at Sly's first meeting with him. The fighter was more forgiving then, more inclined to blame himself for not grasping the good intentions of a difficult man:

"My father—we called him Tony even though his name was Arthur—was tough on us. He was physical with the boys—smacked us or used the strap. He was a big man—six-foot-three, two hundred and twenty pounds. A construction worker. Very strict. Set in his ways. I just didn't realize he was trying to make me better. It wasn't until I worked construction with some of his steelworker friends that I found out how he'd talked about his sons, about how good they were doing. I love my father very much. When he was alive I couldn't tell him that. I realize now how stupid I was for not being able to."

With time passing, breast-beating no longer served, apparently. Cooney saw hard love as limited love. In Lancaster, he would say: "I didn't get attention from my father that a child should get. So I like to give people attention."

Conversations with Cooney constantly turned back on tangents of the same theme—that he, Cooney, was ready and eager to be the shining example that heavyweight champions used to be.

"I want to get that [heavyweight championship] belt," he said. "Hang it out on the fireplace and let everybody look at it. Invite the neighbors."

With that ambition, Cooney seemed to be harking back to a simpler time when the athlete was idealized, more concerned with heroic acts than with renegotiating his deal or checking the latest stock market quotations. Yet in Cooney's case that assumed role was, if studied long enough, a trick mirror as shot through with contradictions and complexities as Cooney himself.

For in projecting himself as Cooney/Lancelot, he was at the same time separating himself from other practitioners of the sport—in effect, making the case for Gerry Cooney as an exception to that clichéd yo-Adrian image of the fighter. "Hey, boxers are living with the stigma of being slow people," Cooney would say, before enumerating the ways—his pay phone business, the real estate investments, his acting lessons at the Lee Strasberg Theatre Institute—in which he was not.

Back in 1980, Sly had written these words about the fighter: "In person, he turns out to be a sunny, accessible individual, with a straightforward outlook, accentuating traditional values—God, family, concern for others."

What struck Sly now was how twisted that prototype Cooney had gotten in those six years. For Cooney seemed to be as extreme a case as Sly had met of an athlete coveting approval. After a long day in which Cooney had run, trained, sat and answered questions for hours, then talked in more relaxed circumstances over dinner, Cooney was computing what the affect of fighter on writer had been. Such was his need for affirmation that toward the end of Sly's first day in Lancaster, Cooney, while driving his cream-colored Cadillac, took his eyes off the road to say: "I can't tell whether you like me or not."

For Cooney, boxing was a necessary evil. It was his only means to what he wanted most to be: a hero. Think of Mickey Mantle, who makes his way through the world these days trading on the importance of Mickey Mantle, and you get the agenda Cooney coveted more than socking grown men in public.

A few years before, Cooney's friend Richie Minervini, who was a comedian, got time off from a club in Fort Lauderdale to go with Cooney to a fight in Miami. After the match ended, the comedian tried to get back to Fort Lauderdale in time to do his act. "I drove like a banshee," said Minervini. "And Gerry: 'You had the night off. Why are you doing this?' He couldn't understand. I told him I loved what I did for a living. And he said, 'Jeez, man. Boxing's not like that. The best part about boxing is the five minutes after the fight.'"

Butch Lewis was keenly aware of how Cooney felt when Lewis was negotiating the Spinks-Cooney fight. In working out the deal, Lewis insisted that in the event Cooney beat Spinks, Lewis would have promotional interests in Cooney's next two fights. According to Cooney's attorney, Neil Gerst, "The deal was written so that if Cooney won, a portion of his purse—one million—would be escrowed so Butch Lewis would have the benefit of Cooney's future earnings. That was part of the contract."

But Lewis was realistic enough about Cooney's priorities to know that once Cooney got the title, he might go into the hero business full-time. As Lewis told boxing people, he foresaw Cooney giving up boxing to do commercials, movies, charity benefits, the Letterman show—the whole circuit of the Gentleman Gerry trade. So Lewis took the precaution of writing into the contract a stipulation that gave him a percentage of Cooney's subsidiary incomes if Cooney beat Spinks and chose not to fight again.

There was no crime in standing as a hero or even profiting from it, particularly when a man felt as Cooney did, that "I have something to offer people." Cooney was a teddy bear of a man, amiable and outgoing, eager to please—perfect traits for the hero business. But the athletic hero, like John F. Kennedy's political hero, was defined by grace under pressure, not the escape from pressure.

All world-class fighters have ego. Ego is obligatory. Without it a fighter will not have the authenticity to do what he must: dominate another man by as naked a show of force as his society permits.

The other side of the proposition is that unless he wins, he stands a chance of being exposed as inferior stock—exposed in a way that is as brutally direct and unadorned as any that exists.

In defeat, a fighter is forced to confront his limits, an objective exercise that clashes with a quality of soaring faith that the mortal borne along by ego has. A boxer needs his illusion of supremacy to do what he does. As a consequence, rarely is a match fought for which the loser doesn't have an explanation for the baffling turn of events. In defeat there are the usual suspects: personal problems, managerial problems, injuries, I-got-thumbed, I-got-screwed, I-got-a-ways-to-go. Excuses are the means to make the fighter whole again.

So Cooney, with The Story, was hardly on the lunatic fringe. He was only doing what fighters do. Yet there was a subtle difference in how he saddled up his excuses and proceeded.

Where most beaten fighters are eager to try again and willing to step in the ring against any opponent, Cooney seemed to hold himself out as a special case, one who needn't trouble himself with the quality control the sport applied to his peers. Pinklon Thomas? Tony Tubbs? Cooney made them out as generic-brand champions, hardly worth the bother of fighting. HolmesHolmesHolmes was the objective. But that objective was elastic enough when Spinks beat Holmes for Spinks to become his Holmes substitute. That M. Spinks, who appeared to be the sorriest and scrawniest of the reigning heavyweight champions, would do where Thomas and Tubbs would not struck the boxing press as one more instance of Cooney's playing the sport cheap.

Item:

> Harrisburg, Pa., Dec. 9 [1985]—The heavyweight boxer Gerry Cooney was arrested this morning on a disorderly conduct charge that grew out of an incident at a hotel bar. Four companions of Cooney's were also arrested. One of them, Robert G. Wesnofske, 37 years old, of Huntington Station, L.I., was knocked unconscious and charged with aggravated assault on a police officer, a felony.
>
> Cooney later said he had come to Wesnofske's aid when the latter was being assaulted. The fighter, who had been training in nearby Lancaster, blamed a "misunderstanding" for the incident.
>
> Cooney and his party had been asked to leave a bar in a suburb in Harrisburg shortly before midnight when they became disorderly, according to Joe Sweeney, assistant to Harrisburg Mayor Stephen R. Reed. . . .

The day following the Harrisburg skirmish, with the story Big News across the country, a downcast Cooney spooned in his breakfast in grim silence. Afterward, he began pulling aside the waitresses and cashiers to rebut the press's account of events in Harrisburg.

"Don't believe that stuff you read," Cooney said.

He was, he told hotel personnel, a victim of circumstances. A terrible misunderstanding it was.

Pretty soon, the Harrisburg redress, like The Story, had the sound of a set piece. Victim of circumstances. A terrible misunderstanding. Dah-dah, dah-dah. "You know me. . . ."

A strange thing to watch Cooney go to the lengths he did to explain himself to people who ordinarily were not tendered such explanations. What did it say about Cooney? Sly was not sure at first. The answer seemed to be that any man who felt obliged to maintain the good opinion of people on the fringe of his life was either a sensitive soul or damn insecure. Perhaps a little of both.

The longer Sly was around Cooney the stronger was his impression that Cooney was in a perpetual conflict with Gerald Anthony Paul Cooney. Beyond the ambiguity he showed about having to fight for his living, there was the burden of hero quest. Being a hero, it seemed to Sly, should, like the weather, just happen. When sought as it was by Cooney, it was a form of egoism a little like declaring oneself an offshore deity.

Before he fought Holmes, the comics had given Cooney a "roast." ABC-TV had filmed the event, intending to use excerpts of it later. No footage of the roast ever made it to the screen, though. The night had not been quite what the network expected.

Cooney, quaffing vodka without apparent restraint, occasionally would lurch to the microphone and ask the gathered assemblage was everything okay. Then he would return to his seat and, as the comics performed, goose them from behind.

When he did it to a young black named Eddie Murphy, Murphy was not at a loss for what to say.

"Go 'head," Murphy told Cooney. "Do it again. Won't it look great for ABC to show Gerry Cooney grabbing Eddie Murphy's dick?"

By the end of the night, Cooney was unable to negotiate the walk to the microphone to say his parting words, and his brother, Mike, had to extend thanks on his behalf. *You know me. . . .*

The Cooney that Lee Jay Nelson knew would swig down

the vodka, bum cigarettes and then act as though he hadn't. Nelson, the entertainment director at Americana Host Farm Resort, spent more than a few evenings in Lancaster-area bars and restaurants with Cooney and his cronies. Then a few days would pass without Nelson's seeing Cooney. The next time the fighter surfaced he would say something like "You still drinking?" in a way that never failed to amuse Nelson. It was as though Cooney were a teetotaler, a Boy Scout, and possibly a saint when in fact he more nearly resembled an amnesiac.

It seemed positively in character. Here was a fighter with a left hook that could put a dent in a Mack truck. Yet so conflicted was he about his business that he existed in it now like banished royalty, a forlorn figure groping toward an uncertain future. That was, in its way, a sad and affecting image. But Sly could understand the impatience of the sporting press toward Cooney. For all the softly spoken explanations—given in that wispy nasalized voice of his—Cooney did not want to fight. Not really. Sit long enough with him and a man heard the whirring of a state-of-the-art self-denial mechanism.

The days went on. Cooney kept training. And explaining.

Finishing a workout one wintry afternoon, he told the small crowd:

"I'd like to thank everybody for coming. It's been a hard road. Lots of ups and downs. Back in 1982, I fought Larry Holmes and was so concerned about going the distance, I forgot to fight. I didn't put out to the limit. The better man didn't win. That's easy to say. But it's true. I . . ."

Whether or not Cooney got a chance to fight for the heavyweight title against Michael Spinks was now Butch Lewis's call.

If Lewis chose to take Spinks into the HBO unification series, Cooney would probably have to wait out the year or so it would take for the series to run its course.

While Lewis was negotiating into Spinks's deal with HBO a provision that would allow his man to fight Cooney during the series on a more lucrative closed-circuit/pay-per-view basis— millions more dollars could be made there than by fighting on HBO—there was a hitch. In return for giving Spinks and Cooney the chance to get rich while boxing off HBO's screen, the pay cable service demanded a written guarantee from Cooney that should he beat Spinks he would take the other

man's place for the rest of the series. It was a contractual assurance that HBO would exact from every fighter, champion or
challenger, who became part of the unification package. The
worst nightmare for HBO was to have a series that dead-ended,
for whatever reason, before a single undisputed heavyweight
champion was crowned.

But Cooney's comanager, Dennis Rappaport, had his own
ideas about Gentleman Gerry's value to a promotion, and he
felt that if he defeated Spinks, Cooney would be worth more
than HBO could afford. A white heavyweight champion, Rappaport figured, would be a closed-circuit attraction, capable of
making far more than the $2 million or $3 million that was big
money in HBO's top per-fight price for the series.

So while Don King was urging Lewis to sign a deal that,
even if Spinks were defeated by one or another contender,
would leave Butch copromoter with King of the entire HBO
series, Rappaport was pressing him to forget HBO and King
and strike it rich with a Spinks-Cooney match.

For his part, Lewis was working out details in both deals,
and reserving judgment on which one he would take. But on
January 9, 1986, as Lewis's attorney, Milt Chwasky, and his
business associate, Don Hubbard, met with Rappaport and
Rappaport's attorney, Neil Gerst, in Gerst's Garden City, Long
Island, office, ostensibly to finalize a Spinks-Cooney deal, Rappaport knew Lewis was seriously considering putting Spinks
into the HBO series and that this meeting might be nothing
more than a ploy by Lewis to drive up his price with HBO.

Dennis Rappaport had not become a millionaire realtor by
slipping up on the angles. Yet there were certain details that
made Rappaport think that Lewis just might be wary enough of
King to opt instead for the one-shot windfall of Spinks-Cooney.
For starters, Lewis had had Rappaport bring Cooney in from
Lancaster to New York so the fighter could be available to sign
whatever documents were necessary to the deal. Then as the
actual negotiations began, Rappaport sensed that Chwasky and
Hubbard were in earnest. Had they been there only to use him
to exact a better price for the heavyweight unification series, he
figured they would have made a token appearance and been
quickly gone. But as the hours ticked away and the temperature
in Gerst's building plummeted—the heat was turned off soon

after the 7:00 P.M. start of discussions—Rappaport thought Chwasky and Hubbard meant business.

It got to be 3:00, 4:00, 5:00 A.M. The various parties alternately stretched out on the floor of Gerst's office as they pushed the deal forward and, in their overcoats and gritting their teeth against the cold, checked the language of the various contractual stipulations that typists put to paper. By 5:30, the typists had gone home, and two hours later, the meeting was ended, with, it seemed, a deal ready for signing.

All that was left was for Rappaport to go to the Garden City branch office of Merrill Lynch and, tapping into his Cash Management Account, draw a Merrill Lynch check in the amount of $500,000—payable to Butch Lewis and nonrefundable if for any reason the fight was canceled because of Cooney.

Against that dark prospect, Rappaport had set into motion the process by which Lloyd's of London would protect him through an insurance policy. Between that insurance and the hefty check he handed to Chwasky and Hubbard later that day he could not help but feel he had attained his objective—another title shot for Cooney.

That was when he was told Lewis wanted his $500,000 in a certified check, and precisely then did Rappaport get the sinking feeling that he'd been had. For it was clear to him that Lewis's request was the sort of nitpicking done by a man who had no intention of concluding a deal.

"I was in a state of shock," Rappaport said. "If Butch Lewis had been in front of me, I'd have strangled him."

That weekend, Lewis left for Atlanta, where King was promoting the WBA title defense of Tubbs against Tim Witherspoon, a fight HBO was televising separate and apart from its envisioned series. On Monday, January 13, Bob Greenway, HBO's vice-president of sports programming and the man monitoring the progress of the King-Lewis talks, awoke in his Darien, Connecticut, home and found that while he was asleep King had left a message on the answering machine in his den.

King's recorded voice had that wee-hour fog on it, which for Greenway augured important developments. When they finally connected, King told him: "Butch and I were up to the middle of the night. I think we can get this done. I think you'd better get down here right away."

Greenway booked the first flight to Atlanta; by midweek

he, King, Lewis, and Lewis's father, the car dealer John L. (called "Boss"), quickly resolved the stickier points in the four-page deal memo that had been their reference text.

On Friday, January 17, Abraham flew to Atlanta and announced to the press that King and Lewis, as Dynamic Duo, Inc., would copromote a series of seven heavyweight bouts for whose live TV rights HBO would pay around $16 million, with a single undisputed heavyweight champion to be the end result.

In formalizing the arrangement, King, Lewis, and Greenway had initialed the amended deal memo, which would now be worked up into a long-form contract. Whether that paper would withstand the intrigues and politics that routinely unraveled boxing's best-laid plans remained to be seen.

That night Tubbs and Witherspoon fought a bout that was distinguished by its mediocrity and a scandal. The question became: would anyone care who won the heavyweight championship? Tubbs entered the ring looking like the Pillsbury Doughboy. A suety 244 pounds he was—or fifteen pounds more than when he won the WBA title—and with each step he took his pectorals shook like a cooch dancer's. Oh that the rest of Tubbs had been nearly as lively. Against Witherspoon, Tubbs fought with a fat man's reluctance, as if each aggressive move was a threat on his limited reserves. It made for dull sport—boxing that more nearly resembled a rugby scrum or the final hour of a marathon dance contest. The body of Tony Tubbs was the very expression of the lost passion among the heavyweights.

Witherspoon beat him, but barely. Two of the judges awarded the decision to him, the other called the fight a draw. A majority decision that was diminished almost immediately by the contents of the urine specimen that Witherspoon submitted after the fight. Laboratory analysis revealed traces of marijuana in Witherspoon's system, a violation of the rules and, had the WBA chosen to enforce its regulations strictly, grounds for overturning the decision.

Witherspoon would deny having taken a toke of the iniquitous *cannabis* and claim that as best as he could figure he had ingested the smoke while hanging around with pothead cronies of his.

Prodded by King, the WBA chose to be forgiving and ordered Witherspoon to give Tubbs a rematch.

Consider the plight of Seth Abraham. Having committed all those millions of HBO's good money to heavyweight boxing he could now contemplate a year of clowns like Tubbs and Witherspoon. Televising sluggards like these was hardly a programming coup. Abraham could be forgiven if it crossed his mind that now might be the opportune time to begin sending his résumé out.

But life, as it happens, does not unfold a straight or logical line, and at a far curve along the bumpy road Abraham seemed headed down came a new man, a fighter now stealing toward the heavyweight spotlight.

Just under six feet tall, he was all bunchy muscle—from a neck that measured more than nineteen inches around to the tree-trunk legs from which emanated the torque that gave his punches their authority. From certain angles he was so extreme a muscle mass that, with his slightly stooped shoulders and the arms hanging off to the sides, he evoked—indiscreet as it might be to say it—the primordial men who preceded the rest of us centuries upon centuries ago.

That was the visual impact of all that body density. To act otherwise was to pretend.

Of itself, of course, disproportionate muscularity was not the advantage it might seem to a layman. In fact, thickly muscled men often were more susceptible than most to fatigue. This fighter, though, had an aura about him. From the moment he entered the ring, with a deadpan expression that sometimes turned at its corners into a self-absorbed scowl, he was the very picture of a gladiator. He did not trouble with a robe; he appeared without fanfare, oiled and greased and ready to go, a stark hulk in black trunks and black high-top shoes with no socks. It was the throwback look of Jack Dempsey, the very image of a man with, in the phrase the fighter himself used, "bad intentions."

Ladies and gentlemen, say hello to Michael Gerard Tyson.

4

Sly saw Tyson for the first time on an undercard in Atlantic City, strictly by chance.

On October 25, 1985, just a few weeks on the job for the
Times, he went down to Atlantic City to cover a match between a
pair of featherweights, Calvin Grove and Dana Roston.

Tyson fought in one of the prelims against a rangy opponent named Robert Colay. With twenty pro fights (14-5-1, 8
knockouts), Colay had double the recorded experience Tyson
did, but it was of no help that night.

Thirty seconds into the first round, Colay threw a left hook
and missed. Moving forward, Tyson countered with a left of his
own. The punch was off target, but as Colay threw the left and
missed again, Tyson sprang up and slammed the business end
of his left hand flush on Colay's jaw.

Colay went down hard on the seat of his white satin trunks.
As the referee bent over the supine fighter, Colay brought both
gloves to the side of his head as if he had ringing in his ears. By
the count of five, Colay was rising up to a sitting position. His
face had the look of a man who had been brought out of sleep

with too little civility, an expression that Sly last had seen during his residence in army barracks.

Colay got to his feet before the count reached ten, but the referee waved his hands across one another—the international signal of a terminated fight—and ruled his erect position irrelevant. Colay was on shaky legs, and in no condition to continue.

With that knockout, Tyson had put together a professional record that looked like this:

1985

March 6	— Hector Mercedes, Albany, N.Y.	TKO 1
April 10	— Trent Singleton, Albany, N.Y.	TKO 1
May 23	— Don Halpin, Albany, N.Y.	KO 4
June 20	— Rick Spain, Atlantic City, N.J.	KO 1
July 11	— John Alderson, Atlantic City, N.J.	TKO 2
July 19	— Larry Sims, Poughkeepsie	KO 3
August 15	— Lorenzo Canady, Atlantic City, N.J.	TKO 1
September 5	— Mike Johnson, Atlantic City, N.J.	KO 1
October 9	— Donnie Long, Atlantic City, N.J.	KO 1
October 25	— Robert Colay, Atlantic City, N.J.	KO 1

Ten fights, ten knockouts. He was nineteen years old.

Early in a career, boxing records often represent managerial art more than a fighter's merit. Yet in putting his man down, Tyson had shown an efficiency and poise that a fighter of his limited experience did not usually have. It caught the attention of Sly, who knew that Tyson was being handled by Constantine (Cus) D'Amato, the septuagenarian boxing man. A few weeks later Sly drove up to Catskill, New York.

Tyson was living at the end of a dirt road in Catskill in a white fourteen-room Victorian house that sat on a bluff overlooking the Hudson River. A picture-postcard view it was. But on this cloudy yet mild November afternoon, Tyson was more interested in looking after his pigeons.

In a crewneck sweater and gray leather trousers, he stepped briskly across the front lawn to the raised coop he had built months earlier. He climbed up a ladder and stood on the platform outside the coop shooing the more than one hundred birds. In formation, the pigeons flew with a gentle whooshing sound broken only by the papery flapping of wings as one of the creatures broke ranks and headed back to homebase.

To make his birds climb higher, Tyson took a red flag on a long wooden pole and began waving it while he shouted, "Harrh, harrrh!" He stood there awhile watching the pigeons' circling flights before turning to say: "Doesn't that look beautiful?"

But a few minutes later, he began to fret as he spied a hawk loitering close by. "Drop down," he said to his birds. "Don't let this guy get you." As the last straggler slipped back to the coop, he relaxed. A bird was safe there. And in Tyson's awareness of this, there was a connection to his own situation. For like those birds, this ghetto kid who had made his way to Catskill five years and countless troubles before found, through D'Amato, that the place at the end of the dirt road was a safe home for him too.

Tyson's unusual odyssey began in Brooklyn's Bedford-Stuyvesant section, where the soft-spoken and timid boy was a target for neighborhood toughs who taunted him by calling him a "little fairy boy."

When Tyson was ten, his mother, Lorna, moved her three children to the Brownsville section of Brooklyn. Here young Tyson was marked as a soft touch, and was beaten and sometimes robbed of his pocket money. It was not until a bully tried to snatch one of the pigeons he was raising on the roof of his tenement building that Tyson fought back. For not only did the older boy grab the bird, he tore its head off. Enraged, Tyson threw himself at his tormentor, battering him into a hasty reassessment of the Brownsville pecking order. In fighting back, a new Tyson emerged.

He soon was hanging out with older boys, twelve to fourteen years of age, for whom crime was the daily curriculum. Against his mother's wishes, he would sneak out of the house and join up with his merry band in robbing people and places.

"The others would have the guns," said Tyson. "I'd go through the pockets, and would take the people's jewelry. That was the life. I didn't know better. I was getting things I liked. I was poor. And I didn't want to be poor. I'd rather have some money. It was exciting. A lot of fun. I liked doing that stuff."

The hard cash was converted to dress suits and top-of-the-line sweat clothes, $200 Pierre Cardin and Fila apparel that gave standing out on the streets.

He was twelve years old the first time he was caught while trying to pickpocket a man in the lobby of a movie house on 42nd Street in Manhattan. Tyson was sent to a juvenile lockup in the Bronx for the weekend. It did not deter him. By thirteen, Tyson had been arrested thirty-eight times, having made a specialty of mugging women whose packages he offered to carry from supermarkets to their apartment elevators. Tyson would later equate the pleasure of criminal victory with a sexual thrill.

His criminal activity eventually led to his doing time at other juvenile detention facilities including, by age thirteen, a stay at the Tryon School in Johnstown, New York. Bitter about being there, he rebelled, making enough trouble to be isolated in a cottage reserved for hard-core cases. At that low moment, he met a Tryon staff member, Bobby Stewart, who had been a professional boxer. Tyson expressed a desire to become a fighter. Stewart gave him his first hard lesson.

"I had a reputation for beating up other students," said Tyson, "and when we boxed each other he would humiliate me so the other kids would see I was nothing. He hit me in the body and I went down. My air stopped. I thought I was dead."

But Tyson fought back. "The next day," said Tyson, "I told him, 'I want to learn, I want to learn. Can we box?' He was surprised. He thought the humiliation would stop me. But every day: 'I want to box.' Bobby Stewart became my teacher. We boxed so much he began to like me. Like a father. Or a brother. He saw boxing was making me a better individual.

"I was becoming a more respectable person. I didn't have to be a bully. If somebody was an idiot, go ahead and be an idiot. I didn't have to punch him in the face. I had my mind made up I was going to change. I wasn't going to stay corruptive. There were some guys that'd been in there for years. I didn't want that with my life. I had ambitions to be somebody. I wanted respect. Power. I wanted to be independent. So I wouldn't have to depend on anyone. To have money was power. To walk around with a bulge in the pocket."

Some nights, after lights-out, Stewart would discover Tyson with the sweat pouring off him practicing the moves the older man had shown him earlier in the day. Tyson absorbed his ring lessons so well that eventually Stewart decided to introduce him to D'Amato, who ran a boxing program in a gym over the Catskill police station.

D'Amato had credentials. He had once trained and managed the heavyweight champion Floyd Patterson and the light heavyweight champion José Torres.

With those and other fighters of his, the Bronx-born D'Amato wanted more out of a relationship than the few business hours most managers shared with their pugs in the gym. D'Amato's impulse was to build a fighter from the inside out, which meant imparting to him a sense of the world beyond boxing, the world according to Cus.

For example:

"I believe nature's a lot smarter than anybody thinks. During the course of a man's life he develops a lot of pleasures and people he cares about. Then nature takes them away one by one. It's her way of preparing you for death."

"There are no stupid people. There are only uninterested people."

"People who are born round don't die square."

"Fear is like a fire. If you control it, as we do when we heat our houses, it is a friend. When you don't, it consumes you and everything you do and everything around you."

"People, especially if they come up in a rough area, have to go through a number of experiences in life that are intimidating and embarrassing. These experiences form layer upon layer over their capabilities and talents. So your job as a teacher is to peel off these layers."

D'Amato had his share of detractors, who saw the philosopher stance he took as phony baloney, a pose that was calculated to create a Cus who stood larger than by strict merits he deserved. Yet of those who heard him out, many swore by him as an exemplar of common sense and compassion, a man to whom they felt an allegiance that brooked no criticism from others.

What the adherents and critics could agree on was that, like him or not, D'Amato was a man who was single-minded.

From a press release in June 1959, prior to the Patterson-Ingemar Johansson heavyweight title bout:

D'Amato, a stocky man in his late forties, who wears his prematurely white hair in a crewcut, has dedicated his lifetime to boxing.

He recalls having had only one other job, that for but a few days when he was in his teens.

Cus boxed a bit as a boy but had to give it up because of an injury.

For the past twenty years, except for a World War II stint as an MP, he has taught boxing at a little gymnasium in downtown Manhattan.

So thoroughly is boxing his life that he never married and for a long time lived in a small room connected to the gym. . . .

In that "little gymnasium," the Gramercy Gymnasium, at 116 East 14th Street, D'Amato slept in a cot in the back with a police dog for a companion. It was the picture of a man who had his own idiosyncratic way of seeing and doing things. Newsmen reported that he feared snipers, and had never married because he believed a wife might be duped by his enemies into doing him in.

Unlike most boxing men, D'Amato was not ruled by money. José Torres says he made "close to one million dollars" during his career, and D'Amato (who never had a contract with the fighter) "took zero." "He told me," said Torres, "I don't want to take any money from you. I make enough from managing Floyd [Patterson]. What am I gonna take it from you for? I'd only have to give it to the IRS. I'd rather you have it."

Although he admired his manager for his principles, in time Torres became desperate for his chance at a title fight, a chance that D'Amato's constant battle with the boxing establishment impeded.

One day in the early 1960s, Torres drove to Boston and knocked at the door of Paul Pender, who was then world middleweight champion. Torres asked Pender if he would fight him for the title for a purse of $75,000. Pender said he would.

D'Amato had intended to give Pender the $75,000 from his managerial share of the purse from a 1960 Patterson fight. But when that money was frozen by the IRS, Torres was out of luck—the shot at Pender fell through.

Years later, a Brooklyn real estate developer, Cain Young, offered to put up $100,000 as a guarantee to Willie Pastrano, then the light heavyweight champion, if he would agree to defend his title against Torres. But as a condition Young insisted that Torres get a release from D'Amato so Cain Young could be Torres's manager of record. Torres refused, out of loyalty to D'Amato, then called his friend Norman Mailer, the writer, to tell him what had happened. Mailer offered to put up $40,000 to $60,000 of his own to lure Pastrano into the ring.

"When Cus heard about it," said Torres, "he said, 'No, I'll give you a release. You can't allow a friend to put up money.'"

Young got the release from D'Amato and Torres got his shot at Pastrano. On March 30, 1965, he stopped Pastrano in nine rounds to win the title.

By then D'Amato was engaged in a dispute with the Internal Revenue Service about a tax debt of more than $250,000. D'Amato, a forceful and opinionated man, would not accept the IRS view of the situation. But rather than take on the agency in lengthy court proceedings, he decided to exist as a revenue cipher, denying the IRS the cash pool from which to draw. On leaving his West 57th Street apartment in Manhattan, he moved to upstate New York in the 1970s and ceased making money.

Even after he settled into the big white Victorian house in Catskill, owned by a congenial woman named Camille Ewald, he continued to claim no income. But through his Catskill Boxing Club, he remained active in the fight game; the expenses for his program were absorbed by a pair of New York businessmen, James Jacobs and William D'Arcy Cayton.

Jacobs's connection with D'Amato went way back.

In 1960, Jacobs was a twenty-nine-year-old sales manager for a business machine and supplies company that he would in later years say was owned by his father in Los Angeles. He was also an avid collector of fight films. In June 1960, Jacobs was invited to show films that he owned of fighters like Sam Langford, Joe Gans, and Jim Corbett to boxing writers in New York. "I showed the films," said Jacobs, "and Cus was there. Cus adored looking at old fight films, and I had five thousand fight films ranging from 1894 to 1953. It was a hobby. I'd started collecting them at twelve years of age."

Their mutual interest in boxing led them to share quarters for ten years in D'Amato's New York apartment. Many nights, said Jacobs, were spent watching fight films. Once D'Amato moved on to Catskill, Jacobs and Cayton (who became partners in a company that commercially exploited a large collection of boxing films) assisted him. "We helped pay bills for twenty years on the fight camp there," said Jacobs.

The countrified Catskill setting did not change D'Amato. He remained a man of contradictions. While some thought him suspicious to the point of paranoia, others knew him as a thoughtful man, a reader of Thoreau, a fisherman and the owner of a large telescope through which he regularly gazed at the stars in the skies over Catskill.

But even in Ewald's home he remained secretive and watchful.

A young trainer who worked under D'Amato, Teddy Atlas, recalled: "Cus didn't let you see into his room. He'd put a match on the door so that if someone opened the door, he knew someone had been in the room. Without making him sound too crazy he was very secretive about his room, and personal about it.

"Once in a while a visiting fighter, he'd get a little wise with Cus, and say, 'What you got in the room? I can go in there and you wouldn't know it.' And Cus: 'I'd know it.' 'What you have in the room?' 'Don't worry what I got there. I have a gun.' And he did. He had rifles over his bed, and he didn't hunt. They were there for pretty clear reasons. If there was a problem, he had a gun."

At bottom, D'Amato was a flinty individualist. When a film-maker named Michael Marton approached him in 1982 about shooting a documentary on D'Amato's boxing club, the first question D'Amato asked was did Marton work for an organization. Marton assured him he was self-employed. D'Amato said, "Okay, then. You've got my permission."

As D'Amato explained to Marton, he had the maverick's faith that one good man working alone could get better results than the poor slob who was beholden to a multitiered organization.

In Catskill D'Amato became a kind of boxing Father Flanagan, welcoming the outcasts from the neighborhood, and sometimes from beyond. At any one time there were usually a select few who were invited to stay in the Ewald house. Most of the lodgers were amateurs, and before Tyson, only Kevin

Rooney would go on to fight professionally for D'Amato, while being managed Cayton and Jacobs.

Rooney was a street-tough kid from Staten Island who had won a New York Golden Gloves title in the 147-pound novice class and then decided to go to Catskill.

Despite the title and by his account, Rooney was inexperienced in the ring and a chronic troublemaker out of it. "Just hanging out," said Rooney, "drinking beers and stuff like that. It was a bad neighborhood—a lot of drugs around and trouble was easy to find. We'd get into fights—fight with other neighborhoods. We thought we were tough. They thought they were tough. We'd have a fight and get arrested."

Under D'Amato, Rooney would change. In the gym on Catskill's Main Street, he learned to box. To cover his living expenses, he worked as a recreation leader in a juvenile facility in Brooklyn. Gradually, he took on a new outlook. "I went to the other extreme," said Rooney. "I became disciplined. I took care of my body." Encouraged by D'Amato, he pursued and finally obtained a two-year associate degree at a community college in Hudson, New York.

"Cus tricked me to go to college," said Rooney. "In Catskill, there wasn't a lot of action. Cus said to kill the boredom and as a chance to meet people I should go to college. So I did it. I did whatever Cus said. It turned out to be the high school I never had."

Mike Tyson was only thirteen years old when Stewart brought him to the Catskill gym on a day release from Tryon. With D'Amato and Rooney watching, Stewart boxed with and even bloodied the thirteen-year-old. But Tyson got his licks in, and his brute power made an impression.

"When I looked at this kid," Rooney recalled, "I didn't believe he was thirteen. He looked older—maybe nineteen, twenty. I wondered if he was lying about his age, so he wouldn't have to go away to jail. I asked Bobby Stewart about it. He said no, he'd checked it. Anyway, they boxed and Mike Tyson was a good aggressive fighter. I remember afterward Bobby Stewart saying: 'I've got to really hit him. The kid is so strong.'"

D'Amato liked what he saw. So in the months that followed, on Fridays Tyson would be let out of Tryon for a day trip to the

Catskill gym. There he would work with D'Amato or Teddy Atlas, while other inmates sat on the sidelines and watched.

"It was the only way that Mike was allowed out of the institution," said Atlas. "Bobby Stewart, because of the rules, would have to take other inmates along. They would sit as I'd work with Mike for an hour or so. On the rudiments. Slipping punches. Punching with proper shortness and form."

From early on, D'Amato prophesied a grand future for Tyson. "Mike had been working with Cus for just a few months," Jacobs recalled, "when Cus, who was supercareful in giving a compliment, told me over dinner in New York one night, in the same tone you might order a cup of coffee, 'Mike Tyson is going to be the heavyweight champion of the world.'

"And I looked at him. Because this is not something Cus would routinely say. Cus was not one for small talk. He never told jokes. In all the years I knew him, Cus's conversation was strictly meat and potatoes.

"I looked at him and I said, 'Cus, how can you say such a thing?' And he said, very seriously, 'I've never seen a kid who hits this hard. I've never seen a kid with this aptitude. He has extraordinary intelligence and he desperately wants to learn.'"

Soon he had a place where he could learn. After spending two weeks living in the Ewald house as a sort of test run, on September 2, 1980, Tyson, now fourteen years old, was paroled to D'Amato and moved back into the Catskill house.

As he put it, "My life begins here."

It was life that took getting used to. Tyson was not communicative at first. He was wary of D'Amato and others. When he spoke to people he would stare at the ground, refusing eye contact. And he was keenly aware of being an outsider in Catskill's small-town setting. One evening, when he and another amateur boxer walked into an ice-cream parlor for a one-dollar cone, Tyson tipped the store owner two dollars.

"Why'd you tip so much?" the other youth asked.

"Cause I could see he was afraid of me," said Tyson. "So I wanted him to know I'm a good guy."

Though he may have felt ill at ease on the streets of Catskill, he was right at home in the Main Street gym. D'Amato's emphasis was on defense. He wanted his fighters, even a puncher like Tyson, to be elusive. "So it was hours of boxing with little and fast fighters, without being allowed to hit them back and trying to make them miss," Tyson recalled. "And if a hundred-forty-pounder jumps up and punches you in the face, it's not going to tickle."

D'Amato soon had Tyson fighting on nonsanctioned fight cards known as "smokers" in venues where the crowds, wagering on the bouts, would scream epithets at the boxers and sometimes settle their differences with knives and other persuasive instruments.

In such settings, Tyson had to learn to deal with wild-swinging and often much older opponents—as well as with his own fear. In his first trip to a Bronx smoker, he excused himself to get a pack of gum. Standing alone in the street, in the shadows of elevated subway tracks, he almost bolted. "I thought to myself, 'What the hell am I doing here? These guys'll kill you.'"

The boxing club was located on Westchester Avenue, and when trains rumbled by on those elevated tracks, the building shook. Very often, though, it did not take an uptown local to create a commotion.

"There was a little bar there," recalled Atlas, "and they charged three bucks at the door to get in. The Latins bet heavy. The neighborhood would come out. A couple hundred people in there. Betting side bets. A very exciting atmosphere. In his first fight, Mike went against a Spanish kid who was seventeen years old. In the third round Mike hit him with a tremendous shot. The other guy dropped to the bottom rope and sat there like Ken Norton when he fought Gerry Cooney. The opponent was helpless. Mike hit him with another shot and put him out on the ring apron and launched his mouthpiece six rows back into the stands and off the wall. Why I remember that is one of the drivers—we took two cars down from Catskill—he was sitting back there. He told me after: 'My God, the people around me looked like you had unveiled some kind of new weapon.'

"The fight was obviously over. Tyson was standing over the guy. And what was happening was that people had lost money because of the ending, which they perceived as a foul. Because Mike had hit this other guy while he was on the lower strand of rope, the people thought Tyson should be disqualified. Well, the fella who ran the show, Nelson Cuevas, saw the situation and jumped into the ring. 'This fight is a draw!' he announced. Even as the other guy was still laying on the canvas. Unconscious. Cuevas called the bout a draw, it meant all bets were off, the money went back into everybody's pockets. Peace and calm were ensured. As for Mike Tyson, the legend was begun."

Tyson kept fighting in smokers (and, eventually, more genteel amateur competitions), with his progress closely monitored by D'Amato, who tutored him in the mental phase of the sport as well, even addressing the fear that Tyson confessed he had experienced. "Heroes and cowards feel exactly the same fear," D'Amato would say. "Heroes just react to it differently."

"People," said Tyson, "think that when you're afraid, you're a coward. I'd tell Cus, 'Cus, I was so scared.' 'It's natural,' he'd say. 'That's how come you're so good. When you're afraid, you're faster, you punch harder. It's just an aspect of what you do.'"

While words can prime the mind, in the end they are only words. The fighter either comes to terms with his fears or he finds other gainful employment. At fourteen Tyson had the body of a man. When he would leave Catskill to box against peers, Atlas had to bring the fighter's birth certificate to assure rival trainers of Tyson's age. More and more, as his reputation spread, Tyson was obliged to fight older men in what he called "these bootleg fights."

Atlas describes one of these early fights. "In Scranton," said Atlas, "on a night Rooney was fighting as a pro, Tyson wound up on the undercard as an amateur. The opponent that night couldn't fight much, but he was a big strong kid. Tyson knocked him down three times the first round, and the fight should have been stopped. But it wasn't. And the kid kept getting up. In Tyson's mind it became a tough fight. He came back to the corner before the second round, and told me his hand was broke. My instinct was that it wasn't. I squeezed his hand to satisfy myself. He never reacted. I had a minute to talk to him. Told him: 'What's broken is your spirit. You'll never be a success if you don't go in there and overcome yourself. You're giving yourself a hard time. Don't let your feelings control you. Get out there and be a man and fight.'

"It sounds crude, but it wasn't. The same thing happened between the second and third rounds—he said he was fatigued. By the third round, he was lunging. They were like two novice heavyweights. At one point, the other guy hit him on the shoulder. Tyson looked at me like he was thinking of going down. I took a chance. I could have been disqualified. But I got up on the ring apron and said: 'Look, you so-and-so. I know what you're doin'. You fight him!' Well, he didn't fall apart. He didn't go down. He floundered but he stuck in there and won. Afterward he said to me, 'Thanks.' Nothing else. When it was all over and we had the solace of the locker room—I didn't want to demean him—all I said—I couldn't let it pass—was: 'The way you felt out there is not important. What's important is what you did. You didn't give in to the feeling. You thought about it, but you didn't. You faced fear, you faced yourself, and you triumphed.' It never happened again. He grew up that night."

D'Amato did not neglect life beyond the ring, trying to educate Tyson to a world far removed from that of Brownsville and juvenile correction facilities. Matters taken for granted elsewhere—like, say, table manners—were not in Catskill. Shortly after arriving there, Tyson joined several others of D'Amato's amateur boxers as they celebrated the sixteenth birthday of one of their own, John Chetti. Chetti's mother took the group to a Chinese restaurant and ordered for the youths. When the waiter brought out a tray of spare ribs, Tyson asked for a knife to cut them. Told that spare ribs were regarded as finger food, he replied: "No no. Camille said never to eat anything with your hands."

While Tyson was shown the right way to do things, he sometimes proved resistant. "At first," said Camille Ewald, "Mike was very rebellious, very angry. He wouldn't listen. But Cus spent hours and hours explaining everything. When he had to, Cus was the boss. He would scold him. Then Mike would come to me for sympathy."

In the beginning, said Tyson, "if I got upset, I'd get nasty. Cus would take me aside to warn me. If I did it again, he'd warn me out in the open—put me in my place. 'I warned you about that already. You're not back in Brooklyn with those tomato cans and bums.' I wouldn't say nothing."

Torres recalled: "One time very early on, Mike acted up and Cus told him: 'You think you're tough? Let's go outside. I'll knock your fucking brains out.' I saw and heard this. Mike didn't go outside."

In time, Tyson came to regard the house in Catskill as home, and became deeply committed to fulfilling D'Amato's vision of him as the youngest-ever heavyweight champion. In his room up on the third floor, he would watch old fight footage from the Cayton-Jacobs collection of more than seventeen thousand boxing films and he would read incessantly about the sport.

"I read all the books," said Tyson. "This is how boxing became important to me. I loved reading about the old fighters."

Boxing boxing boxing: sometimes there were two workouts a day, and when he got home, D'Amato might ask him to demonstrate the moves he had worked on in the gym. Then there would be the endless talk about the mental side of the sport.

"There is no such thing as a natural puncher," D'Amato would say. "There is a natural aptitude for punching, and that is different. Nobody is born the best. You have to practice and train to become the best."

Or: "When a fighter no longer wants to fight, he finds a convenient corner to lie down in. It's all psychological."

Or: "No matter what anyone says, no matter what the excuse or explanation, whatever a person does in the end is what he intended to do all along."

Then back to the gym Tyson would go. There, Atlas, who had trained under D'Amato until an injury had forced him to quit fighting, guided Tyson through his workouts while D'Amato watched, or waited at home for a progress report.

Whatever Atlas did with Tyson, it was by D'Amato's methods. For instance, when D'Amato had been with José Torres, he had developed a punching instrument known as the Willie Bag, after Willie Pastrano, from whom Torres would win the light heavyweight title. Willie was made of five mattresses wrapped about a frame. On the exterior of the front mattress was a rough-hewn sketch of a man, with his body demarcated by numbers that served as targets for particular punches. #1 was a left hook to the jaw; #2 a right hook to the jaw; #3 a left uppercut; #4 a right uppercut; #5 a left hook to the body; #6 a right hook to the body; #7 a jab to the head; and #8 a jab to the body.

D'Amato had created Willie to encourage his fighters to punch in rapid combination and had made tape recordings, in his voice, of varying sequences of numbers. When the fighter stepped up to Willie, he would respond to his master's voice by delivering the mandated combination punches.

For Tyson, there was also the sand-filled "slip" bag, a tear-drop-shaped black bag about the size of a fist that would swing from a length of rope as the fighter stood directly in its path. To avoid being hit, Tyson was taught to move his head from side to side and dip down, the prescriptive maneuvers for avoiding actual punches. Through his work on Willie and the slip bag, and through sparring, Tyson was acquiring the means to activate his power without its backfiring on him.

Through their talks D'Amato tried to impart to Tyson a larger vision—of success far beyond Catskill. "Cus would tell me," recalled Tyson, "'You know every punch in the book. The only reason you're not champion is you don't have the confidence and experience. With enough experience, you can do anything. Success breeds confidence and confidence breeds success.'"

Tyson first experienced success on a national level when at age fourteen he won as a heavyweight in the U.S. Junior Olympics in Colorado Springs, Colorado, in June 1981. Three fights, three first-round knockouts. "He loved the attention, the response he got from achieving something worthwhile," said Atlas. "He was proud. He wanted to be liked. And boxing gave him that."

Imagine, though, the mind of a fourteen-year-old who has gone virtually overnight from the harsh realities of juvenile lockup to the familial setting in Catskill and a touch of success in the world beyond. It did not take keen insight for Tyson to recognize how fragile was the line between the loneliness and deprivation of Tryon and what he had now. The differences were too stark not to inspire flickers of doubt and fear that for an abruptly wrong turn the whole shebang could go up in smoke, leaving him in a world cold to that burning desire of his to be connected, respected, loved.

At fifteen, when he returned to Colorado Springs to defend his Junior Olympics title in June 1982, that emotion was close to the surface. Through Michael Marton's documentary on D'Amato's boxing program, film footage exists of what Tyson, less than two years out of Tryon, was like then. Marton had begun shooting at a time when Tyson was but one of many young fighters reaching for success. Yet during the course of filming, as Tyson's star ascended, Marton was there to observe him under pressure.

For instance, before his semifinal bout in Colorado Springs in '82, Tyson was seen pacing up and back saying, "Not going to take my title. No way."

A few frames later, Tyson rushed out to center ring and hit his opponent flush on the chin, dropping him where he stood. Minutes later Atlas was on the phone to D'Amato with the results:

"Hey, Cus. Eight-second knockout first round . . . eight-second knockout. Yeah . . . the right hand . . . yeah, he did. And he set a new record. The official came over, told him, said, 'You just set a record . . . fastest knockout ever. . . .'"

It was a striking scene, but what the camera recorded just before Tyson went out to fight for his second Junior Olympics title the next day was far more revealing. On a street near the arena where the fight was to take place, Tyson, in a blue robe with a gold belt, began to pace back and forth. "Just relax, Michael," Atlas said, sensing Tyson's nervousness. "Just relax."

As the trainer put his arm around the fighter's shoulder, Tyson began to cry. On the soundtrack, amid his snuffling, only snatches of Tyson's conversation were audible. "When we first started . . . come a long way, remember? . . . Everybody likes me . . . I'm proud of myself. . . ."

It was, as it turned out, but one of several crying jags Tyson had had while awaiting his title fight, and the only such moment that made it into the film. "What he was saying to me," Atlas recalled, "was that he had come a long way. 'People like me. I've done good. And people like to know me.' He was afraid of losing all that and he felt that if the guy beat him, he *would* lose that."

Inside the arena, Tyson went to work. With practically his first barrage of punches, a white towel, sign of surrender, flew from the other man's corner. As the referee signaled the end of the fight—KO 1—Tyson raced back to his corner, jumped into the air, and pumped his gloved fist into the air. Still delirious with joy, he dropped to the canvas and rolled along it, the way children do in piles of autumn leaves.

For most fighters, boxing starts out as a means to establish self-worth. In Tyson the impulse was more acute. Nor did it appear to have slackened when, three years later, Sly saw the fighter flatten poor Robert Colay. That night, and on nights to follow, Tyson would offer the one element that heavyweight boxing had lacked for too long: passion.

In the ring, he fought with forward-march aggression. He was a bobbing, weaving torpedo with an urgency about him that was impossible to miss. Much as the style had evolved from the fighter's physical structure, and D'Amato's measured calculations about bringing out the considerable talent—making it flash like a jewel lifted from the mother stone—what caught a viewer's eye was not technique so much as attitude: the fervor of the crouched figure who sprang at opponents like the great cats of a *National Geographic* TV special.

The casual observer could easily miss what an insider saw—that there was art in the brawler's aggression of Tyson, that with his head constantly moving from side to side and with the quickness of his feet, he was an elusive target in spite of his seemingly reckless rushes forward.

But in the whir of the typical Tyson bout such fine points were lost to the visceral spectacle a fight of his became. The Tyson who now was a wage-earning professional lit up fight arenas by the sheer abandon with which he offered himself to the fray. That full-tilt aggression of Tyson's was a heavyweight attitude change fast becoming a commodity. As Sly would write that December:

> He is nineteen years old and is yet to be ranked by the governing bodies of the sport. Most of his opponents are men who will never advance beyond the agate print of their defeats. And not until his next bout Friday [December 6, 1985] against Sam Scaff in Madison Square Garden's Felt Forum will he fight a ten-round match. Despite all that, the three major television networks are already after Tyson to make his network debut in February for them.
>
> The reason is simple: Tyson punches so hard that opponents take the kind of half gainers to the canvas that leave a usually rational observer with only a comic-book vocabulary of wow-geez-&-ohmygod. Nine of thirteen opponents developed arrested consciousness before the first round was over, and one of them, Sterling Benjamin, stated afterward: "He have a sledgehammer," which he meant apparently in a figurative sense.

Three days after Tyson knocked out Benjamin, on November 4, D'Amato died of pneumonia at age seventy-seven. "Coming back from Cus's funeral," said Camille Ewald, "Mike broke down and cried. He said: 'Camille, I never knew what love was until now. He taught me so much.' It was the first time I ever saw him cry."

Less than two weeks after D'Amato's death, Tyson fought in Houston, taking with him a photo of D'Amato and himself. "And he told me," said Ewald, "'A lot of people would think I'm crazy. But I talked to Cus. I talked to him every night.'"

5

H BO's unification series opened in March in Las Vegas with a fight that offered not only twelve rounds of spectator sport but an object lesson as well. The lesson was to pay attention to business.

Pinklon Thomas learned the lesson at the cost of his WBC heavyweight title, which by the end of the night was the possession of the challenger, Trevor Berbick.

Going into the bout, Thomas had been regarded as the best of the reigning heavyweight champions—Witherspoon (WBA), Spinks (IBF), and him. He figured to easily beat Berbick, a sturdy but awkward fighter. But the Pink Man, as he was known, succumbed to the malaise so many recent heavyweight titleholders before him had. He showed no spark.

What happened?

Well, there was no empiric science of analyzing the mind of a fighter. But in the days before the fight Thomas provided a pretty fair clue that he might not be taking Berbick all that seriously. In the lobby of the Riviera Hotel and Casino, he spent hours selling audio tapes of himself crooning an easy-listening ballad written for him, called "Hanging on to Promises."

This was, as an HBO profile would suggest, but a facet of some multidimensional Thomas, who not only handled silky lyrics but, as his own manager, had branched out to where he was managing the careers of other fighters as well.

The problem with Pinklon Thomas the manager, it became clear, was he had not been supple enough to kick some good sense into Pinklon Thomas the boxer. That would have helped with a man who had not troubled himself to get in shape, under the illusion, perhaps, that he could con his way against Berbick.

Berbick was deceptive. He lacked the textbook fluidity, yet he had a strong blockish body and a survivor's wits: with a minimum of art, he forced the other man to work, and if he found weakness there, he was opportunistic enough to keep the pressure on.

In the end it was quite simple. Thomas, like a slowly deflating beachball, ran down, as Berbick hammered him with short choppy blows, bereft of elegance but insistent enough to put a look of sheepish forbearance on the Pink Man's face.

Probably there was a song there. Somewhere.

By the time Trevor Berbick took Thomas's title, Mike Tyson had become, in the street lingo of Don King, "SKD— some kind of different."

Since pulverizing Robert Colay in October, Tyson had been fighting more regularly than church bingo.

November 1	— Sterling Benjamin, Latham, N.Y.	TKO 1
November 13	— Eddie Richardson, Houston, Tex.	KO 1
November 22	— Conroy Nelson, Latham, N.Y.	TKO 2
December 6	— Sammy Scaff, New York, N.Y.	TKO 1
December 27	— Mark Young, Latham, N.Y.	TKO 1

1986

January 11	— David Jaco, Albany, N.Y.	TKO 1
January 24	— Mike Jameson, Atlantic City, N.J.	TKO 5
February 16	— Jesse Ferguson, Troy, N.Y.	TKO 6
March 10	— Steve Zouski, E. Rutherford, N.J.	KO 3

In all, nineteen fights, nineteen knockouts.

By now, a good portion of continental America was becoming aware of the Tyson story; with the Ferguson fight Tyson had made his network TV debut—the first bout of a five-bout deal with ABC worth about $1 million. There had been a story on him in *Sports Illustrated,* an early-morning appearance on December 10, 1985, on the *Today* show. In the offices of The Big Fights, Inc., on East 40th Street, where Cayton and Jacobs ran their film business, calls for Tyson interviews and appearances were piling up.

Among the earliest callers was HBO's Abraham. If Tyson continued cutting a swath through the heavyweight division, there would come a time when HBO subscribers—not to mention the sporting press—would look at the unification series and see it as the marketing coup it was for Don King and his menagerie of heavyweight retreads. But if, like a *deus ex machina,* this destroyer, Tyson, were suddenly to *materialize* in the series, the dramatic possibilities were enhanced, as was the market value of HBO boxing.

The problem was timing. It was too early in his career for Tyson to make the jump up to the caliber of competition that was in the unification series. Abraham was obliged to shift to Plan B: sign Tyson to a deal separate and apart from the unification package, a transitional step, perhaps, toward easing him later into the series.

The talks between HBO and Cayton and Jacobs began around January. Tyson's managers were asking for a three-fight deal at $450,000 per bout. HBO wanted to pay less. Meantime Tyson was practically a movie montage of a busy fighter—one fight after the other, and with each bout he was adding value to his name. For HBO, it was like negotiating with a moving train. On March 12, the pay cable service surrendered: Tyson signed a three-fight deal for $1.35 million—or $450,000 per bout.

Meanwhile another heavyweight provocateur, out there on the flanks, made his move too. Gerry Cooney signed to fight Eddie Gregg that May in San Francisco. For Cooney, it would be his first fight since December 1984. Between Tyson and Cooney, the division threatened to cease being a public nuisance.

6

For several weeks, during a long-ago summer, the teen-aged Sly and his friend Gutman had talked of trying out two pairs of boxing gloves that had found their way into Gutman's possession. On this day, they slipped into the thickly padded mitts and stepped down from Gutman's flagstone patio onto a grassy back lawn that sloped gently to a river below.

There, in nervous anticipation, they stretched, flexed, and threw practice punches before they turned and moved toward each other. Raising their hands, they took up fighting stances. Then, in the instant before they let the punches go, they glanced into one another's eyes. When they did, a strange thing happened. They laughed.

Not a snickering what-the-hell sort of laugh, followed by roundhouse punches, but rather a more convulsive outburst that prompted them to drop their clenched hands and disengage, and left them pacing about, trying to figure what to do about this notion of punching each other. At that moment of eye contact the idea dematerialized. But they eventually tried again. Moving to close quarters, they began to bounce soft punches off each other's arms and shoulders, steadily increasing the intensity of the blows until the discomfort touched aggression's nerves and put them, like the werewolf at the moonlit hour, in a darker region.

There was nothing extraordinary about what followed. They went at each other in earnest, huffing and puffing through five to ten minutes of boxing, their fatigue more a factor of inexperience and lack of ring savvy than of their actual physical condition. In other words, it took a helluva lot of work to be a horseshit boxer.

Sly learned another revealing truth: a punch for punch's sake was not the same as the usual schoolboy's games. In that moment in which best friends caught each other's eye, there was a recognition of the difference. Laughter had been the expression of that—an involuntary response to the ambiguity they felt about what they were about to do. A punch was rawer than a straight-arm, or a cross-check. A punch was personal, and its consequences were a dimension beyond that of other sports.

It was not just a matter of pain—there was more to it than that. Being struck a blow was an insult to a man's dignity, and later, as a ringside regular, Sly would find the effect easier to apprehend. Up close, that look of sheepish dismay that a fighter got when he was hit with startling abruptness and force registered, and more vividly, certainly, than it did for the patron in the cheap seats or even the viewer at home in front of his TV screen. Television obscured some of boxing's three-dimensional spectacle—it reduced its emotional content.

There were moments in other sports—an airball, a dropped forward pass, the ground ball through the legs—when the athlete was mortified, but in boxing the consequences of a mistake were more insistent. A fighter had to stay and defend his bad choices, while in team sports a player had others on the field who could take up the slack for him.

So when two pros boxed, they worked closer to the hard edge than other athletes did. It was the recognition of that that made fight fans of some people even as it appalled others. Boxing was less the jerry-built diversion of team sports than a ritualized version of life's perpetual conflict. And as in all conflicts, there were winners and losers, and sometimes there were even sore losers.

*   *   *

On April 19, 1986, moments after he lost his rematch to Michael Spinks on what would be a disputed split decision, Larry Holmes stared straight at the TV camera and told the world:

"The judges, referees, and promoters can kiss me where the sun don't shine—and because we're on HBO, that's my big black behind."

As exit lines go, Larry Holmes's was a beaut. Right up there with not having Richard Nixon to kick around anymore. By later that night, in his suite on the twenty-seventh floor of the Las Vegas Hilton, Holmes had calmed a bit. In announcing his retirement from boxing, he said, "I'd like to go out clean. Not with negative feelings."

He sounded like the child who, having slain his parents, threw himself on the mercy of the court because he was an orphan.

Spinks-Holmes was the second bout of the HBO heavyweight unification series, and in its way the little fuss about the decision was good for the pay cable service, creating a controversy in the press that lasted for days and gave the fight an importance that the series itself did not yet have. For with a trio of champions that included a pothead (Witherspoon), a plodder (Berbick), and an overblown light heavyweight (Spinks), what was there to compel public interest? What did HBO have to offer?

A: About as much punch as diluted Kool-Aid.

Yet of the three men calling themselves champion, one of them intrigued Sly. Michael Spinks did not fit the popular notion of the heavyweight champion as a man who brimmed with confidence—either the measured assurance of a quiet destroyer like Joe Louis or the brasher airs of Muhammad Ali. Compared to Ali, who easily pronounced himself "the greatest of allll tiiime," Spinks was a virtual quiche-eater of a champion. Real heavyweight men conveyed an invincibility. Not Spinks. With him, an opponent, any opponent, was a calamity waiting to land on him. At least that's what he projected before his bouts.

But Spinks was deceptive. He had a chameleon knack for changing his colors to blend into hostile surroundings. He had needed that guile against Holmes in the rematch. For the Holmes who had been so lethargic in September this time was grimly determined. Moments before the opening bell, Holmes faced the ringside section where his wife, Diane, sat and shouted: "I kick his ass. I kick his ass." Then, at the opening bell, Holmes rushed out, grabbed Spinks, and threw him to the canvas, hollering as Spinks fell backward, "Come on, get up."

Holmes, it was clear, was working from emotion. But Spinks would not be drawn into that mindset. As the referee, Mills Lane, warned Holmes to cut the rough stuff, Spinks climbed off the canvas and, his expression utterly calm, told Lane: "That's okay, ref. That's okay."

As Sly would write the day after the fight:

> With his hands held high at the sides of his head and utilizing feints and upper-body mobility, Spinks ducked and dodged and ultimately absorbed the adrenal fury of Holmes's opening attack. Though Spinks's backpedaling was so pronounced that the crowd of 8,328 at the Hilton Center booed the champion in round three, and though he lost the first four rounds, Spinks stayed with his strategy. He waited for Holmes's early charge to play out.
>
> From the fifth round on, tentatively at first, the 29-year-old Spinks began to mix it up with Holmes, who was now fighting at merely mortal pace. On the cards of the judges, Jerry Roth and Frank Brunette, both of whom awarded Spinks the victory, the champion won rounds eight through thirteen. The other judge, Joe Cortez, who voted for Holmes, gave Spinks five of those six rounds.

Spinks would now move onward in the unification series, while Holmes headed back to Pennsylvania to tend to his various business holdings. The wheel turned on results.

Tyson's numbers were 19 and 0.

They signified results-plus. The plus was the aura of danger that Tyson brought. In a heavyweight, there was nothing more appealing.

But the learning phase that allowed a youngblood like Tyson to consort with soft touches was passing. Tyson was beginning to advance his claims for legitimacy as a contender, a quest that required him to meet accomplished fighters or, in the jargon, live bodies.

One such live body was that of Tyson's next opponent,

James (Quick) Tillis, a fighter who once had shown great promise. In October 1981, as an undefeated (20-0) heavyweight,
Tillis fought Mike Weaver for the WBA title.

It was to be Tillis's first title fight, and his irrepressible
trainer, Angelo Dundee, had spent the days before the bout
trying to lighten his fighter's mood with silly jokes (Tillis's
hometown, Tulsa, Oklahoma, was described as "population
327 . . . and that's counting the cows") and worse jokes ("When
you were born," he told Tillis, "the doctor slapped your
mother").

On the night of the fight Dundee told Tillis sincerely,
"Mike Weaver doesn't have the glow of a guy who's ready to
win. You glow."

That night the luster began to fade from Tillis. Dundee's
strategy was for Quick to circle Weaver, hit him—bang bang—
and retreat before the champion could unload his heavy
punches. Stick-and-move is what fight people call the tactic.

But by the ninth round, Dundee sensed that Tillis was
fighting too defensively, that he had to risk more if he wanted
to persuade the judges that he was dominating the action. For
Dundee, the time for being companionable was over. "Go to
work, for Christ's sake," he hollered. Tillis, however, continued
to play safe.

Before the tenth round, the trainer screamed at him:
"Weaver ain't got nothin'. *Show me! Show me!* You got to push
him." He slapped the fighter's legs and shoved him into the
ring. For the rest of the fight, Dundee berated and beseeched
Tillis. "Fight him, Quick, goddammit."

Between rounds, he smacked Tillis's face and legs and
cursed him. Sweat streamed from Dundee as he tried to
galvanize his man. Down the stretch, Tillis landed stinging
blows on Weaver but failed to follow his advantage. In the end,
Tillis's caution cost him the fight. Weaver won a unanimous decision.

In the dressing room, Dundee told Tillis: "You're a baby,
son. You'll get better and better." But moments later, he was
muttering: "He could've won it. He could've won it."

By 1985, could've-could've was Tillis's epitaph. In four
years he had gone from the title shot to being strictly an opponent for ranked and rising fighters.

1984

| October 22 | — Carl Williams, Atlantic City, N.J. | L 10 |
| December 15 | — Bashir Wadud, Waukegan, Ill. | W 10 |

1985

| May 20 | — Marvis Frazier, Reno, Nev. | L 10 |
| September 7 | — Gerrie Coetzee, Johannesburg | L 10 |

1986

| January 25 | — Tyrell Biggs, Lancaster, Pa. | L 8 |

It was the record of a hardcore opponent. That was what it had come to for Tillis. It was a job, and someone had to do it. And in fact Tillis did it well. Sly had seen the fight against Biggs. Tillis stood his ground and gave action for the dollar. He just could no longer remember how to win; that made him attractive to fight managers seeking to add quality names to their boxers' records without incurring undue risks. Of course, a fight, any fight, made in the abstract was, when live and in color, not bound to expectations. There was no law of perpetual decline in boxing. Opponents had rights too.

On May 3, Tillis fought Tyson in Glens Falls, New York. With his nineteen straight knockouts, Tyson had become that figure of intrigue lacking for so long in the heavyweight division—a fighter who could punch his foes to the horizontal while seeming to have smoke curling from his ears. A bona fide hitter, this *shtarke* from the darker precincts of New York's juvenile justice system.

That afternoon he gave every indication that he would not disappoint expectations. In the fourth round, Tillis missed a left hook and Tyson didn't: the punch landed flush on Tillis's jaw and sent him sprawling onto the seat of his shorts. Tillis arose quickly and took the mandatory eight count from the referee, Joe Cortez, seconds before the bell ended the round.

Routine business for Tyson, it seemed, auguring another quick bout. Tyson kept after Tillis, bloodying his nose and mouth in the sixth round and pounding the other man's body with heavy punches. While the blood was visible to the crowd, to Cortez's discerning eye the reaction of Tillis to those thudding body blows was more revealing. As Cortez saw it, Tillis's eyes were registering pain beyond the call of duty. Between the sixth and seventh rounds, he walked to Tillis's corner and asked him whether he wanted the fight to go on. Tillis said he did.

It seemed only a matter of time, though, before he would not be so eager to press on. For Tyson was, if anything, unrelenting. Or had been until the bell for round seven rang.

Then, suddenly and without explanation, he was not unrelenting. Tillis began to beat him to the punch. With his gloves held close together at his chin, Tyson slackened his pace, standing and eyeing his opponent rather than punching him. The crowd booed. For the first time in his pro career, Tyson was forced to go the distance. He won a close but unanimous ten-round decision.

Immediately afterward, Tyson would say he had been looking to land the big punch but that his diminished pace was no big deal—he had the fight won anyway. The words struck ringside reporters as hollow-sounding; Tyson's fade in the late rounds seemed to owe more to fatigue or confusion.

Tyson would admit as much a week or so later when Sly met up with him back in Manhattan. Tyson conceded his passivity through the late rounds had occurred because he was, as he put it, in "untested waters."

"I wasn't really sure about going ten rounds," he said. "I felt the pressure of the fact that it was ten rounds."

Whatever the reason, the lapse in perpetual aggression persuaded some in the boxing press that Tyson was not the holy terror he had been proclaimed. They saw the Tillis fight as a clue to Tyson's future. Under pressure, their theory went, Tyson was not the swamp monster he appeared to be when things went his way.

While such opinions could be arrived at with objective clarity, it seemed to Sly that with Tyson, there was more going on. Tyson had risen from the pack with such startling abruptness that he already was beyond boxing. He was in that company of the highly prominent whose success begets a perverse skepticism.

Some two weeks after he beat Tillis, Tyson sat in the backseat of a limousine that wended its way through mid-Manhattan traffic. He tried to put the next appointment on his busy calendar in perspective.

"From Brooklyn to the David Letterman show," he said, his

tone of voice suggesting he was pleased and maybe just slightly incredulous at how quickly his career had turned him into a star.

That night, as he left the studio where the Letterman show was shot, he was reminded of the allure that his rapid-transit celebrity held for those without it. As Tyson headed for the elevator and back by limousine into the night, one of Letterman's many pretty staff associates slipped him her phone number on a scrap of paper that he discarded before he was back out on the street.

Dealer's choice: earlier in the day, out in front of the Penta Hotel while he waited for his limousine, he had tugged at the pigtail of another girl and, when she looked over, had given her a shy smile to indicate his interest in her.

So accelerated was Tyson's fight itinerary that he was practically a perpetual warrior, minding the rites and rigors of training. A few days later and a little more than two weeks after he beat Tillis, Tyson was booked into Madison Square Garden to fight the main event against Mitch Green, a four-time New York Golden Glove champion with a 16-1-1 record.

Green, who was ranked number seven by the WBC, was nicknamed Blood, a tag he claimed to have acquired in gang fights on city streets, where, as he put it, "I'd be making guys bleed."

"So the name kinda fit me," he said.

Green's trademark was a toothpick that perpetually jutted from his mouth even when he ambled into the ring, a look that wasn't calculated to endear him to polite society. "I had managers that didn't like me to do the toothpick," Green would say. "So naturally I just kept on doing it."

The words pretty well conveyed the character: Blood was your basic agitator, stirring shit wherever he went, in his boxing life and out. Police blotters had featured Green in various "incidents," and as a fighter he had managed to pick a quarrel or two along the way.

During the time the Bronx-born Green was managed by Shelly Finkel, Finkel said his fighter frequently complained about the progress and profits of his career compared with what other fighters of Finkel's had.

"Mitch would say, 'Alex Ramos is making this. I should be making this,'" Finkel recalled. "I'd say, 'I don't tell you the money. The network makes the offer. Then it's my decision to pass or accept.' I tried to convince him he should take what was out there and get to the next stage of his career. Otherwise, a fighter's skills dilapidate, and he ends up making less money. By staying active, his name is in the newspapers all the time."

Green was a tall man, six-five. He had a mustache, chin whiskers, and chaotic hair that fell to his shoulders. A strut in his walk reinforced the effect that toothpick meant to create: he was Street Kid all the way.

A day before Green and Tyson were to fight, Green shook things up when he sought to renegotiate his deal. That was hardly protocol, and less so when Blood chose to do it in public—at the weigh-in at Madison Square Garden. "They ain't been paying me," he said, almost to himself at first.

But the hint of grievance in his voice caused reporters to draw near. It was all the encouragement Green needed.

"Everybody knows about Don King," he said, his voice rising. "I have no manager to negotiate for me. I've got Don King's son as a manager. Whatever Don King decides to give me is all right with my manager. And whatever they give me, I have to take it. That's why I don't fight that much."

"This man isn't keeping my money anymore," he said, referring to Don King. "He said he was going to do me right. And he hasn't."

Soon after, Carl King appeared at the weigh-in and Green began to harangue *him*. The fighter waved his finger at King, who pushed Green's hand aside. "You're going to pay me, one way or another," Green said, with a threatening tone.

Carl King would tell the press that the fighter had known for some time the size of his purse ($30,000). But Green contended that King had told him he was being paid roughly what Tyson was receiving, and had learned only recently of the wide variance: his $30,000 against the $200,000 guarantee Tyson was getting from the Garden, out of which would come certain expenses, including a maximum of $30,000 for the undercard. In addition, Tyson was to receive $450,000 more from HBO, which was televising the bout.

Toothpick dangling from his mouth, Green went on and on about his money his money his money; soon enough he was threatening to pull out of the fight if the purse wasn't sweetened. In the end, his talk, like his purse, was cheap.

Green would fight Tyson, but with less overt aggression than he had shown trying to roust the Kings for a better deal. In fact, he spent most of the night holding Tyson whenever Tyson got near him, the clinches being his only resort against the explosive bursts of punches Tyson repeatedly got off.

Twice in the early rounds, Tyson's punches sent his opponent's mouthpiece flying, and on several occasions his jarring blows caused a halo of water to shoot off Green's long stringy hair.

While Green was never staggered by Tyson, he absorbed plenty of punishment and fought most of the bout with a bloody mouth. The most vivid image of Green's problems was the piece of his dental work, complete with strand of wire, that Tyson blasted from his mouth in the third round. It landed on the ring apron, several feet from where Sly sat.

The next day's headlines would read: *Unanimous Decision to Tyson/Green Lasts 10 Rounds.*

For Green, the defeat would earn him that thirty grand and an adios from the Kings, who released him from his contracts with them.

For Tyson the beat went on.

1986

May 20	— Mitchell Green, New York, N.Y.	W 10
June 13	— Reggie Gross, New York, N.Y.	TKO 1
June 28	— William Hosea, Troy, N.Y.	KO 1
July 11	— Lorenzo Boyd, Swan Lake, N.Y.	KO 2

"Cus's basic philosophy," said Jacobs, "was that whether you were a brain surgeon, pianist, or fighter, you've got to do it frequently to do it at your best."

As the lively instrument of that precept, Tyson, just turned twenty, was moving hard toward the goal that D'Amato had set for him—boxing's youngest-ever heavyweight champion. But just how that opportunity would arise was, by the summer of '86, uncertain.

There were two routes that Tyson could take to a title shot—he could jump into the HBO series or keep beating the best names his network and cable patrons could buy and fight the undisputed champion from the HBO series after it was over.

If he elected to step into the HBO competition, he would—according to HBO—fight the WBC champion, Berbick, that fall. But like all boxing schemes, HBO's was no better than its ability to withstand the nefarious designs of its adversaries. It was a bit like that old 1960s saw that the hippie/liberal axis used to spout: what if they gave a war and nobody came? What if HBO's Abraham declared Berbick would meet Tyson and found that "the Fighting Preacher" had the heretic notion of bolting the series for a more fiscally sound opportunity?

In this case, the what-if was no matter of galloping paranoia. Berbick was bent on doing what he had all his career, muscling his modest talent to the best dollar he could get. In 1986 that meant allowing himself to be wooed by Dennis Rappaport, comanager of Gerry Cooney.

On May 31 in San Francisco, in his first bout in eighteen months, Cooney had scored a one-round knockout over Eddie Gregg. For reasons not clear to anybody conversant with boxing talent, Gregg was ranked number three by the WBA and number nine by the WBC at the time he fought Cooney. That meant that in demolishing him, Cooney was forgiven his past inactivity and gained the pedigree of the man he had vanquished. And for all the critical prose written about him, he still had puncher's mystique. Against Gregg, he had landed the kind of booming left hooks that leave stretch marks on an opponent's psyche.

While Berbick was contractually bound to remain in the unification series, Berbick had a history of never letting the fine print get in the way of a better deal. Lawyers could always sort out whatever mess his me-first methods made.

Cooney was as attractive an opponent as was out there—a hard-punching white heavyweight who still intrigued the public enough to ensure cash guarantees that would make Berbick's end in a bout against Cooney easily exceed the $750,000 that had been penciled in as his purse for his first title defense in the HBO series, the one for which Tyson was now being proposed as the opponent.

That meant that once again Rappaport would be negotiating with a man who, as Butch Lewis did earlier, had a fallback position. Whether he fought Cooney or not, Berbick was going to be in business. If his purse for fighting Tyson was now only

$750,000, who was to say Berbick might not improve his price by merely threatening to bolt the HBO series to fight Cooney? That left Rappaport in tricked-up circumstances. But he was a clever man, with a solid understanding of the marketplace.

A fighter was a property, a free-floating muscular body seeking value in a hostile world. For his traditional 33 1/3 percent cut, the manager was charged with raising the fighter's skill by finding him a compatible trainer and then by laying out a progression of matches that would educate the boxer to his game. But it was not enough for a fighter just to sharpen his talent: a boxer was, after all, a commodity whose value was based on the public's perception of him.

The public's regard for, and interest in, a fighter was what kicked his purses upward. So a manager who wanted to get best value on his property was perpetually weighing the risk of matching him "tough" against the commercial advantage of extending the illusion of his fighter's invincibility.

Nor was Rappaport apologetic if, in the pursuit of Cooney's interest, he had sought the opponent who might no longer have the skills to test his fighter but still had the name that added to the fighter's reputation. His job, Rappaport would say, was to maximize earnings and minimize risks. By his own standards, he and his partner, Mike Jones, had done fine, just fine. Such was the popularity of Cooney by the time he was matched against Holmes for the title that Rappaport and Jones could demand—and get—parity with an undefeated champion which forever after embittered Holmes, who felt that white made fiscal right.

There was more to it than that, though. Cooney had, as Tyson later would have, the puncher's big chill about him—an image that, in part at least, managerial cunning had built. But in every fighter's career there is a night he goes into the ring, as they say, "for real." The risk of matching a fighter against too many easy opponents is that when the midnight hour is at hand, he will lack the depth of experience on which to draw.

In his constant narration of The Story, Cooney time and again would say he had been "buffaloed" into measuring out his aggression against Holmes by the press's repeated reference to the fifteen-round distance and its doubts about his ability to last it.

That Cooney would say that with a straight face—and apparently mean it—suggested he was a long way from the complete fighter the night he went for the title. For any boxer whose tactics in the ring could be influenced by the Big Cigars of the boxing press had to be a mite thin on self-awareness. And if G.A.P. Cooney did not know his limits and strengths by the time he came to blows with Holmes, then serious miscalculations had been made in the lead-up to that moment.

By 1986, Rappaport was the surviving member of the managerial team that had started Cooney in the pros in 1977. (Cooney had ousted Jones after he decided that Jones was no longer in synch with him. Jones then sued Cooney and Rappaport for his fair share.) Once the unification series was in place, Rappaport was put into the position of trying to persuade Berbick to risk HBO litigation and possible WBC punitive measures by tiptoeing away from that series.

Rappaport's only other choice, it seemed, was to knuckle under to HBO and agree that Cooney would stay in the HBO series in the event he beat Berbick. Had he done that, Abraham and King would have backed the Brink's truck up to Rappaport's North Shore Towers apartment building in Great Neck, New York, with his guarantees.

But Rappaport was still not disposed to deal on HBO's terms. So Rappaport made a business decision he tried to cloak as a moral stand, depicting HBO's parent company, Time Inc., as Goliath and Cooney and himself as David. He fantasized aloud about how public indignation would not allow the corporate colossus to keep his fighter from getting his shot at the title. His was the sort of gall that got Rappaport's critics in the boxing press—and they were legion—crazy. Cooney the misbegotten was, like Nixon the misunderstood, a concept that took some getting used to.

Yet Rappaport had an instinct for grabbing attention for his fighters; he was consistently wittily imaginative. With undefeated middleweight Ronnie Harris, he had shown a public relations man's ingenuity for creating interest in a fighter that boxing people knew as a "stinker," a boxer whose concern for self-preservation made for dull fights.

"When I got Harris in 1976," Rappaport recalled, "I was new to boxing. I didn't know anyone. Now I have a fighter. What do I do with the fighter? I called everywhere. Nobody wanted to use Ronnie Harris. Mike Jones knew somebody who knew somebody who knew Bob Arum. Bob Arum quickly dismissed us. He kept insisting our Ronnie Harris was the Ronnie Harris from Detroit, another fighter than ours. Our best offer came from a promoter in Orlando, who said, if we paid for the opponent, if we paid for Harris, if we paid all expenses, he'd let Ronnie fight on his card in Orlando. From business experience even I knew that was an untenable situation. I then decided the only way to approach a business where I had no contacts was to stir up and generate excitement."

Rappaport did that by giving Harris a nickname, Mazel, from the Yiddish word for good luck. Then, claiming Harris was a black Jew, he asked the New York State Athletic Commission to allow Harris to wear a yarmulke, a skullcap, when he fought. In pursuit of that objective, Rappaport would even go to court. When the commission got the decision in Harris's favor overturned on the day Harris was to fight at Sunnyside Gardens in Queens, Rappaport kept the story going.

"I now found a song from forty years before—'All You Need Is Mazel—Mazel Means Good Luck,'" said Rappaport. "And the night of the fight I handed out sheet music. I hired a band to play and had the crowd, a mostly Latin crowd, sing the song. It was hysterical: they pronounced mazel 'may-zel' rather than 'mah-zel.'

"But the real challenge was to get Teddy Brenner, who was a matchmaker at the time for Madison Square Garden, to use Harris on the Garden fight cards. He'd promised to, but eventually he told us, 'I can't use Harris. Nobody wants to fight him.' I was really down about that. So the question was how to force a big company to use a fighter that (a) didn't want to use him, and (b) told you they didn't want to.

"After realizing how much publicity I generated by the court case with the yarmulke, I said to myself, let me try to embarrass Gulf & Western, the parent company of the Garden, and generate publicity. I called up every newspaper and TV station and told them, 'Be at the Garden tomorrow at one o'clock.' At one o'clock, Ronnie Harris and I showed up at the lobby of the Garden with a gorilla. John Condon, who was with Madison Square Garden Boxing, was so annoyed by the scene we created he threatened to have us arrested and was taken aback by our readiness to be arrested. Teddy Brenner calls Mike Jones at home. 'Get this crazy man outta here—he's embarrassing Gulf & Western. I'll give Harris a fight against Sugar Ray Seales for three thousand dollars.' Mike Jones said, 'Five thousand.' Brenner said, 'I'm hanging up.'"

The type of hoop-de-doo he generated for Harris was by no means alien to Rappaport's nature; this millionaire businessman had risen in the world through creative finagling.

By the time he was sixteen and attending New York University, Rappaport was working for a real estate firm in Hempstead, Long Island. "They were using me to put circulars under doors. I remember the first time I sold a piece of property. A drunk came into the office. And since I didn't have my driver's license, the only place I could show him was walking distance from the office. So I took a walk with the guy—eight, ten blocks—and showed him a place. I came back. I look up the monthly payment book. It's nine hundred dollars down. He told me he didn't want to put nine hundred down, he wanted to put twenty-five hundred instead. The experienced men in the firm are laughing. 'He's loaded,' they're telling me. 'He won't come back.' Two hours later, the guy came back with a paper bag and twenty-five hundred in one-dollar bills. My first sale.

"Because I was a kid I was not able to take leads, which were called 'ups.' In other words, when customers called about houses they had seen in advertisements, the salesmen got to pitch them on a rotating basis. I couldn't get any ups. The only customers I was allowed to handle were the ones I brought in myself. So I'd put pictures in the window. If somebody would look, I'd go out and talk. But that wasn't all I did. After a while I was selling three times as many houses as the next-best salesman. What I was doing . . . I went over and saw where my first sale, the drunk, lived. It was a housing project in Hempstead, mostly blacks. I started knocking at every single door. I printed a circular: 'Dream of Owning Your Own Home,' with pictures and color.

"Now during this period of time, there was a lot of turmoil in the streets, the early 1960s. I was so hungry that what I used to do, if there were riots in Harlem or Bedford-Stuyvesant in Brooklyn, I'd take my literature and, in the middle of the riots, I'd be giving out my literature, figuring people in these areas, a lot of people, would start thinking of moving to the suburbs. I recognized that there was an emerging middle class in black communities."

Like Cooney, Berbick had a manager. But that manager was Carl King, the stepson of Don King. As Berbick saw it, Carl was unlikely to help support any move that would lead Berbick out of a unification series that Don was copromoting. So if Berbick meant to explore the possibility of fighting Cooney, at the start at least he was on his own.

On the face of it, that put Berbick at a disadvantage. The average fighter simply hadn't the background in cutting deals to go up against a keen business type like Rappaport. But Berbick was hardly a typical fighter.

In the summer of 1985, Don King was in Las Vegas, feeling apprehensive and low-down about a tax-evasion case the government was about to bring against him.

A glimmer of hope would reach him, however, on a daily basis: "Every morning at six-thirty A.M. there'd be a knock on my hotel door," King said, "and here would come Trevor Berbick carrying a Bible and a cross.

"'While everybody may be your enemy, the Lord is on your side,' he'd tell me. I'd be sleepy and half groggy while he'd preach. Two, three weeks in a row, he'd be there first thing in the morning, reading the Ninety-first Psalm: 'He that dwelleth in the secret of the most High shall abide under . . .'"

King referred to Berbick as "The Three Faces of Eve"—he was that mercurial a man. Yet while Berbick was sometimes indecipherable under ordinary circumstances, sometimes inconsistent in the ring, and sometimes buccaneer in his business practices, he could prove an engaging character with a shrewd sense of boxing's backstage maneuvers.

When Berbick fought, the question was always which Berbick would stand up that night. Would it be the Berbick who against just average opponents had stumbled (he was knocked out by Bernardo Mercado in one round in 1979, fought to a draw against Leroy Caldwell the same year, and in late 1982–early 1983 suffered successive losses to Renaldo Snipes and S. T. Gordon), or would the opponent be up against the Berbick who, though never an overpowering puncher, had a durability that enabled him, when he was right, to power his way to victory?

Berbick, with his 31-4-1 record, had made a habit of raising the level of his talent when least expected. Against favored opponents—John Tate in 1980, Muhammad Ali in 1981, Greg Page in 1982, and, the past March for the WBC title, Pinklon Thomas—Berbick prevailed with pressuring tactics that eventually wore down his big-name opponents.

Berbick was a curiosity to boxing people, who marveled that ten years into his career a man with his limited skills was not just a factor in the heavyweight division but was one of its champions.

"He is a strange figure," said Mort Sharnik, the CBS-TV boxing consultant. "Nobody has ever been able to get a grip on him. The most clever, the most ruthless of the sport. None of them have been able to tie him down. He seems to be impervious to threat, or anything."

After meeting him that June, Rappaport would describe Berbick as a "likable rogue."

"He's unpredictable," Rappaport said. "During a period of negotiations he's on the verge of a breakdown, talking to himself. Yet by the same token, Trevor can be very charming. He's bright, though capable of a lot of con."

Berbick was said by those who knew him to be a dedicated family man (he had two daughters and a son), and he could sound like Henry David Thoreau when he extolled the virtues of picking fresh fruits from the trees in his backyard in Miramar, Florida.

On his two and a half acres, he grew oranges, grapefruits, grapes, and sugar cane, and it was there that Berbick felt closest to his origins: he had grown up in Port Antonio, Jamaica, where he would climb coconut trees for the fruit and dive in nearby waters to haul up fish from nets and traps. He claimed to have had a religious experience at the age of sixteen, and he led a life that was relatively simple for a world champion.

Just the same, he could turn strange, acting as though his frequency was jammed when others sought to communicate with him. For instance, after Berbick beat Thomas for the WBC title, Larry Merchant, HBO's boxing commentator, said to Berbick in the postfight interview that few people had expected him to win. A straightforward comment it was that elicited this rather disjointed response: "Well, Mr. Merchant, I say this to you. That many people don't understand what mysteries I've been through. But I think right after this fight, and pretty soon . . . I won't say too much, but when I build my church and the gates of heaven, hell will not prevail against it. You don't understand that. People will understand it soon."

When Rappaport and Berbick met in June to discuss a match against Cooney, the fighter's opening words were: "I need money. A hundred-thousand-dollars deposit."

"I said, 'What?'" recalled Rappaport. "And he said, 'I got a message from God. He said to ask you, and you'd give it to me.' I said, "When did you speak to God?' He said, 'About twenty minutes ago.' I told him, 'Trevor, He changed His mind. He spoke to me about five minutes ago and told me not to give you twenty dollars.'"

Berbick would acknowledge asking for $100,000, but said what he had told Rappaport was that if he wanted the Berbick-Cooney fight as much as Berbick did, then that meant that God wanted it too.

In any event, it was clear that Berbick was no novice, as fighters were, when it came to getting the Almighty dollar. He had the blessed ability to take good care of Trevor.

For instance, when he won his first major fight by knocking out Tate in June 1980, he refused to renew his contract with Don Kerr, an attorney who had managed him since 1976.

Kerr said that he and his business associates had gone $250,000 into debt to keep Berbick's career afloat, and called Berbick's refusal to re-sign "desertion."

For his part, Berbick said that if there were losses, which he doubted, they would amount to a tax write-off for Kerr and his colleagues and that, nice man though he was, Kerr had neither the time nor the connections to get a fighter big-time purses.

Berbick had signed with and then shed a brigade of managers, advisers, and attorneys, many of them leaving in disharmonious and litigious circumstances usually brought on by Berbick's reluctance to pay. Yet Berbick not only endured for his unorthodox tactics, he profited from them.

In pursuit of financial security, Berbick had repeatedly signed and then renounced contracts, sometimes even amending the purse to his advantage. Before going into the ring against Ali, he demanded, and got, a letter of credit from the bout's promoters when their finances turned shaky, and more than once he had improved his original purse for bouts under Don King.

Now as champion, Berbick meant to get his money's worth from his title. But in their first meeting that June in New York, Rappaport sensed that Berbick was a slippery character. The $100,000 that Berbick claimed by divine decree was a pretty fair clue, as was his fuzziness about certain elements essential to locking in a Berbick-Cooney deal.

"At that first meeting," said Rappaport, "Berbick makes like there's no contract [for the HBO series] with Don King. He tells me, 'I have an out. I'll work it out with Don King.' He says Don King is afraid of him."

King claimed that when he had flown to Nassau for Berbick's fight with Ali, he was beaten up and threatened with death by James Cornelius, the bout's promoter, and four other men. Now meeting with Rappaport, Berbick implied King had gotten his comeuppance because of Trevor Berbick.

"It was almost like he was taking credit for the beating King got," said Rappaport. "'You know what happened to Don King. That was me.'"

Yet at the same meeting, held at a restaurant at the Penta Hotel, Berbick had nervously looked around to make sure the meeting was not being monitored. "That first time with Trevor," said Rappaport, "there was a lot of secrecy, innuendo, and vagueness."

Yet among the reigning champions, Berbick appeared to be Cooney's likeliest prospect. Witherspoon was signed to a potentially lucrative title defense against a popular British fighter, Frank Bruno, for that July. Spinks's promoter, Lewis, somehow had convinced HBO that a Norwegian fighter, Steffen Tangstad, was a suitable opponent for the IBF heavyweight championship in September.

Soon after, Tangstad, who had not been in the IBF's top twelve—a prerequisite for any IBF contender's being allowed to fight for a world title—ended up being ranked number twelve. Magic.

Understand this: the governing bodies of boxing, the WBA, WBC, and IBF, each separately ranked fighters by weight classification. By these ratings the most worthy fighters were, in theory at least, given the means to be recognized and then speeded to their rightful opportunities, including the chance to fight for world titles.

Between the letter of the law and its implementation, there was a more than occasional left turn from accepted practice. It was not unheard of for a fighter who had qualified for a shot at the title to be passed over while an obscure gladiator with a suspect record materialized suddenly at the bottom end of one or another of the governing bodies' rankings and fought the champion instead. It sometimes left the unhealthy impression that the ratings were a promoter's convenience and that any politically connected fighter, regardless of merit, would find securing a rating about as difficult as landing a mail-order divinity degree.

There was nothing mystical in these occurrences. Since a champion was usually linked by contract to a promoter and since the governing bodies tithed only world title fights (cutting shares from the boxers and the promoters), it made good business sense for the WBA or WBC or IBF to get along with a promoter, particularly a successful one.

So while there might be rules and regulations, these were susceptible to back room politics and, it was said, to the persuasive fat envelope. As HBO's Abraham had put it, "The state of boxing is as close to sixteenth-century buccaneering as anything on the planet today."

That fast-and-loose atmosphere gave Rappaport a fighting chance at getting Berbick to snub his nose at HBO and box Gerry Cooney instead.

7

Tyson seemed to have emerged practically overnight; to the public, one morning this phenom who made grown men drop like Sequoias was suddenly there. In fact, though, when Tyson started his pro career in March 1985, he had not been a special case at all.

That was no shock. For amateur boxers did not routinely strike it rich when turning pro, as, say, the stars of college football and basketball did year after year. That kind of cash-rich transition and spotlit recognition were far more rare for the amateur fighter, coinciding usually with the Olympics, held every four years.

As great as an amateur fighter might be, if he did not make it to the Olympics and then win a medal, preferably a gold one, he was unlikely to earn the big dollars at the start of his pro career.

While Tyson had won junior Olympic titles as an amateur, he failed at the next level, in his bid for the 1984 Olympic team. Whether he was, as he would later claim, a victim of amateur boxing politics was beside the point. In losing his Olympics berth to Henry Tillman, he'd blown the star-spangled advantages an Olympics medalist had.

Starting with the 1976 Olympics at Montreal—the Olympics of Sugar Ray Leonard, Leon and Michael Spinks, Howard Davis, and Leo Randolph—television networks had signed Olympic boxing stars to six- and seven-figure contracts, unheard-of in the past for boxing beginners.

By contrast, Tyson got $500 for his first fight, a sum that Cayton and Jacobs anteed up because if they had relied on what the promoter could afford, their fighter would have ended up with pocket change. By contract they were not obliged to sweeten Tyson's purse. But their sense was that the more generous paycheck would encourage Tyson.

Beyond that, there was a bond between D'Amato and the managers that was not based strictly on business principles. Tyson was not merely a signatory to a contract but a fighter on whom D'Amato, their friend, had lavished time and affection. In the years during which D'Amato was shaping Tyson—he eventually became his legal guardian—Jacobs and occasionally Cayton would take the New York State Thruway to Catskill and spend time with the two men. D'Amato had an understanding with Cayton and Jacobs. For their support of his Catskill boxing operation, they got to manage whatever professional fighters emerged from the program.

The common thread for those who formed the inner circle of Tyson's camp was that allegiance to D'Amato. It explained how Kevin Rooney, another pro of D'Amato's, would end up as Tyson's trainer.

Early in Tyson's amateur career, Teddy Atlas had been his trainer. But Atlas argued with D'Amato over what he claimed was lax disciplining of Tyson, who, he said, was accorded a latitude other fighters were not.

D'Amato loyalists had another version of the split. They claimed that when Atlas got married he chose to leave Catskill for New York City and, without telling D'Amato, tried to induce several of the older man's amateurs to leave with him.

Atlas denied this, but about midway through 1982, D'Amato called on Rooney to take over the training of Tyson. Rooney worked with Tyson throughout 1983 and continued training him even when he resumed his own boxing career in

1984 after being inactive for nearly a year and a half. By 1985, Rooney twice headlined on cards that had Tyson in his first professional fights; on those occasions, Rooney would work Tyson's corner and then hurry to the dressing room to get ready for his own match. In June of that year, he retired for good.

Part of the intrigue that boxing held for Sly was precisely in the piecing together of how disparate types like those in the Tyson camp came to be collaborators. To track the converging lines of biography, as, say, in the cases of Cayton and Jacobs, was fascinating in just the way that following the different narrative lines of a wide-ranging novel is.

Cayton, for instance, was graduated from the University of Maryland in 1937 with a degree in chemical engineering; he went to work for Du Pont in Wilmington, Delaware.

As the newest arrival there, he inherited the lowly task of writing technical reports. It was a job he performed so well that he drew the attention of the advertising agency of a rival of Du Pont's. At four times the salary he was making in Wilmington, Cayton was invited to New York to try it as an advertising copywriter.

By 1948, Cayton, now running his own ad agency, was asked to devise a sports show that would promote a hair-tonic account. The ad man first thought about football for his format but decided that on a five- to seven-inch TV screen, the game would look more like a Jackson Pollock painting. To his mind, baseball suffered from the same problem.

The image of two prizefighters having at it was quite another story. Cayton believed that boxing would sell enough Vaseline hair tonic to keep his client happy. So it came to pass that Cayton created a fifteen-minute show, *Greatest Fights of the Century,* that from 1948 to 1954 followed *The Friday Night Fights* on NBC.

"Enormous ratings," said Cayton. "More than the live fights even. Our ratings back then were sometimes in the nineties, which makes the Cosby show look anemic."

By the 1950s, Cayton had moved on. He was buying fight films for international distribution. Those films were not widely available in this country, for reasons that were rooted in America's troubled racial past. On July 4, 1910, Jack Johnson, a black heavyweight champion who was perceived as being an "uppity sort," knocked out James J. Jeffries, who was white. Johnson, of course, would become the inspiration for the Broadway musical (and later film) *The Great White Hope.*

When the film of Johnson's victory was shown in Southern movie houses, riots ensued. That led soon after to the passage of a law by Congress prohibiting interstate commerce in fight films.

"From that point on," said Cayton, "the people who dealt those old fight films were the same people who bootlegged whisky."

More recent fight films were the property of the International Boxing Club, a powerful promotional organization in the 1950s that eventually would be declared in violation of antitrust laws.

To the IBC and to the dealer who represented the bootlegger crowd, Cayton paid more than $100,000 ("a lot of money in those times") for a package of boxing movies that ranged back to the early 1900s.

But well before the prospering advertising executive found value in fight films, Jim Jacobs was amassing his own collection. As a boy growing up in Los Angeles, he had accompanied his father to live boxing cards and there, hearing of past great champions, was curious enough about them to buy whatever Castle Films 8mm footage there was, and soon after was adding 16mm films to his collection.

"I adored boxing, and I became a serious fight film collector," said Jacobs.

Jacobs was himself a skilled athlete. For more than a decade, beginning in 1955, Jacobs was the most successful player in the United States Handball Association championships—the Babe Ruth, so to speak, of his game. He won six singles and six doubles titles. As he dominated handball, Jacobs continued accumulating fight films, pursuing them with the sort of passion he would later characterize as "compulsive." "I'd think nothing of jumping on an airplane and going anywhere for a film," he said.

Once, hearing of a British collector who had the film in which Jack Johnson won the heavyweight title from Tommy Burns (December 26, 1908), he wrote the man asking to see a frame from the film, an accepted practice among collectors that assured the buyer of the footage he sought.

When this particular collector declined to send the frame,

Jacobs flew to London. By the time he got there, the owner of Johnson-Burns had encountered a few problems with the law and was in prison. It would be two years before Jacobs finally secured the Johnson-Burns footage for himself.

In 1956, by chance, Jacobs came upon a 65mm nitrate film that was, as he put it, "like the Hope Diamond to me." It was the film—or excerpts, at least—of the March 1897 heavyweight title fight between James J. Corbett and Bob Fitzsimmons— footage that had been stored away for forty years in shoe boxes belonging to a car dealer from Multnomah, Oregon.

"I was giving a handball clinic there," said Jacobs, "and he brought down these shoe boxes of Corbett-Fitzsimmons. To him it wasn't valuable. He knew I was a collector, so he just gave it to me."

Their mutual interest in fight films brought Cayton and Jacobs together in the late 1950s. By then, Jacobs had more than five thousand films in his collection and Cayton was about to produce a five-minute TV series called *Knockout.*

The two men hit it off: Cayton invited Jacobs to work for him. And in time they became partners in The Big Fights, Inc., which quickly became a profitable operation. In the mid-1970s, the company struck a deal worth $4 million with ABC-TV that gave the network exclusive rights to use The Big Fights' film library on the air. A renewal of the deal in the early 1980s was worth $6 million more.

That kind of success left Cayton and Jacobs with the resources to obtain attention for the fledgling Tyson that was disproportionate to the standing he had in the business. Tyson's Olympic failure did not dissuade the two men from believing that their fighter was special and merited star treatment.

At their expense the managers had decided to film every one of Tyson's fights.* In the beginning, this meant sending crews to small and sometimes poorly lighted arenas, then having the footage edited overnight onto videocassettes. The cassettes were shipped to leading television broadcasters so that on the next day's 6:00 news, another opponent of Tyson's, live and in color, would fall horizontal, bouncing off the canvas like a pink spaldeen.

---

*The only fight not to be filmed was Tyson's sixth pro bout—against Larry Sims in July 1985. Cayton: "The camera crew we hired didn't show up."

Because these poor bastards hit the deck like time-speeded lessons in gravity, they made for good TV—hot footage with which to top off the night's more crucial sports stories.

The same cassettes were mailed to a list of elite boxing writers on the theory that they would be impressed enough to jot a line or two about this rising young fighter from Catskill. A little bit here, a little bit there: it added up, enabling Cayton and Jacobs to ask—and get—$95,000 a bout from ABC-TV by February 1986 for a fighter who was unranked and just beginning to box main events.

Of course, there were no blinders on Bob Iger, the executive at ABC-TV who cut the deal. A heavyweight who could chill opponents with a single punch was a rare commodity. Clever as Cayton and Jacobs were in exposing their fighter, they also had a man who emanated a presence, an authority, uniquely his own. On ABC-TV, Tyson had stopped Jesse Ferguson in six rounds in February, then beat Tillis in May.

Now, in the summer of '86, as Cayton and Jacobs were poking and prodding at the marketplace, Tyson was readying for his next opponent—the best-known of all the men he had fought to date, Marvis Frazier.

Frazier was a gilded boxing name and, in this case, was connected by blood to one of the sport's great champions. For Marvis was the son of Smokin' Joe Frazier; he was Joe's very own kid and, some said, too much his very own fighter.

To the passing Amtrak commuter it looks like just another old creaking building in this run-down North Philadelphia neighborhood. The upper floors of the three-story building at 2917 North Broad Street sport gray-white stucco patches where windows used to be; the rest is brown brickface.

But the designation on the exterior—"Joe Frazier's Gym"—is a good clue that this place is no candidate for the wrecker's ball. It is, in fact, a kind of boxing landmark, a gym where fighters have been training since 1968, when Cloverlay, Inc., the syndicate sponsor of the heavyweight contender Joe Frazier, bought the gym for him. Smokin' Joe used it well: he became the world champion and, on retiring in 1976 (there was a one-fight comeback, a draw against Jumbo Cummings, in 1981), bought the gym from Cloverlay for $75,000.

These days Frazier had offices up a flight of stairs at the

back of the gym. From the elevated spot, through a wide window, he could gaze down onto the gym floor, and watch a second generation of Fraziers have a go at the manly art. Since 1980, when Smokin' Joe's oldest son, Marvis, a six-foot-one, 210-pound heavyweight, turned pro, he had presided here over a corps of fighting Fraziers. Beside Marvis they were Rodney (13-3, 10 knockouts), a heavyweight who was the son of Frazier's sister; Mark (10-3-3, 9 knockouts), a super-middleweight who was the son of Frazier's brother; and Hector (15-4-3, 13 knockouts), a junior welterweight who was another of the former champion's sons and who fought under the name Joe Frazier, Jr.

Of them all, only Marvis (16-1, 7 knockouts), ranked ninth at the time by the WBC, was regarded as a world-class fighter.

If he could beat Tyson (and the consensus was that Marvis was overmatched), it would redound to Smokin' Joe's credit too. For many fight people contended that the full-bore aggression Joe brought to his own bouts, and his complete assurance in his talents, well suited the fighter he once was, but were not necessarily an advantage for a boxing manager—in whom discretion was often more valuable.

In 1976, when Smokin' Joe bought the gym, its sidewalks had been lined, daily, with the long sleek cars of the city's boxing establishment. Inside, in the evening particularly, the place would swarm with activity, fighters shoulder to shoulder in the noisy, square-built room.

But by '86 Frazier's gym no longer knew that kind of bustle. A clue to why could be gained from a sign that had appeared at the entrance of the gym a few years before: "Starting January '83, any trainers that do not have fighters for Smokin' Joe Frazier must and will pay $250 for gym dues. Thank you. Joe Frazier."

At the time, other major gyms in the city, such as the Percy Street Gym and McCall's Gym, did not charge trainers dues. Was it the Frazier cachet—as if it were the Gucci's of gyms—that prompted Frazier to raise the ante?

Not really, said Frazier's critics. "Eventually, we got the point," said one manager, Gary Hegyi. "Joe wanted the gym to himself. His own fighters. You don't have to hit me in the head with a two-by-four to make me understand."

In 1983, Hegyi took his business elsewhere, as did George

Benton, the trainer who had worked with Frazier and later with Marvis. Other boxing men left too, including Milt Bailey, who had been a cut man in Frazier's corner when Smokin' Joe was active in the ring. "I couldn't see a trainer paying to train a fighter," Bailey said then. "That was a new one on me."

New or not, Frazier stood by his methods. "You don't go to General Motors, build a car, and say it's yours," Frazier said. "Same thing at my gym. If you come here and learn, I want to make money back. You belong to us."

By his own words, Frazier showed that the no-nonsense directness of the fighter he had been had filtered down to the businessman he'd become. But was that ham-fisted approach suited to the world beyond the prize ring? "He's a stubborn, opinionated guy," said Lou Duva, a trainer and manager. "But a good guy. I love Joe."

"But the question is, does he book his fighters' matches from here," said Duva, touching his heart, "or from here," tapping his head. "Who's fighting the fight? Joe Frazier or his fighter? He'd like them to fight as good as Joe Frazier could. But there's only one Joe Frazier."

Yet another manager, David Wolf, who took Ray (Boom Boom) Mancini to the WBA lightweight title, credited Frazier with doing the job a manager is supposed to: making a handsome living for his charges. "People underestimate Joe as a manager," Wolf said. "I say Marvis exceeded his potential in the purse Joe got him to fight Holmes when he was the champion."

In November 1983, Marvis reportedly received $500,000 to fight Holmes, who knocked him out in one round. Afterward, Joe was criticized for rushing his son into a title fight for which he was not ready. Wolf disputed that assessment. "Anytime you're offered the amount of money he got to go after Holmes in what was a no-lose situation, you take it," Wolf said. "Marvis was not a whole lot less marketable afterward, because nobody had expected him to win. And beyond that, he hasn't matched Marvis poorly in any other fight. He successfully resurrected his career by picking good opponents."

For fighting Tyson, Marvis would earn $250,000, and though Smokin' Joe had been criticized for mismatching his kid against Tyson, Wolf again disagreed. He said that for Marvis to earn $250,000 he would have had to fight five bouts against quality opponents, any one of whom might lick him. Besides, said Wolf, there were not so many network fights these days that Marvis could say to himself, "I'll fight every other month because I'm Marvis Frazier."

Just who Marvis Frazier was these days as a fighter (and who he might have been) raised questions about Marvis's development. When Marvis first came to the North Broad Street gym as a sixteen-year-old, it was George Benton who shaped the youth into a defense-oriented operative—a boxer type. "Then somewhere down the line he became more a brawler-type fighter," said Benton.

Toward the end of Marvis's amateur career (he had a 56-2 record, losing to Tony Tubbs and James Broad), Benton said that Smokin' Joe gradually assumed control of his son's training. "The air got a little thin. It was hard for me to breathe in that relationship. One day, Joe just said, 'I'll train the fighter when I'm here. I'll handle the boxing.'"

The version Marvis and Joe told was that Benton was often on the road with his other fighters, and that because he couldn't give his full attention to Marvis, it behooved the son of Smokin' to have the old man—or Pop, as Marvis called him—take over. "Besides," Joe said, "there was the basis of the bloodline."

The fact was that the fighter Marvis had been as an amateur and the fighter he became once his father mobilized him were different creatures. Under Benton he was an agile, quick-handed boxer-puncher, a defense-minded amateur good enough to beat Tubbs, Mitch Green, David Bey, Tim Witherspoon, and James (Bonecrusher) Smith. "The word about the kid as an amateur was extravagant," said Sharnik of CBS-TV. "From the most critical sorts I'd hear that he was the best-looking amateur in the world."

Under Smokin' Joe, the style changed. As Marvis told it: "The only thing Pop added was my standing my ground a little firmer. Rather than my being defensive, a little more offense was added." That "little more offense," which in Marvis's account sounded rather like a quarter-turn of the wrench in a subtle mechanical refinement, had struck others as radical retooling—a change of psyche and outlook.

"Joe's only fault," Duva said, "was trying to make a replica of himself rather than letting the talent come out of the fighter's own style. George had Marvis cuter, more defensive.

See, a guy like Marvis Frazier shouldn't be going into a fighter and trading punches. He should box and be cute. It would make him a better fighter."

Talk to Joe Frazier about how he had influenced his son's style and he would deny molding him in his own image. "You can't make guys like yourself," he said. But in the next breath: "Sure, you have to move around the ring, but when you jump in a guy's face, you got to get the job done."

When Marvis sparred, his father was wont to bark commands like "Breathe on him," which meant he wanted Marvis to fight his man at close quarters. Or "Fall down," shorthand for Marvis to throw the left hook. Smokin' Joe's jargon reflected the attack-minded approach he had had as a fighter and seemed to have retained as a trainer. Why wouldn't he? When Joe Frazier threw the left hook, "fall down" was an appropriate tag line. Opponents went horizontal when struck by that blow.

In contrast, Marvis's biggest victories as a professional— against Broad, Joe Bugner, Tillis, and Bonecrusher Smith—all were fights that went the distance. Marvis, with a longer, leaner physique than his father's, had never shown the force as a puncher that his father did. Instead, he had been a limited version of Pete Rose, a scrappy performer relying on drive and superior conditioning. A recurring comment from boxing men on the subject of Marvis was: "The kid has heart."

The kid also was uncommonly close to his father. "Dutiful son" were words with which others frequently described the relationship. Marvis captured the underlying spirit when he said: "When we come in the gym, I'll holler to Pop, 'Heyyyyy,' and he'll holler back, 'Heyyyyy!' We say it real loud. I don't know what it means. But it feels real good."

Though Marvis grew up in a sixteen-room stone split-level house in a predominantly white suburb of Philadelphia, he was not, as Hegyi put it, a spoiled brat. "This kid," Hegyi said, "was one of the nicest, most decent young men you'll want to meet."

Sharnik concurred. "Boxing is so remote from his character and instincts," he said. "He is such a gentle man. Such a godly man." (Marvis was a deacon and a member of the choir in the Faith Temple church in North Philadelphia.)

After Frazier beat Smith in February, he stopped by to see the promoter of the fight, Sam Glass. "He thanked me," Glass said, "for having him on the card and said he hoped I was satisfied with how he fought. He was uncommonly gracious. Fighters just don't do that sort of thing."

Marvis's upbringing apparently instilled that instinct for doing the right thing.

"We called the cellar of our house the Zoo," Marvis recalled. "When I was ten, I got into a fight with my sister Jacqui. My mom said, 'Up to your room, wait till your father gets home.' Pop came home. I heard Mom say, 'I want you to talk to Marv.' *Poom poom poom*—he bangs at the door of my bedroom. 'Get up, boy. You ain't asleep.' I was trying to act asleep. 'What's this I hear about you hitting girls? We're going to the Zoo. Get the gloves.'

"There were two pairs of boxing gloves in his room. I'm going, 'I'm sorry.' Crying and all. And Pop: 'Put them gloves on.' He started jabbing me. I covered up. 'You want to hit girls, huh?' Jab jab. 'You know how much strength you've got?' 'Sorry, Daddy.' 'I'll teach you what to be sorry for, you sissy.' He got mad. I haven't hit a girl since."

Marvis did not take up boxing until his parents, hoping to remedy their son's bad grades, sent him as a tenth-grader to a private school that had no varsity sports. Marvis, who had wrestled and played basketball, baseball, and football as a schoolboy, asked whether he could use his father's gym to keep active. "I knew after three months in the gym that it was boxing for me," he said.

It took his father longer. "When Pop realized I wanted to fight, he said no," Marvis recalled. "Gave me a lecture: 'This is nothing to play with. You have to be serious. Guys are in there to tear your head off. No one gets in there unless he's serious.' Then one day after that, me and my cousin Russell came in. Russell boxed too. Pop liked him. Russell had a style like Pop's. Russell and I worked out together. But Russell had been slacking . . . while I'd been working.

"Anyway, one Saturday we come in, and Pop says to me, 'I want to see what you've got.' Got in the ring. I started tagging Russell. And then got out of the way of his left hook. Pop hadn't expected it of me. So Pop said to Russell, 'Don't want to do your roadwork?' Then he said to me: 'Hit him to the body.'"

The first time Sly saw Marvis Frazier was in the late 1970s. Marvis was leaving his father's gym. It was winter; Marvis was bundled up, but the unmistakable Frazier features registered, despite the hooded parka.

"A Frazier?" Sly asked George Benton as they entered the gym.

"The kid, Marvis," explained Benton.

"Fighter?"

"Gonna be a damn good one."

So it appeared then. By 1986 it was clear that Marvis Frazier was a proud, spirited professional, but that he lacked the physicality that his old man had had. In a weight division rooted in power, that was a terrible deficit to have.

As the match between Tyson and Marvis neared, and the elder Frazier repeatedly sneered down at Tyson's burgeoning legend, a listener couldn't help but feel that the sight of Tyson had activated the ego of the fighter Joe Frazier rather than the manager/trainer of the same name.

If there was a genius fight prognosticator, Sly had never met him. While most boxing guys fancied themselves as having an informed opinion, there was no proof he had seen that they were any shrewder arriving at the result than the man in the street. A boxing guy might have a keener eye for what fighters did in the ring, but anticipating that action was another sort of puzzle, too full of variables to yield any quasi-science.

Even so, there were times when a man on the boxing beat felt plugged into the future, when he padded into the arena on fight night sure that the bout he saw in his mind's eye had come straight from the same deity that told Trevor Berbick to hit Rappaport up for a $100,000 advance. Sly felt that way about Tyson-Frazier. Not that it took any genius to handicap the outcome. It was not so much that Tyson would knock Frazier out that he foresaw, but that Marvis, too brave for his own good, could end up badly hurt.

So convinced was he that when Patti Dreifuss, a boxing publicist working for Frazier, told him just before the bout that Frazier had been persuaded by a stir-crazy sparring partner to go for a brief training run near midnight the night before, Sly began trying out leads in his mind that took note of the fact. ". . . should have kept going, due west to his hometown of Philadelphia and out of harm's way." And so forth.

Then came the fight.

Tyson was primed for action. On entering the ring, he

stalked about with a scowl on his face, stealing glances at his opponent. So eager was he to get the fight going that the referee, Joe Cortez, waiting for a signal from an ABC-TV official to start the bout, had to motion Tyson back to his corner as he inched toward center ring.

When the opening bell finally did sound, Tyson backed Frazier against the ropes and hit him with a powerful right uppercut. Then he maneuvered Frazier into a neutral corner. Another uppercut hurt Frazier, and a flurry of lefts and rights put him on the seat of his trunks.

Frazier, whose head hung forward, was in bad shape. Cortez's count got to three. "Then," the referee said afterward, "I saw it was not worthwhile continuing the count. I saw Marvis Frazier was out of it. His eyes rolled inward. I was more concerned about his safety."

Seated glassy-eyed, his head drooping like a wilted flower, Frazier was an alarming sight—one that for a flickering moment made Sly fear he had been all too prescient. He was relieved when Marvis proved only a victim of the moment's damage, and stirred from that sedentary position, eventually to be propped up on a stool for medical inspection.

The beaten fighter was okay, but the reaction of Poppa Joe surprised the press. In the news conference following the bout, Smokin' Joe repeatedly said he would not believe Tyson had real "kick" in his punch until the old man—Frazier's reference to himself—tested it. "I'd like to see what he's got myself," he said. "What is the guy, an animal? I want to make a date to go down and work with him. I want to check him out myself. I don't believe he can hurt me."

Whatever.

For Tyson, the next fight would be waged over phone lines and in face-to-face negotiations by Cayton and Jacobs, who now wanted to resolve whether Tyson's approach to the heavyweight title would be through the unification series or not. On August 7, 1986, after a fourteen-hour meeting between the managers and HBO ended with both sides, in Abraham's words, "seven figures apart," Cayton and Jacobs reported they would summon Larry Holmes from retirement. They would proceed with a bout against him, then try to fight the eventual winner of the unification series. Abraham did not believe Tyson's managers were bluffing; as far as he could see, the negotiations were "deader than a mackerel." It remained for Holmes to sign, and Tyson and the former champion would have themselves a fight.

But Holmes became a moving target. Every time his price was discussed, it went north: from $1.5 million to $1.7 million to $1.9 million. Yet Cayton and Jacobs believed that if they worked the deal long enough and hard enough, eventually they would reel in Holmes. Holmes's equivocation encouraged another player, the promoter Bob Arum, who stepped forward with a $2.2 million offer for Holmes to fight Tyson on November 6 at Caesars Palace in Las Vegas. For $2.2 million, Holmes said, he could see his way to fighting Tyson.

But as far as Cayton and Jacobs were concerned, if Holmes were to fight Tyson for $2.2 million Arum would be no part of it. There was history there. For seventeen years, Jacobs said, he and Cayton had been good friends with Arum—until Arum tried to steal a fighter of theirs, Wilfred Benitez. While Arum conceded that he sought to become involved with Benitez, he claimed he did so only when the fighter and his father questioned whether Jacobs's option on an expiring contract was valid. "Eventually Jacobs and Benitez argued it before the New York State Athletic Commission," Arum said, "which upheld their option."

Marvin Kohn, a deputy commissioner for the New York organization, said that Benitez had signed a six-year contract with Jacobs, even though the commission usually permits managerial contracts to run for only four years. "But Jack Prenderville, who was chairman at the time, allowed the six-year term because Jacobs paid the fighter a seventy-five-thousand-dollar bonus for the extra two years," Kohn said. "Prenderville felt the fighter was getting fair return. At the time of the dispute, Benitez wanted to break the contract and he said he never had signed it. But I had witnessed the signing and the commission ruled for Jacobs."

Jacobs had a deep abiding distaste for Arum. Not a man ordinarily given to petty gossip, he was only too pleased to make an exception in Arum's case. A line of D'Amato's was a special favorite of his. "Someone," recalled Jacobs, "once asked Cus to compare Arum to another promoter. 'I don't know the promoter you're talking about,' Cus said, 'but I do know Arum.

The other guy couldn't be as bad as Arum. Because God couldn't make the same mistake twice.'"

For his part, Arum depicted Jacobs as a rich man so consumed by amassing money—as he had amassed fight films and a collection of more than 800,000 comic books he kept in storage in Los Angeles—that he was an Ebeneezer caricature. By Arum's account, Jacobs lived well beneath his means and would turn rhapsodic about a particularly keen bargain he had gotten.

Confirmed as their enmity was, still they had dealt with one another early in Tyson's career. Arum had a long-running boxing program on TV—a weekly card that had appeared on ESPN since 1980. With Tyson's objective to fight once, twice a month, Arum's ESPN outlet offered regular exposure before a national television audience.

In spite of what Cayton and Jacobs might have thought of Arum, they were not about to let personal feelings stand in the way of an opportunity for their fighter. Tyson was put on the ESPN card. But according to Cayton, dates that were later promised to Tyson abruptly dematerialized. And when Cayton complained, Arum told him he could not interfere in matters his hirelings were charged to conduct. So the dealings with Arum ended. A new promoter, Jeff Levine, was located, and he did what Arum would not: he gave Tyson regular work in venues in the Albany area.

Presumably, by August 1986 Arum knew that he was not exactly the promoter of choice for Cayton and Jacobs. And with a star of Tyson's magnitude, the two men never had to do business again with Arum. What Arum accomplished in upping the ante for Holmes was to make future negotiations with Holmes more difficult for Cayton and Jacobs. He had raised not only Holmes's price but his expectations as well, and he had done so, they felt, for petty mischief—to screw them up by forcing them to pay Holmes more than they would have had Arum not indulged in his bit of harum-scarum. The more Holmes got of the available monies for the bout—live site fee, TV, foreign sales—the less there was for Tyson, and that galled Cayton and Jacobs.

A few hundred thousand, more or less, might not seem a major issue to the civilian unaccustomed to dealing in the finances of big-time boxing. But Cayton and Jacobs took pride in making the best deals possible—the dollars and cents were tantamount to keeping score. They shared a reputation for being negotiators who, as one man who had dealt with them put it, "leave no crumbs on the table."

For Don King, the idea that his archrival, Arum, *might* infiltrate a division, the heavyweights, that had been his purview through the 1980s was enough to make him take another stab at getting Tyson into the HBO series he was copromoting with Lewis. Never mind that Cayton and Jacobs had made it clear that their future course was Tyson-Holmes. King trusted King to do what he did best: talk his way toward a solution. The problem was how to resuscitate negotiations that Cayton and Jacobs had declared terminated.

"King was over at my office that day, August 14," recalled HBO's Abraham. "At the time he had to give Jacobs a ten-thousand-dollar check for training expenses for a fighter of his, Edwin Rosario. So he called Jacobs and said, 'Come up to my office and I'll give you the check.' Jim suggested he just send it by messenger. 'No, no,' said Don, who was acting as if he were in his office. 'You got to come up to get the check.' After he hung up, Don said, 'I got to talk to Jim, got to keep the deal alive.'"

King rushed from the HBO office at Sixth Avenue and 42nd Street to his office at 69th Street, off Madison Avenue, roughly a mile in distance. By then it was 5:30 P.M. With a phone call, King dispatched Abraham and another HBO executive to his office.

Abraham said: "Jim saw us walk in and said, 'What are you doing here? I'm not here about Mike Tyson.' That's when Don walks in. Jim says, 'I've been tricked.'"

For the next four hours, negotiations resumed in King's office, followed by a dinner that ran past midnight. By the wee hours of the morning, a "frame of a deal," as Abraham put it, was in place.

Soon after, the *Times* headline would read:

TYSON TO JOIN
HBO'S SERIES

FIRST FOE
IS BERBICK

*   *   *

Berbick was as finely tuned an agitator as there was in the boxing business; he was not going to let the formality of a contract disturb his latest notion of his net worth to a promotion. As the WBC heavyweight champion, Berbick had more than a little leverage.

Not only that—he knew that with Tyson's entrance into the series, the economics had changed. HBO had agreed to pay Tyson $5.5 million for a projected three fights, including $1,550,000 to fight Berbick. That was twice as much as the $750,000 Berbick was supposed to get, and the disparity struck him as being way out of line. It made Berbick willing to continue his dialogue with Rappaport about a fight with Cooney.

In August, Berbick and his Las Vegas attorney, Marc Risman, flew to Kingston, Jamaica, to confer with Rappaport and his attorney, Neil Gerst. On arriving there, Berbick made himself scarce, leaving Risman to get the negotiations rolling. But Risman, who drove a gold Rolls-Royce and carried a cordless telephone, could not make much headway with Rappaport, who kept wondering whether Risman was proceeding from Berbick's instructions or just winging it on his own.

Rappaport's antagonism toward the lawyer was further fueled by the bills he was paying in Kingston for Risman's room and board—a tab he said was topheavy with dining costs because Risman, Rappaport claimed, was enjoying lobsters virtually around the clock—breakfast, lunch, and dinner. Had Rappaport paid as much mind, Risman insisted, to an equitable distribution of the wealth for Berbick-Cooney as he did to the consumption of Jamaican lobster, he might have been in more harmony with the tropical setting. Risman was asking for an advance of $300,000 and for additional guarantees in case Cooney pulled out of the fight, leaving Berbick possibly stripped of his title and without anything to show for it.

Even when Berbick deigned to appear, he had a way of disconcerting the other side with his changing moods. "He was," said Gerst of Berbick, "extremely erratic. One day during discussions, I was watching Trevor. What he was doing, as we negotiated, was looking at a stack of pictures. He'd look at a picture, really study it, and finally sign it. For forty-five minutes this went on. A long careful look, sign it. A long careful look, sign it. Eventually, as he saw me staring at him, he showed me what the pictures were. They were postcards of him with a label on it, something like 'Jamaican Hero' or 'Young Tiger.' Some kind of hero picture that he was autographing. *But* . . . they were all the same. Every one was the same shot. Yet he'd study each one of them before signing."

It was not until Berbick brought another man into negotiations that Rappaport, Gerst, *et al,* began to feel some progress was being made. He was Lucien Chen, a Chinese-Jamaican who had grown up in the slums of Kingston. Chen was a legal bookmaker in Jamaica with a chain of fifty betting shops; he owned a video rental store in Miami.

Chen was a congenial man who lived in the fast lane: he had owned horses, gambled heavily, and never been averse to a party. He had married a former Miss Chinese Jamaica and had even produced a film in Jamaica, *The Marijuana Affair.* Although it was, by his own admission, a commercial flop, for redeeming social value it could boast the screen debut of one Bob Arum. Arum, a friend of Chen's, had played Stokes, a high-level bureaucrat who turned out to be a conniving dope dealer.

To Rappaport, Chen was a "charming guy." More to the point, he was a man who got negotiations on track. Risman did not disappear from the daily discussions, but with Chen involved Cooney's people felt they were moving forward.

"One day, toward the end of our week in Kingston," said Gerst, "the meeting broke up. We felt we were starting to get close. To keep things going, Dennis, Risman, and I kept talking. And from being close to a deal all of a sudden Risman started to impose unilateral terms that Berbick had not mentioned. Dennis was questioning him when Risman started pointing a finger and yelling. I'm disgusted. I get up from the conference table and start walking around. The next thing I know Dennis is on top of Risman's chair and is choking Risman. There is a lot of yelling and a few four-letter words."

Risman's version: "We were discussing terms in what I thought was a businesslike manner when suddenly Rappaport rose up and . . . I don't know whether he was trying to choke me or push me out of the chair. But he went on the attack. Cursing as he did. I was shocked. I'd conducted a lot of business negotiations and had never seen anything like that. As bright as he was in real estate, he had trouble concluding a deal fair to all parties. He could not perceive someone else was in the driver's seat."

Gerst moved to break up the fight, but without great urgency. "I walked around the table the long way," he would joke later, a pointed commentary on his feelings about Risman.

As August wound down and the fight crowd headed to Las Vegas for the next bout in the HBO series—Spinks vs. Tangstad on September 6—Rappaport had acquired powerful allies in his efforts to persuade Berbick to fight Cooney. With Arum agreed to copromote the bout and Caesars Palace to serve as the live site, Berbick knew whatever offer Rappaport or his negotiator, Loren Cassina, made had real weight behind it. On an airline ticket sent him by King, Berbick made plans to go to Vegas.

To flee or not to flee—that was the question. Berbick could jump the series and, for a price, fight Cooney, or he could renegotiate with the cagey King and avoid the political waves that his defection might trigger. (It was rumored that the WBC would strip him of his title if he fought Cooney.) In the days before he was to leave Florida for the Nevada desert, Berbick scrambled to find his answers. He knew he might never have an opportunity like this to strike it rich; that was making him edgy. On Wednesday, September 3, Berbick twice phoned Seth Abraham and asked him to be in Las Vegas to lend his support to whatever deal he might strike with King. "If you come out and guarantee my purse won't be cut . . ." said Berbick to Abraham. At the same time, communications with Cooney's people continued.

On September 5, Berbick headed to Las Vegas from Florida, accompanied by Chen. Berbick was due to check in at the Las Vegas Hilton, where the Spinks-Tangstad bout was being staged and where King was staying. But in midflight the plans changed.

"We had to switch planes on the way to Vegas," said Chen. "So from an airport phone I called Rappaport. 'Listen, Dennis, we're supposed to go to the Hilton. But Trevor doesn't want to go to the Hilton. He doesn't want a confrontation with Don King.' And Dennis: 'No problem. We'll send the limo for you.'"

On landing, Berbick was whisked away by limousine to Caesars Palace. He and Chen went straight to a suite without troubling to check in. The paperwork was done in their rooms, Berbick registering under the alias T. Brown.

Late that Friday night at the Hilton, Abraham turned up for a meeting at which he and King expected to see Berbick. But in his place Berbick sent Risman, who set up a meeting for the following morning in King's suite.

Meanwhile, back at Caesars Place, negotiations with Rappaport's man, Loren Cassina, went on far into the night. Cassina awoke early Saturday morning and called Rappaport to tell him if he wanted a deal with Berbick, he would have to up the ante.

"We'd been talking of two million for Berbick," said Cassina. "I told Dennis the deal could be made at three million. By this time, what King was offering was one point six million for Berbick, with Carl King getting a managerial share of that."

That morning, Chen received a firm offer of $3 million for Berbick to fight Cooney. With that offer in mind, he proceeded from Caesars Palace to the Hilton. There, joined by Risman, he met with King and, from HBO, Abraham and Greenway.

Abraham asked Chen: "Do you have the authority to sign for Trevor Berbick?"

Chen said, "No. I negotiate for him."

"Then this is a waste of time," said Abraham, who departed with Greenway.

That night, Spinks stopped Tangstad in four rounds. By morning, Chen was having second thoughts about Berbick vs. Cooney.

"All night I couldn't sleep," said Chen. "I got up Sunday at six, seven A.M. and spoke to Trevor."

Chen expressed concern that the combined forces of King and HBO might litigate the fight out of existence, and damage Berbick financially in the process.

With Carl King owed one-third of the $3 million purse, Chen wondered aloud, might Berbick be at less risk fighting Tyson if a deal could be cut to improve the $1.6 million that King had out on the table?

With a letter from Berbick authorizing him to negotiate, Chen met King at midday in a coffee shop at the Hilton. At that time, King raised the $1.6 million offer to $1.8 million. With King's stepson, Carl, taking a 33⅓ percent managerial share of Berbick's purse, that left Berbick with a cool $1.2 million.

"Don," said Chen, "let's not waste time. You know that's unacceptable."

Back and forth they went, King sticking to 1.8.

"If that's your best offer," said Chen, "I'll pass it on to Trevor."

"Hang on," said King. "You're not going without me. You started it with me and you've got to finish it with me."

When they arrived at Caesars Palace, rather than going up to see Berbick they detoured instead to a coffee shop and resumed their talks there. $1.8 million transmuted into $2 million, with Carl King still due his 33⅓ percent share. Again Chen said no deal.

"Imagine, Lucien," said King, "two of the greatest negotiators in boxing . . . and this son of a bitch—I'm running after him."

"Don, this man is so mad," said Chen, "he'll go back to Port Antonio and fish for a living. He'd cut his nose to spite his face."

Shaking his head, King left the table. "I'm gone, I'm gone," he said.

Chen watched and waited as King wandered into a sundries shop in the hotel and eventually back to the coffee shop. With a new deal. The offer was now $2.1 million with $500,000 set aside for Carl King's managerial share; the net purse for Berbick was $1.6 million.

"I'm going to let Trevor accept this figure," said Chen.

Chen brought King up to the suite he and Berbick shared and had the promoter wait in his room while he laid out the deal for Berbick. When Berbick learned that King was there he excused himself on the pretext that he had to shave. To Chen it seemed the fighter was "terrified" at the prospect of facing King.

Eventually he finished shaving; when he and King saw one another, they embraced, as if long-lost buddies.

A meeting was arranged for later that afternoon at King's suite in the Hilton. Soon after, Berbick tippytoed out of Caesars Palace for the Hilton, again not bothering with the usual registration procedures. In King's suite the formalities were done. This time Berbick was checked in as Lawrence Welk.

Chen had insisted that the particulars of Berbick's purse be amended *on* the original contract, figuring that that would serve as a precedent if Berbick were to beat Tyson. As the conqueror of Tyson he would be worth more than the $1 million the contract called for him to receive for the bout that followed the match against Tyson.

With King, Chen had come to an understanding that the promoter would exert "best efforts" to sweeten that purse. In truth, Chen was not overly concerned that HBO would pinch pennies with the conqueror of Mike Tyson. But Risman was not so sure. He believed that what gave Berbick the bargaining power was the importance of the opponent, Tyson, and that, win or lose, Berbick would never again have the market value he did as of this moment. What's more, it was naive, he thought, to expect that if, say, Berbick later fought Witherspoon, or even Spinks, King would feel any urgency to lobby on his behalf for more money.

It was at this moment in the negotiations, as the deal was moving smoothly to a conclusion, that Risman chose to point out to Berbick the paradox of his getting $2.1 million to fight Tyson and not even half of that as the man who beat the scourge of Catskill. If there was one thing Berbick could fathom, it was his best interest. Quicker than you could say "deflationary market," he was threatening to bust the deal.

King went crazy. To be so close to a deal and then . . . Out of his chair he bolted, straight for Risman, to do him bodily harm. Poor Risman, who had gotten his degree thinking lawyering was a noncontact sport.

"I've never seen a man so mad," said Chen. "'You motherfucker.' And he was going after him. Even when Trevor held him, Don went on, trying to push Trevor away. Screaming at Risman, 'You motherfucker. I never want to see you again.' Risman turned white. He was backing off."

Risman's version: "King's outburst, compared to Rappaport's, was more controlled, maybe even planned as a negotiating tactic. King used the outburst to his advantage in the negotiations. He changed the tempo, it was a matter of distraction, of turning attention away from an important negotiating matter. He was screaming profanities, and 'I'm going to get you.' Both Carl King and Trevor jumped in between Don and me to stop any type of altercation. And Trevor: 'Don't worry about the options.'"

King's version: What Risman incident?

Anyway . . .

"I told 'em," said Chen, "'I can't deal with you people. This is like a street market. Let sanity prevail.' I started to leave. Don's attorney, Charles Lomax, and Carl King came after me. 'Without you, this deal will not go through.' I came back. I said to Trevor: 'Let King sign you and he'll do his utmost best to up the ante. Because if you beat Tyson, you'll be in a position to bargain.'"

Berbick saw the sense in that, and initialed the changes in the original contract.

Berbick versus Tyson was on.

8

Even though Berbick was the champion, he was going into the fight as the backdrop to Tyson's story. Most people were interested in whether Tyson, who had turned twenty that June, would become the youngest-ever heavyweight champion.

Big fights, and Berbick-Tyson was that, had a voltage that the routine matches didn't. The time leading up to such a bout unfolded with a ritualistic familiarity that heightened anticipation. A week before the match the press would begin to arrive; behind them would come the assorted other Boxing Guys—managers, trainers, cornermen, cut men, promoters, booking agents, commission members. In the lobby of the Hilton, they would mix and mingle, trading gossip and opinions and checking up on the latest odds.

For the writers, there were workouts to watch, a final press conference to attend. After sending their daily quota of words back to their home offices, they could find solace and sun poolside or continue to the Hilton lobby for a crack at the gaming tables. In a town that did not encourage early-to-bed, the boxing crowd would loiter in the lobby late at night, talking fight talk amid the constant paged searches for parties real and whimsical: *Telephone call for Don King, Don King. Telephone call . . . Telephone call for Dorsal Fin, Dorsal Fin. Telephone call.*

In the final day or two before the bout, civilians and celebrities streamed into the Hilton. As a rule of thumb, the center of attention in any prefight hotel lobby was slow-walking and soft-talking Muhammad Ali. Said to suffer from Parkinson's syndrome, Ali was patient and pleased with the very fond attentions. He signed autographs, hugged strangers, kissed babies.

In the forty-eight hours leading up to the fight, there was a festive air at the bout site. Evenings, women in slit skirts and revealing necklines were all about the lobby and casino: Prefight strut, Sly found, was directly proportional to the perceived glamour of the bout. The casinos understood that: their sports books established betting lines to encourage action on the fight (and not coincidentally compound the vigorish the house got with each bet). The big fights were a magnet for the action crowd; from all over the world the sporting sorts came, packing the tables the night before, and the day of, a bout. Cries of pleasure and disappointment, the physical density of that collective wagering creature, added to the feeling of big doings.

What was it about boxing that, more than any other sport, hooked the casinos' heaviest players? Probably the raw spectacle of risk. A fight's psychological core appealed to the competitive nature of the gambling man who would buck house odds for twenty, fifty, a hundred grand of play over a weekend.

In those forty-eight hours before the fight during which the casino's VIP crowd descended, so too did the hustlers and hookers and petty thieves slip into town. In some casinos, at elevator banks unsecured earlier in the week, uniformed guards now asked to see a room key as proof that the ride from the casino floor upward was for the right reasons.

The night of the fight, Sly would make his way to the arena early to reconnoiter the ringside setup and make sure he had a working phone and an electrical outlet to accommodate his computer typewriter. Gone were the days of tearing sheets of copy from the carriage of a manual machine and handing them to the Western Union man to send along. Once the fight was over and his account of it written, in this electronic world Sly would press a button that locked his story into the machine's brute memory and then would dial a phone number that connected to the *Times'* receiving apparatus back in New York.

With another flourish of buttons, he would be set up to transmit, and he would do so by slipping the phone receiver into two round receptacles built into his machine. Then, holding his breath, he would wait to see if this was the night his technology would rebel.

That was a horror. It was trying enough to think straight and write the King's English on deadline amid the noise and commotion of a big fight. To somehow muddle through and, with six hundred to one thousand words combat-ready, be sabotaged by machinery was an unimaginable insult to a man's nerve endings.

Soon after his ringside check, Sly would settle in for the early bouts, and as the arena gradually filled up over the next few hours, feel the excitement that a fight like Berbick-Tyson created. In the hour before the main event went off, the VIPs and celebrities made it to their seats. For Berbick-Tyson, on this night in November, 1986, there were Hollywood types—Kirk Douglas, Rob Lowe, Tony Danza, Robert Duvall, Mr. T, Sylvester Stallone, Eddie Murphy; television types—Heather Thomas, David Hasselhoff, Lisa Hartman; Vegas stars—David Brenner, Norm Crosby, Engelbert Humperdinck; and fighters—Ali, Hector Camacho, Thomas Hearns, Holmes, Michael Spinks. King, like a Catskill *tummler,* worked the ringside area, shaking hands, grinning, and intoning his signature line: "Only in America."

By now, Berbick and Tyson were in their dressing rooms, waiting. When Jacobs stopped in to see Tyson, Tyson asked his manager, "How do you feel?"

"My palms are sweaty," confessed Jacobs. "I'm nervous."

"That's very normal on the day of a title fight," Tyson assured Jacobs, in a tone so detached that Jacobs was taken aback.

Some experts had anticipated that Berbick might taunt and push Tyson to unnerve him, as he had done to Holmes, with whom he had gone the distance while losing a decision in 1981. But from the earliest moments of the bout, it was Berbick who was discomfited.

Berbick's face registered alarm, his movements turned herky-jerky and unsure, from the shock, it seemed, of the punches Tyson landed from the start on him. With twenty-six seconds remaining in the first round, Tyson hit Berbick with a jab, then threw a right-left-right-left combination, the last two punches of which landed on Berbick's jaw and sent him lurching backward toward the ropes, in imminent danger. Tyson dug two left hooks to the body to lower Berbick's defenses, classic finishing technique. But when he shifted his assault to Berbick's head, he was off target with most of his blows, and the champion had the good sense to hold on to Tyson until the referee, Mills Lane, broke them as the bell ending the round rang. As though to convince himself things were not so bad as they seemed, Berbick threw Tyson a baleful look and then stuck his tongue out at him.

That hardly deterred Tyson. As the second round opened, he began throwing punches with, as he put it later, "bad intentions." Some landed, some did not. But the final right of a seven-punch sequence knocked Berbick backward onto the canvas. Berbick got to his feet quickly, bouncing in place and nodding to Lane that he was all right.

He was not all right. The end came late in the round. Tyson had a unique combination: he would throw a right hand to the opponent's ribs and then, in a flash, rip the same hand in an upward arc, to the jaw. Against José Ribalta that August, he had landed the two-punch shazam perfectly, the uppercut lifting Ribalta off his toes before he dropped to the canvas.

Against Berbick, that uppercut missed. But the next punch, a left hook that Tyson bounced off Berbick's temple, did not. As Tyson landed the punch, he stepped in, gloves reaching for Berbick's arms to balance himself for his next thrust. But before Tyson could unload, Berbick, in delayed reaction, tumbled butt-first to the canvas.

Trying to regain his feet, Berbick went sprawling backward into the ropes near his corner and onto the canvas, his head going through the bottom two strands of the ring ropes while a glove brushed against the chest of one of the ringside photographers.

Berbick's arms flailed as he sought to right himself. He lurched back toward where he had fallen originally, in the center of the ring, and dropped again. This time he stabilized himself on his left knee and, getting himself erect, stumbled toward a neutral corner. By now, Lane's count had reached nine and Berbick was on his feet. The referee took a quick look at Berbick and, seeing he was in no condition to continue, threw his arms around him and stopped the bout.

At two minutes and thirty-five seconds of the second round, Mike Tyson became the youngest heavyweight champion in the history of boxing. As King, José Torres, Rooney, and others streamed into the ring, Tyson sought out Jacobs, saying to him: "Do you think Cus would have liked that?"

The impact of Tyson's blows that night went beyond the nearly comic loop-the-loop that Trevor Berbick's legs had executed.

With Tyson as champion, the heavyweight division was brimming with opportunity. All matter of gain seemed possible, as Berbick's maneuvers indicated. A onetime cruiseship waiter, he had huffed and bluffed his way to three times what HBO originally had intended to pay him, $1.6 million net. Berbick's fiscal derring-do stirred hopes in the hearts and minds of heavyweights everywhere: HBO, a component of the Time Inc. empire, and Don King had capitulated against Berbick's gimme-gimme, and visions of sugarplums must have danced in fighters' heads that night Tyson ascended. For they knew Tyson was the ghost of Ali and Leonard and, for that matter, of Elvis too. Tyson was show biz.

It was a rare fighter that managed to excite the public appetite for heroes, but when it did happen, it was more often than not the heavyweight champion who created a stir. Heavyweights had the knucklescraper appeal—they satisfied that place in the psyche that was roused by dominance. Tyson in his black trunks, the glistening body without robe, the shoes without socks, the close-cropped haircut, embodied the notion. In fact, the look of him was almost extreme, as if he had come off the drawing board of a cartoonist. Captain Mike, arms akimbo, scowl cutting laserchinks of fear into the hearts of merely mortal prizefighting men.

He was the compleat destroyer. It was not just that he had learned the Xs and Os of beating grown men up: he had the primeval passion for, and pleasure in, his task. Back in February '86, after he had stopped Jesse Ferguson in six rounds in his network TV debut, he had told newsmen with a half-smile: "In the fourth round, I saw the opening for that uppercut. I always try to catch them on the tip of the nose because I try to push the bone into the brain."

It was not a shock to reporters that there were practitioners

who worked from the darkest malice—the surprise was that
Tyson had spoken so candidly. For while boxing might oblige
men to be brutal and even cruel in their working hours, it was
customary that when the job was done the recounting of it was
couched in civil tones, with the opponent, however inferior,
praised beyond truth and reality. That was the drill as fighters
through the years had known it. Always the other guy was "willing," "came to fight," "took a helluva shot," "gave it his best,"
and so on and so forth.

That Tyson was not given to such clichés was, for the writers at least, a refreshing change. The bout's publicist, Mike Cohen, would hear more than a few writers remark how pleased
they were to discover the depth of this new phenomenon's
gladiatorial instinct: a three-dimensional character was always
easier, and more interesting, to write about.

Nor had Tyson's brutal imagery been a slip of the tongue.
For as those writers who had been sending early-deadline stories arrived at the press conference already in progress, Tyson
repeated what he had said before, uttering the words slowly,
precisely, as if to allow the slowest of the notetakers to get them
verbatim. So Tyson's wild and woolly words were accorded the
widest circulation, a sorry situation as far as Jacobs was concerned. In the weeks that followed he tried to discount the
quote by insisting it was misbegotten humor on the fighter's
part, or the influence of a karate movie Tyson had seen. He
even temporarily retired Cohen as his publicist.

Jacobs was always dogged in his defense of Tyson, and lav-
ish in his praise of "my little guy," as he called him, doing both
in a style of speaking uniquely his own. There was a pro-
fessorial thrust to his words. The language he used was precise
and sometimes felt as though it were gussied up in ruffed col-
lars. "Cus adored such and such," he would say. Or "Shelly's a
dear man." It was a spoken English given to if-I-mays and al-
low-me-to-suggests—a language that Jane Austen might have
written, and one that the press did not always appreciate.

It was in the nature of their relationship that the press
would want to strip away the masks of their subjects while management would prefer to keep the image of the fighter as sanitized as it could. Both sides understood the other's objective
and usually worked on one another without hard feelings aris-
ing. But between Jacobs and a portion of the boxing press there

developed an antagonism that was rooted in what the scribes—
a word of Sly's sports-page-addicted youth—perceived as the
manager's haughty attitude.

"You and I, my friend, are on tracks that are not converging," Jacobs would say to squelch a conversation he felt was
going nowhere. To Wally Matthews of *Newsday* Jacobs said, "Allow me to add one more tasty tidbit to your already vast storehouse of knowledge because I might know a little more about
this than you do."

Like him or not, whatever Jacobs did he did to protect his
fighter. He had recognized, for instance, the damage that
Tyson's bone-to-brain remark could do to the fighter's image,
and tried to remedy it. Part of the problem, in this instance, was
that with Tyson the callous presumptions of the gladiator did
not vanish merely because the fight was over. He was still
"pumped" in the minutes after the action. So the Ferguson bout
would be a lesson to the Tyson camp. After that, when fights
ended, Rooney and Steve Lott (the aide-de-camp and corner
man) would, so to speak, debrief Tyson. With the opponent still
lying prone, they would be at Tyson's shoulder to reorient him
to polite society, cueing him with the customary phrases that
fighters uttered after hostilities. *Showed a lot of heart . . . My hat
is off to him . . .* the usual la-di-dah. And most times Tyson
would play down the ferocity that made him so intriguing when
it was activated in the prize ring.

In those early days, both Jacobs and Cayton accentuated
the distance Tyson had traveled from his nasty origins. As businessmen, they understood that if Tyson was ever to capitalize
beyond the ring on his reputation, it was imperative that mainstream America feel comfortable with him. While the public
might marvel at the savagery with which Tyson dismantled opponents, it needed to be assured that he was, in a term sports
executives love to use, "good people." Good people, and not
another athletic creep. The impression he made after he
fought, or whenever else he looked at the Cyclops eye of the
TV camera and spoke in that incongruous voice of his, would
influence the corporate misters as to whether Tyson was hero
material.

It was a matter of image. Image was like advertising, a
slick-paper way to deceive. A celebrity's image was the palatable
truth, the cosmetic truth, the reconstructed truth, and a real-

life fucking lie. Just another of life's penny-ante trickerations, to use a Don Kingism of which the scribes were fond.

The Tyson that his managers wanted to convey was the slugger-with-a-heart, Joe Palooka Redux. The real Tyson was more complex—and still evolving, trying to do so as far from the public eye as he could get. As a result, Tyson was becoming the sort of celebrity about whom every development, change, complication was seized upon by curious fans, who computed each detail in their attempt to understand him.

Early in 1987, Sly received this letter from a female reader:

Dear Sir:

    Is there something wrong with Mike Tyson?
    I notice, while watching his last fight . . . a nervous jerking of his head.

    I have read numerous newspapers and have never seen any mention of this affliction.

No fighter in circulation at that time seemed to incite the interest Tyson did, but the question "What is Mike Tyson really like?" was not an easy one to answer. For one thing, Tyson was a private person given, by his own admission, to mood swings. Compared with, say, a Muhammad Ali, who was accessible to the news media and the public and was an extrovert, Tyson kept his distance.

When Sly, visiting him that first time, in November 1985 in the Catskills, asked to make notes on Tyson's room there, the fighter got a sheepish look on his face and politely wondered if the newsman would mind skipping that.

Later on, while training for big fights in Atlantic City and Las Vegas, Tyson would hole up in private quarters rather than in the casino/hotel facilities in which his opponents usually stayed. Where the Bonecrusher Smiths and Berbicks could be seen walking through hotel lobbies, Tyson was tucked away out of sight.

After Tyson's victory over Mike Jameson in Atlantic City on January 24, 1986, he appeared at a postfight interview in a pair of gaudy triangular sunglasses he later would refer to as his "Andy Warhol look." That night he displayed a remote, nearly belligerent attitude toward reporters' questions. When he was reminded of those circumstances much later, he would say: "I just didn't care. I wanted someone to say something about the glasses."

There was a sense back then that Tyson was feeling his way toward his new celebrity. Those were the days when Tyson would attend news media functions and even awards dinners in old street clothes—a denim jacket unbuttoned to the navel—and answer questions as though he were double-parked. "You got enough?" he would ask, easing from the dais before anybody could protest.

Earlier in his championship year, he had experimented with the party life that his success made available to him.

"I went off the track a little when I first became popular," he said. "I wanted to test it out. To try this, to try that. I went on a spree. Girl hunting. Hanging out late. I was really curious what it was like to be a semicelebrity, what it's like to hang out."

Under D'Amato there was not much margin in Tyson's training regimen. "With Cus," said Jacobs, "it was train, fight, train, fight. Cus had no tolerance for three days off and go-have-fun-with-the-guys. But it wouldn't have been any good for Bill or me to tell Mike he shouldn't have been doing what he was. Because I know when I was nineteen, if anybody told me not to do something, I'd go and do it."

On his own, Tyson said, he discovered that party life was "not my style, not really me."

"I'd step back and look at what I was doing," he said. "It was a show, a circus. And the people—not that I feel superior to them—I was just not one of them. They were meant for one another. I am not a weirdo that dresses crazy. So why should I go to those places?"

Tyson seemed to have a distrust of celebrity—and ambivalence toward the acclaim accorded him by a world of strangers. Long before he was Iron Mike he had existed outside the mainstream, just another guy.

What's more, the feeling grew that Tyson's "moodiness" might harbor a darker side. For as time went on, Sly heard ominous rumblings about the fighter's Catskill past. The Cus-and-the-kid tale was not necessarily the idyllic version that was circulated. A few dark patches had been conveniently edited out.

"Mike had problems, lots of problems," said Teddy Atlas.

"He'd verbally, and a little physically, force himself on girls in school. There were a whole bunch of incidents reported, incidents by young girls in school. They'd say no. He'd get emotional. Wasn't good emotion. He felt he had a right to act that way.*

"One time, he wanted to be fed in high school at ten in the morning, and when the teachers told him no, he opened a milk bin and threw pints of milk at them, and all over the place. That night I had a bunch of kids fighting on a card at Columbia-Greene Community College and I told Mike he couldn't go. I got there, I look up. And there's Cus, smiling, with Mike.

"I felt Mike needed to be disciplined like I disciplined others in the gym. Cus was creating a situation where he was allowing him to get away with this. I was the fortress of discipline. I became the guy nobody wanted to hear. Cus would tell me: 'He's from a special background, he has to be dealt with with more sensitivity.' I told him: 'Cus, that's a crock.' Cus was a good man, but he was human. He wanted another champion. Money meant nothing to him. But fame and ego and a place in history mattered a real lot. I understood Cus, I felt for Cus. The guy was under tremendous pressures."

Atlas said that as Tyson's destiny became clearer to D'Amato, D'Amato was more inclined to paper over Tyson's problems.

"Cus allowed Mike to think you can cover things up with friends in the press, radio, and police department," said Atlas. "He was showing him ways to escape. Cus was a great man, but he justified what he was doing for his own reasons. He was afraid to discipline Mike because he could punch so hard. The way of dealing with it was to cover up, to put a Band-Aid on. It was a lesson to Mike, who, with his mentality, figured he could get away with things."

Atlas recalled the time Tyson "put his hands on" a male teacher during a dispute.

"They had a hearing at the school," said Atlas, "and Mike said the teacher threw a book at him. I had three kids from the class who worked out in the same gym with Mike. They told me it didn't happen, the teacher didn't throw a book. But Cus told

---

*On ABC-TV's *20/20* a few years later, a woman named Robin Givens would speak about that troubled adolescence during which, she said, Tyson was "hitting teachers and hitting girls and pulling them into a bathroom."

Mike, 'Don't worry. If they throw you out, I'll get Jim Jacobs to get you a tutor.'"

Because of the classroom incident, Tyson was expelled and D'Amato arranged for a tutor.

"Mike was a ward of the state," said Atlas. "And a lot of the reason Cus would handle situations himself was that under the terms of being a ward of the state, the state could pull him back. The state was paying for him to live at Camille's house. And under those circumstances, he had to keep up rehabilitation. They were supposed to stay informed about school and any incidents, and deal with them accordingly. They could, if they wanted, have put him back in a facility, or a foster facility. Cus was afraid of that. Cus was bright, and charming, and he gained the caseworker's confidence. Basically the line of communication was broken because the system depended on Cus's version. When Mike dropped out of school, the state didn't even know. Cus had gained their confidence, and they didn't check. He'd send them clips about Mike winning fights. Meantime, Mike was being abusive with other students and doing things, and nobody said, 'Hey, you have to learn there's a certain way to behave. And that comes first.'"

It was Tyson's behavior that apparently brought the split between D'Amato and Atlas. For a long time the specifics of what occurred eluded Sly. From Atlas he got a terse admission that there had been incidents involving Tyson. From the Tyson camp there was even less said. The subject of Teddy Atlas was closed to discussion.

In follow-up attempts to pry the information, more details would emerge. Atlas would divulge that in one instance Tyson had abused somebody and that he as his trainer would not stand for it.

Fred Chetti supplied the missing information. Chetti, a fifty-two-year-old management-level worker in the computer business, had two sons who had worked out in D'Amato's boxing club, and he himself had been a member of the village of Catskill recreation commission that had approved D'Amato's conversion of a meeting hall into his Main Street gym.

"There were two incidents," he said, "that led to Teddy's going. The first involved his sister-in-law, who was fifteen, sixteen years old at the time. She claimed Tyson tried to put his hands on her in school. She told Teddy's wife, Elaine, who was close to our family, and Elaine told us.

"The other incident was when Tyson came home from a workout and, without showering, sat on a couch in Camille's house. Camille is fussy about her house. She asked him not to sit there 'til he'd showered. Well, he cussed her up and down— she'll deny it today, but another fighter living there told me about it—and Teddy didn't like it.

"Both of those incidents came at a time when Tyson was walking into the gym when he felt like it, training when he felt like it, even disrupting the schedules of the other fighters. And Cus was letting him get away with it. This kid was doing what he wanted to do.

"Well, Teddy had it out with Tyson, and threatened him.* The kid went to Cus. Cus backed Tyson. 'Leave him alone,' he told Teddy. Cus was afraid that the kid would walk away."

Chetti said that Tyson's reputation in Catskill was never a sterling one. Aside from his problems with co-eds and teachers, he had a reputation for bullying younger boys into giving up their lunch money to him. But Tyson's success after he turned pro in March 1985 changed how he was perceived in Catskill. The same people who had once shunned him now wanted to befriend him. He was not exactly surprised: throughout the loneliness of his incubation period in Catskill, D'Amato forecast the day when the instant friends would materialize.

For Tyson, his extended family would become his anchor in a life grown chaotic with money and acclaim. In news conferences, where he would become visibly bored, he would sink into his chair and rest his head on the shoulder of Jacobs, much as a child might. With the world at large, Tyson kept his guard up, suspicious of what it could want from a once-poor black kid, and determined not to be a captive of his success. At times he would bolt from appointments with the news media or disappear from training camps, his way of not taking things seriously.

"It's nice," said Tom Patti, an amateur boxer who lived in the Catskill house with D'Amato and Tyson, "to be in charge of

---

*Was Atlas's threat backed by a gun? That was the rumor that the boxing press heard. Atlas: "I had something in my hand—let's leave it at that."

your own world. I think that's what it is. Rather than being at everyone else's beckoning."

Now that he was champion, there would be more time between fights. Tyson spent it increasingly in New York, staying at the East 40s apartment of his aide-de-camp, Lott. With a longtime partner of Jacobs's, Marty Decatur, Lott had been the national four-wall handball doubles champion in 1975, and he worked for The Big Fights, Inc., as a film editor. Often unannounced, Tyson would turn up at Lott's door; he would camp out for as long as he had free time to move about the city. In New York, there were movies, concerts, parties, order-in Chinese food. Some nights Tyson would look at old fight films with Jacobs, who lived in Lott's building. Mornings, Lott would wake to find Tyson asleep on his living-room couch, the TV on, a portion of Tyson stranded on the floor, the rest of him holding precariously to the couch. A curious sight, Lott found—the WBC heavyweight champion all pretzeled up like that.

For Tyson it was a time for the fun he had known only in a more limited way as an amateur. His odd-man-out status in Catskill had not made for the sort of bonhomie that Fonz and the guys had on TV, and social life was sometimes so troubling that Tyson would get depressed. Once when Tyson was feeling low-down about the vagaries of his teen love life, D'Amato reacted to it by telling him to buy a bat. "A bat?" said Tyson. "What's that got to do with anything?"

"'Cause when you turn pro," said D'Amato, "you're going to need it to keep the girls away from you."

Sometimes the image of Tyson—willful agent of violent endings—was so vivid that a man could forget the obvious—that the physical fighter and the chronological youth were not yet emotionally integrated. "When I first got to know Mike," said Lott, "he was like any eighteen-year-old boy. Nervous with girls. And so forth. I remember just after he turned pro, Cus told Jim and Bill, 'He wants a car, he wants a Cadillac.' So Jim said: 'If you say he wants it, and it's okay with you, it's okay with us.' They bought him a new car, a silver-and-gray Cadillac. Mike loved it. In that period—we're talking about March, April, May of 1985—he'd sit out in the driveway in Catskill, turn the radio on, and just stay there until he fell asleep."

As a teenager, Tyson had had fantasies of carrying on like

John L. Sullivan, who used to belly up to bars and boast he could whip any man in the house. But as a certified adult, Tyson found that "it wasn't really me—to be insane." Tyson preferred to move about this sweet-swinging sphere in a quieter fashion, trying not to draw attention to himself.

Not long after Tyson beat Berbick, Sly met up with him in The Big Fights' offices, where—strange interview—Tyson seated himself before a TV and answered questions while watching the flickering footage of old fight films on the screen. The questions dealt largely with the state of mind of the new champion. The answers came amid his reactions to the unfolding fight action on the TV. "Boom, boom, boom—oh, what a beating!" he said at one point as Jack Dempsey pounded Jess Willard.

When Tyson talked of himself, though, the mood was more subdued; he seemed energized only when boxing was involved. He was, by his own account, detached from a world that was eager to celebrate him. "I have to have excitement because I'm a dull guy," he said.

Yet the parties and the nightclubs that were the routine diversions of the young apparently went just so far with him. In the weeks following his victory over Berbick, Tyson said that he had looked for fun but "didn't have any—I don't know what to do."

"Those parties," he said, "I get tired of parties."

Eventually, he said he settled for eating out with friends, or just being by himself.

"I watch more TV than I used to," he said. "I don't know why. I guess I'm bored a lot."

Tyson by now had a two-bedroom apartment in Albany that he used on occasion for privacy. But he still considered home to be in Catskill. "I've been places," he said, "and wasn't that impressed."

Wherever he went, he was drawing crowds, attention he did not welcome. "I've had nights where people nag you, nag you, nag you," he said. "I'm twenty years old. And they're talking, talking. Give you no privacy. And I'm a very private person. Can I tell you something? Other than boxing, everything is so boring."

That afternoon Tyson said he had no new friends, and didn't want any. What friends he already had, he insisted, were enough to last him a lifetime. "Lots of guys come around now," he said. "I don't know what they're looking for. But there is nothing they're getting."

Was it a pose—a cynic's posturing? Not really, said Rooney, the trainer, who believed that when his fighter was not in a gym or in the boxing arena he was truly at large. "Other than girls," said Rooney, "he doesn't have a lot of interests."

What he did have was a catalytic effect on the heavyweight division. With Tyson as champion, things began to happen—motion and commotion in a division that he had turned cash-rich. All of a sudden the beggars could be choosy. The season of trickerations was at hand.

The next bout on the unification series docket was the heavyweight title fight between Witherspoon and Tubbs that the WBA had mandated when traces of marijuana had shown up in Witherspoon's postfight specimen. It was a rematch—scheduled for December 12 at Madison Square Garden—that held little appeal for boxing aficionados, the original fight having been a clinker. In a paroxysm of candor, King, the promoter of both fights, would say that pairing those two men again was so limited an attraction that it "couldn't draw flies to a dump."

Curious words to speak aloud just days before the rematch. Yet by then, events were unfolding that would make King and his methods as much an issue as the fight.

The convoluted scenario began on December 4, eight days before the bout, when Tubbs said he had a shoulder injury and King said that that was merely Tubb's way of trying to enlarge his purse, reported to be between $75,000 and $85,000. King used the word "extortion" for what Tubbs was doing. Whereupon Tubbs materialized in New York on December 8, waving medical reports from his Los Angeles physician and agreeing to be examined by the New York State Athletic Commission.

Tubbs asked that the bout be postponed so he would not lose the chance to fight for the title. But after Tubbs dropped out, HBO executives began negotiating with representatives of Tyrell Biggs, an undefeated heavyweight, to take Tubbs's place. When those negotiations broke down over Biggs's asking price, $475,000, King began talking to Alan Kornberg, the comanager of heavyweight James (Bonecrusher) Smith.

At the time Smith was in training for a bout with Mitch Green, the fighter whose tirade on his fiscal abuse at the hands of the Kings, *père et fils*, had enlivened the weigh-in preceding his match against Tyson in May. Like Green and, it would soon appear, virtually every heavyweight contender, Smith had his own grievance against the King household.

In an affidavit given on June 16, 1986, as part of Smith and Kornberg's suit against Don King Productions, Inc., and Carl King, Smith stated that two months earlier, in April, he had gone to Las Vegas for the Spinks-Holmes title fight and had met with Don King.

Smith said in his affidavit, "King told me if I wanted a championship bout I had to enter into a promotional agreement with DKP and also had to sign a managerial agreement with Carl King, his son. If I failed to agree to have Carl King as my manager, there would be no promotional agreement for a championship fight."

In his affidavit, Smith said that because of the "activity" in King's suite he and King took their discussions to the bathroom in the promoter's suite.

"I was presented," said Smith in his affidavit, "with what I thought was a promotional agreement for the championship bout. While I was attempting to read the agreement within the confines of the bathroom, King stopped me and said it was a 'basic contract,' demanded me to 'sign here.' I left the meeting with a contract after having signed the agreement."

Smith's relationship with Kornberg had been a close and mostly satisfactory one. But back in April, Smith, thirty-three years old rather than the thirty-one listed on press releases, had known time was running out on his goal of becoming heavyweight champion. That pressure had led him into an alliance with the Kings that he questioned soon after signing his promotional deal.

"Subsequent to the signing of this agreement, I met with Carl King," Smith said in his affidavit. "I advised Carl that I had no need for his services as I already had a manager. I was advised again that there would be no promotional agreement for a championship bout unless I signed an agreement to have Carl as my manager. I reluctantly signed."

By December, it was not widely known that Carl King was comanager of Smith. Even after Don King and Kornberg struck a deal, Carl King's role was enough of a secret that José Torres, chairman of the New York State Athletic Commission, would profess he was unaware of the arrangement. Whatever. Bonecrusher agreed to take Tubbs's place for $230,000, a sum deemed sufficient to make Kornberg and Smith drop their suit against the Kings. Witherspoon had an opponent. King and HBO had a fight.

Or so it seemed; in fact, things got curiouser and curiouser. Suddenly Witherspoon, who was managed by Carl and promoted by Don, began to question whether he was getting his due. For fighting Tubbs, Witherspoon was to have been paid $250,000. Under pressure to ensure his good patron, HBO, of a fight, King had been obliged to pay Smith a lot more money than he would have given him under normal circumstances. With Smith getting $230,000, that required King to up Witherspoon's purse by $50,000, to $300,000.

But Witherspoon by now was asking in whose interests it was for him to fight Smith. For with Tubbs no longer the opponent, Witherspoon felt the mandate for the bout was lifted and he was free and clear to move on in the series and fight his next scheduled opponent, Tyson, for a $1 million purse. $1 million versus $300,000: the next move was clear. Witherspoon hired a lawyer, Dennis Richard, of Miami.

Richard was a newcomer to boxing, but on Wednesday, December 10, two days before the bout, he would get a seminar in the semilunatic convolutions of the sport.

The day began innocently with a news conference which attorney Richard said he had been told was off until he and King could unravel the paperwork attendant to the fight. As Richard was saying there was no news conference, a news conference of sorts broke out, with Smith and his manager,

Kornberg, huddled with reporters and the Garden's director of boxing, Bobby Goodman, attempting to point the gathered souls to their seats.

When Richard advised reporters that Witherspoon had hired him because King refused to let the fighter look at documents dating back to 1984, an aide of King's accused Richard of holding a news conference at what was not to have been a news conference at all. At which point King, having got wind that the nonevent was rolling of its own accord, arrived, followed soon after by Mitch Green, who launched into a finger-pointing tirade against the promoter.

"For the last time, Don," he shouted, "you done messed up my life! Six years you took my money!"

As King stood behind burly colleagues, Green shouted, "I'm going to break his neck," while a female friend tugged at his arm and tried to steer him away from trouble.

When King cracked an uneasy smile, Green sneered, "Keep laughing, keep laughing."

Green's pique apparently was over his canceled bout against Smith for that weekend in North Carolina. With Smith being released from his contract so that he could fight Witherspoon, Green was out in the cold.

"I'da broken Tyson's neck if you'da paid me," Green now shouted.

"How come there's no security?" King wondered.

"I got more money my first pro fight than I got in six years with you!" Green shouted.

"This is a joke," said King.

"Taking from everybody," said Green. "Nobody wants to speak up. Keep on laughing. I'm going to jump on you. I'm the wrong guy to fool with. I stand up for my rights."

Eventually, Green left, and King, taking charge of what was now definitely a news conference, spoke for seventy minutes, quoting Shakespeare, using street colloquialisms and Biblical allusions. He referred to America the Beautiful, the Constitution, and the Bill of Rights.

"I did not establish the rules of boxing," he said. "I just play by them. But I police myself because I recognize that white America makes the victim the victimizer."

He depicted his operation as doing right by black fighters whom white promoters had wronged in the past. He said he had persuaded the WBA not to strip Witherspoon of his title when traces of marijuana were found in his system after his bout against Tubbs in January; wasn't Witherspoon's implicit threat to withdraw from Friday's fight an odd way of showing gratitude? He said that HBO had given him $750,000 to stage the fight and that his "nut" was already $1 million (which he intimated made a profit as unlikely as Witherspoon's squeezing a penny more out of him). He promised that in the future there would be "no more arm around the shoulder, lovey-dovey" with his fighters.

Witherspoon's attorney, Richard, then got up to say, "The lady doth protest too much."

Three hours and fifteen minutes after the non–news conference was scheduled to begin it ended, with Richard and King adjourning to a meeting at which they hoped to sort out their differences so that the fight could take place.

That left James Smith of Lillington, North Carolina, to conjure with his last big chance as a fighter—and with the improbability of it.

The life of Smith had had the variegated richness that used to be mandatory for any red-blooded novelist.

A college graduate, Smith had been a farmboy, a soldier, a prison guard, a car salesman, and a heavyweight fighter. His was not the usual dossier of a boxer. But then for Smith, the path he had taken to glory in the ring had been anything but typical. To begin with, he did not throw a punch in anger until he was twenty-three years old and stationed in Wurzburg, West Germany, with the army. A file clerk for the military, Smith would wander into the base gym to play basketball—a sport he had lettered in at high school in Warsaw, North Carolina, and at Shaw University (B.A. in business administration) in Raleigh.

"Before then," said Smith, "I hadn't even been in fistfights. I was a big kid and nobody picked on me. Then one day in Germany, the boxing coach there asked me would I be interested in fighting." Smith was interested. Though he "didn't know anything about boxing," he knocked out his first opponent. Success provided its own impetus. Smith began to fight in military tournaments, and when he was mustered out at Fort Dix, he went on to Philadelphia and enrolled at Joe Frazier's gym to find out, in the fighter's words, "how good I was."

"It was a chance to spar with Michael Spinks, with Marvis Frazier, with Jimmy Young," said Smith. "I was star-struck. To be there with Joe Frazier—it was a pleasure to be in the same gym, even though guys were beating me up in the ring every day. But I kept learning."

Eventually, fight managers began to approach Smith with offers to turn professional, but after each offer, the next manager to speak to him would warn him off the fellow before. All the whispers and insinuations made this self-described country boy—Smith grew up on a thirty-acre tobacco farm in Magnolia, North Carolina—uneasy and "all confused."

"Pro, that was all new to me," said Smith. "I decided, 'I'm getting out of here.'"

In 1979, Smith and his wife, Reba, returned to North Carolina, where he began to work as a prison guard for $700 to $800 a month, a job that quickly enough became an inducement to try boxing again.

"It was depressing seeing guys locked up," said Smith. "And for eight hours every day, I was locked up too."

Three nights a week he would drive fifty miles from Magnolia to Fort Bragg in Fayetteville to train at the base gym. It was there, in November 1981, that he heard that Teddy Brenner, the matchmaker from Bob Arum's Top Rank organization, was looking for an opponent for James Broad.

"There was a chance to fight on national TV, on ESPN," said Smith. "Live from Atlantic City."

In his debut as a professional, James Smith was knocked out by Broad in four rounds. "I figured afterward that professional boxing was not for me," Smith said.

Thinking it over, though, he became convinced he could do better. In 1982, he beat Rickey Parkey (who later became the IBF cruiserweight champion) on a decision, then knocked out Mike Cohen and Lou Alexander.

"After Broad, raw strength got me over," said Smith. "Nobody else believed I could do it. I was an opponent. At least they thought I was."

On September 11, 1982, he was supposed to be just an opponent against Chris McDonald, a promising young heavyweight with a network TV deal. Against McDonald, in his fifth professional bout, Smith scored an upset decision.

Two New Yorkers, a real estate broker named Alan

Kornberg and a mortgage banker named Steve Nelson, were watching the fight on TV that night. Both had spoken of taking a fling at managing a prizefighter, and an unknown like Smith seemed just right for the pair of managerial beginners.

Kornberg and Nelson gave Smith a $5,000 signing bonus and put him on a $100-a-week salary, enough to enable him to quit his job as a prison guard. Then they hired Emile Griffith, the former world champion, to train him. "Griffith," said Smith, "taught me to get balance. With that I began getting more power."

After beating McDonald, Smith—called Crusher by his trainer—went on to score nine straight knockouts. In May 1984, he was offered his first main event, against Frank Bruno of Britain. Smith's purse was $60,000, a significant improvement on the $300-to-$500 purses he had received the year before.

Griffith's strategy for beating Bruno was to have Smith bang him to the body and soften him for the knockout. But nine rounds into the fight, Bruno had a commanding lead, was nailing Smith with every jab he threw, and was absorbing Smith's body blows without noticeable effect.

"Between rounds nine and ten," said Smith, "I told Griff, 'Let me do it my way.' I went out and hit Bruno with a left to the body, a right to the head. He went back to the ropes. He was tired. I kept hitting him. Boom boom boom. Finally he fell and didn't get up."

With his dramatic knockout victory, Smith was suddenly in line for a title shot against Larry Holmes, the IBF champion. But from the high of his triumph over Bruno, more difficult times followed. Though he would have Holmes in trouble during their title bout, on November 9, 1984, he succumbed to the champion in the twelfth round. After that, he lost three of his next four bouts, to Tubbs (March 15, 1985), Witherspoon (June 15, 1985), and Marvis Frazier (February 23, 1986).

After the Witherspoon defeat, Nelson, the comanager, suggested that Smith retire. Nelson was so convinced his fighter had no future that he walked out of his dressing room that night and Smith never heard from him again. Smith himself was discouraged enough to quit for a while and sell cars at a dealership in Fayetteville. And then when he decided to try boxing again and lost to Frazier, he consulted a psychiatrist in Raleigh.

"I was depressed," said Smith. "Four out of five fights I'd lost. I thought I was losing it mentally. The psychiatrist told me, 'If you want to win, you'll win.' That made me madder. Paying seventy dollars an hour to hear that." Smith changed psychiatrists. The new one told him, "The ring is your domain. You've got to protect your turf."

In his next fight, on April 5, 1986, he knocked out Mike Weaver in one round. Soon after, Carl King became his co-manager with Kornberg.

Consider, if you will, Rule 208.3 of the boxing regulations of the New York State Athletic Commission:

"No manager is permitted to have more than one boxer, whom he manages compete on any one boxing program without the special permission of the commission."

With the December 12 bout, Rule 208.3 would receive more than its share of attention. Carl King seemed ubiquitous as the manager of heavyweights promoted by his father: in the recent past Carl had managed and Don had promoted Berbick, Tubbs, Witherspoon, and Green. Then there was the Kornberg/King arrangement with Smith. That meant that if Witherspoon went ahead and fought Smith, Carl King would have a managerial cut of both fighters' purses.

Richard, the attorney, was unhappy about King's involvement with both fighters and ended up bringing 208.3 to the attention of Torres on the day of the fight.

"I asked Torres," said Richard, "why he was not enforcing the rule, even as he was telling me I could end up in jail for acting as a manager without a license. I asked why he was not threatening to suspend Carl King. Well, he turned and looked at [deputy commissioner] Marvin Kohn and said, 'Is Carl King managing more than one fighter?' Kohn said, 'Yes. He's managing Bonecrusher Smith.' Do you know what Torres told me? He told me that the rule is not enforced. Like nobody paid attention to it."

Torres would say he did not threaten Richard but rather gave him friendly advice about his potential unlicensed managerial status. He would also dispute Richard's interpretation of

208.3. "The rule gives me the power to reject and accept the manager in such a situation," Torres said. "I chose to accept Carl King because everything was done aboveboard."

If "Terrible Tim," as Witherspoon was known, had elected not to fight Smith he would have found himself in a legal squeeze play. For when Don King signed Smith to fight Witherspoon, Carl had initialed the revised contract that inserted Smith in Tubbs's place. By New York rules, the manager was empowered to do so on the fighter's behalf. Since Torres saw a valid contract, he could insist that Witherspoon was bound to fight Smith. And if a skeptical attorney like Richard might view Carl King as a front for his father and derelict in his duties to the fighter, well, that was the beginning of what he might persuade a court was breach of contract. And worse. Someday. For now, it was saddle up and go: Witherspoon would fight Smith.

And live to regret it.

SMITH FLATTENS WITHERSPOON
TAKES TITLE IN FIRST ROUND

After much sound and fury there was a World Boxing Association heavyweight championship bout after all. What it signified, in the end, was that James (Bonecrusher) Smith could punch big enough to be a champion.

He came out winging from the outset of a scheduled fifteen-round bout last night and knocked out Tim Witherspoon, the champion, at 2:12 of the first round, flooring him three times in the abbreviated fight to take the title at Madison Square Garden. . . .

If King was glad to be rid of Witherspoon, he did not show it. In the past, when he had promoted a fight card, he was never shy about being stage center. He would stride along press row, croon the names of individual writers while emitting his rumbling har-de-har laugh. Stepping up into the ring, he would kibitz from there with celebrities and commoners alike while awaiting the introductions of the night's combatants.

On this night in the Garden, King sat hunkered down in the high-priced seats and did not raise his usual tumult. The events leading up to the fight had opened up a Pandora's box, and King was, in his own words, physically and mentally exhausted.

Nor was the fight to be the end of his problems. Litigation followed—a $9 million suit by Witherspoon against the Kings, Torres, and the WBA and an $11,425,000 suit by Tubbs against the Kings.

Months following the December 12 bout, the methods of King and his operations would still be under scrutiny by lawyers, investigative journalists, and New York State's inspector general. But King, who had been in jams before, was not to be deterred from his appointed rounds.

Nor did the scribes expect he would be. To them he was like Ronald Reagan, a man with the Teflon knack. For instance, the state inspector general, Joe Spinelli, as an FBI agent, previously had been involved in a four-year investigation that resulted in the indictment of King on tax-evasion charges. But in 1985, a jury had found King not guilty, even as it sent a female aide of his to jail on the same charges.

Before that there had been the 1977 ABC-TV tournament of King's that had been plagued by charges of rigged fighters' records and other indiscretions so extensive that the network had terminated its telecast. Yet King had not been injured by the scandalous revelations; his career rolled right along.

The relationship between boxer and promoter was inherently adversarial. Fighters dealing with King were obliged to weigh their aspirations against the hard bargain the promoter drove.

In April, James Smith had been this close to the end of his career. Then, following a conversation in the john of Don King's suite, he had suddenly become one of boxing's anointed, stumbling into a title shot ($300,000), and now a shot against Tyson ($1.25 million).

A fighter's career was like that. There was no telling when by mere chance it would take off as Smith's had, or unaccountably execute a left turn into the shitter. Nor was success any guarantee of continued prosperity. While fighters primed the notion of their invincibility, they did so like the wary pedestrian who whistled as he stepped into the dark, to con himself into equanimity. As that night voyager perceived danger, so did the fighter, for all his bravado, recognize that in a single untended moment an opponent's blow could dent consciousness, not to mention his financial future.

The very transient nature of success, of course, made a fighter half-fucking-crazy to get the most out of his chance while he could. That was only natural, and explained why so many of them were susceptible to rearranging their business setups as Smith had.

In negotiations with a promoter it helped a fighter to know the fiscal parameters of the monies available. Most boxers hadn't a clue. $550,000 might have sounded like a grand sum to Witherspoon for fighting Frank Bruno. But if, as Richard said, King's allocation for the bout was $1.7 million (HBO's Abraham said it was $1.35 million) and Bruno was being paid a larger purse from a separate allocation by *his* promoters, then the purse of Witherspoon, the champion, might be due reassessment.

Some fighters become sophisticated enough to learn the dollars and cents of their business. Holmes, for instance, said that during the early days of his career under King, when his purses were modest, he made a point of saving as much as he could. "If I made fifty thousand, I saved twenty-five," he said. "The next thing you know, I have a bundle of twenty-five thousands. That saved me. I didn't have to ask Don for loans. I could go to the bank."

With a financial cushion, Holmes said, he was not as susceptible to manipulation by a promoter. "Plus," said Holmes, "I learned the value of money. Of what ABC-TV and the other networks were paying, I learned how much the opponent was getting and how much Caesars Palace was putting out. Say there was four million out there and Don wanted to give me two million, and eight hundred thousand for the foe. That left him one point two million for his profit. All that plus ancillary rights for Don. No good. I wanted more than two million. That's when I became a problem for him."

Contrast Holmes—who had substantial financial holdings in and around Easton, Pennsylvania, where he lived—with Witherspoon. Witherspoon, sounding a bit like the character Lenny in *Of Mice and Men,* would say that all he ever wanted was to buy a modest home in the Philadelphia area—a $30,000 house, as he called it. "But I'm scared to try to get the house," Witherspoon said. "I don't know what Don's going to do."

King used to tell a revealing story about himself. In January 1973, more than a year after he had come out of prison, King had gone to Kingston, Jamaica, to see Joe Frazier defend his title against George Foreman.

"I made friends with Foreman," King said. "I'd go to the airport every day to pick up family members of his. I told George: 'You're going to win the fight, you're going to knock him out.' I was just a novice. I was just a fan. But I could see the type of effort George was putting in. Anyway, I told him— the only one who had the confidence in him—'You're going to win.' So I had, like, a nouveau friendship with George.

"But I was already friends with Joe Frazier and his manager, Yank Durham. And the night of the fight, I went to the fight with them. Motorcycle cops. Sirens blasting. Yank gave me a ringside seat on his side of the ring, front row. The first round, George hit Frazier with a devastating punch that sent Joe leaping into the air. Every time he'd strike Frazier, I'd move closer to the end of the row, toward George's corner. By the time the fight ended, a second-round TKO, I was *on* George's corner. When the fight was stopped, I'm into the ring. 'I told you.' And George: 'Come with me.' He was eating ice. He took me to his room. Same thing. Motorcycle cops. Sirens blasting. I came with the champion, and left with the champion."

A metaphor it was for King's modus operandi in the years to follow. Beaten champions of his would remark on how gingerly King would step over their prone bodies in his haste to embrace their conqueror. With business allies, with champions, King had a knack for ingratiating himself: he would extol them in that hyped prose of his for as long as they were of value. When he no longer needed them, *pfft*, goodbye.

Lucien Chen, who had helped keep Berbick in the HBO series and had been lauded by King for it, got no response from the promoter when Chen asked him for a deposition in a suit Chen filed against Berbick, alleging the fighter had not paid him for his role in negotiating the $2.1 million deal. Two years after the fight, King still had not responded. That was King—he was expert at taking care of D-K, as his aides called him.

Whether or not he used the race issue to further his aims was a question that frequently arose when King's methods were under scrutiny. Tubbs would claim that King had slowed his career until he agreed to replace Cary Medill, the white attorney who managed him, with Carl King. Tubbs said that King had told him the white man couldn't do for him what brother King could. King denied saying that and blamed Tubbs's troubled career on the fighter's reluctance to rumble.

Whatever.

As often as King denied exploiting race, the issue arose anew. In April 1987, a few months after Witherspoon-Smith, King tried to enter the ring at the conclusion of a stirring middleweight title fight between Hagler and Leonard, a bout promoted by his rival, Arum. On his way up the ring steps King was interfered with by Arum, who tore the pocket of King's sports jacket to keep him from advancing another step and horning in on a Top Rank promotion.

Sly got a glimpse of the push-and-shove, and of the hasty appearance of a large-sized black Caesars Palace security guard. Caught up in the crush of deadline obligations, he was unable to eavesdrop on the heated conversation. But his *Times* colleague, columnist Ira Berkow, who was within earshot at his ringside seat, heard what was said.

"Arum," said Berkow, "told King, 'You have no business in the ring, it's not your promotion.' King told him: 'Leave me alone.' It's indelible in my mind what King said to the black security guard: 'You motherfucker, you let a white man punch me after all I've done for the black people. You fucking Uncle Tom.' And on and on. And the guy said nothing. He held King back from going into the ring."

By 1987, King had a structure to fit his philosophy of perpetuating Don King. With the unification series, champions could come, champions could go, but the man with the highrise hairdo was always in for a piece of the action. What's more, whoever ended up undisputed champion would be beholden to the Dynamic Duo, Inc., for two title defenses.

Bonecrusher Smith was among those in the HBO series on whom King had a healthy grip, through his promotional contract and Carl's comanagerial position with the fighter. But if the Kings were in for their fair share of the Crusher's loot, Mr. Smith as a paying proposition figured to be a short-term issue—what with Tyson the next opponent. In his demolition of Berbick, Tyson had taken on an aura of indestructibility, as the billboards for his next fight, against Smith, to unify the WBA and the WBC crowns, suggested.

The Tyson depicted was a man chiseled from hard ore, the sculpted planes of his face conveying a no-nonsense character. High above Las Vegas's streets, he loomed like RoboSlugger, a mythic quality resonating from the words that accompanied the billboard's graphic:

> Your grandfather wished he'd seen Dempsey.
> Your father wished he'd seen Marciano.
> Don't you miss Iron Mike Tyson,
> March 7, at the Las Vegas Hilton.

But if that Godvoice sound was meant to inspire awe, it failed to have that effect on Smith. He was a bright and unpretentious man, at ease in company, as well-spoken as the only college graduate to win the heavyweight title might be expected to be. Where Berbick had sounded like a snake-oil salesman when he predicted he was going to give Tyson a "whupping," Bonecrusher came off more rationally in speaking of his chances against Tyson. At a press conference in New York to formally announce the bout that January (1987), Smith would sound entirely credible in claiming to be immune from what King had termed "Tysonitis." "I plan to win the fight," Smith said. "Mike Tyson hasn't faced the caliber of guys I have."

Never mind those fearsome images of Tyson that confronted Smith on billboards all over Las Vegas or even at reduced poster size in the lobby of the hotel where he was staying. James Smith wasn't having myths, fairy tales, or exaggerations. At the final news conference days before the bout, he would say, "When I was a kid, I believed in Santa Claus. When I grew up I realized who Santa Claus was. The media has made Mike Tyson invincible. Most of his opponents believed that. I don't. Half of his fights, he's won when he stepped into the ring. I see fear in his opponents. But for the first time, Mike Tyson should be fearful."

Again, the tone was that of a reasonable man, without any objective other than to set the record straight, lest the public and its scribes be taken in by this so-called Iron Mike.

The fight that Smith projected would be that classic

punchout that devotees loved. No holds barred. A Big Guys version of Hagler-Hearns. So Bonecrusher said. And so the press—Sly among them—believed. That prospect had them rubbing their inkstained hands in anticipation. The idea of Tyson's being obliged to face up to the blows that a man bigger—Smith was six-foot-four and 233 pounds—and possibly stronger than he would fetch him was a lively vision.

While few among the scribes felt Bonecrusher had the staying power to beat Tyson, it would be enough if, as he promised, he stood and whaled away with Tyson in a compressed show of force. It would be the brand of intense confrontation that was the epitome of boxing's man-on-man format and, when played out by willing and spirited fighters, could be an exhilarating spectacle.

But the drama that Bonecrusher promised, and the emotional release it portended, fizzled away with practically the first blows that Tyson smote him that night. In the Hilton's outdoor stadium, under desert skies, a look of high alarm suffused his intelligent face as Tyson began to assail him. At which point Smith made a business decision. That decision was to survive— as opposed to fight, a distinction that had everything to do with the boxer's code of conduct. For in adopting the plan he did, Smith was resigned to wage a nonfight—to grab and hold Tyson at every chance and merely last out the twelve rounds for which the bout was scheduled. Coping with Tyson that way minimized his risks and nullified the spirit of combat, which was built on having the courage to rub up against danger.

To circumvent that precept and not be exposed for a faker required an accomplice—another fighter who, for whatever reasons, was not disposed to press the issue. That was a working definition of two fighters just going through the paces. But what made Tyson a unique viewing experience was his ultra-aggression. With every punch he intended harm.

Had Bonecrusher punched back on occasion while moving in and out of range of Tyson's power, he would not have incurred the displeasure of the crowd, as he did. Stick-and-move was an accepted form of dealing with a slugger like Tyson. Spinks had used it to good effect twice against Holmes. And while usually not as visceral a pleasure for spectators as the brute force that Smith had promised, it could make for a stirring evening, especially when its objective was to confound an

opponent and beat him. But Bonecrusher became Bone-
clutcher; when Smith gave up on the idea of winning the bout,
he resorted to encircling Tyson with his arms and squeezing
him against his body every chance he could. He did so far too
often to suit the crowd, which booed, or the man officiating the
bout, Mills Lane, who deducted a point from Smith for excessive holding in rounds two and eight.

Tyson played into Smith's plan by (a) not varying his tactics
and (b) becoming frustrated when Smith repeatedly smothered
his wide-arcing lunging blows. Had he jabbed more and
switched the angles and pace of his thrust toward Smith he
probably would have opened the other man up to the third,
fourth, and fifth blows of his volleys. Instead he was predictable
enough with his exertions for Smith to anticipate and immature
enough at this stage of his career to let emotion get the better
of him. Tyson began roughing up Smith, banging him with
forearms and on more than one occasion hitting him after the
bell. It was a stinker of a fight, and nobody much liked it, including the victorious Tyson.

The irony was that in the twelfth and final round, when
Smith elected to let a real punch go, he landed a right hand
that stopped Tyson dead in his tracks. It was as good a punch
as Tyson had been hit with in his career, and back in Lillington,
Smith must have thought about it in the months that followed.
When Sly talked to him nearly a year later, he said, "I should
have thrown all caution to the wind. I just didn't do it. I don't
know why."

What was there to say about that lack of nerve? That it was
subject to massive hindsight by Smith, and derision by those
who bore witness to it? That it was easier to be bold at a dais
than in the ring with Iron Mike tattooing your vulnerable hide?

In the lobby of the Hilton the next day, Sly shook hands
with Smith and said quietly, "Take care, James." As soon as he
had, he realized that it was the first time in the months he had
known Smith that he'd called the fighter by his Christian name;
he wasn't Crusher, or Bone, or Bonecrusher, as Sly had ad-
dressed him before.

What the hell: Mr. Smith had earned his James.

10

Las Vegas, Nev., May 30—Mike Tyson successfully defended his heavyweight title when he knocked out Pinklon Thomas here in two minutes of the sixth round of a scheduled twelve-round fight.

The end came on a five-punch sequence that was vintage Tyson—powerful, and sprawling. A right uppercut landed flush on Thomas's jaw, but with it Tyson's weight shifted onto his heels so that when he threw a snappy left hook, it was while drifting backward—a brush stroke. Even so, it hurt the Pink Man.

Tyson corrected his balance and let fly the last three punches—a short left hook that landed flush on Thomas's chin, a right that didn't, and, with his legs spread wide, a final left hook to the chin that had the full measure of his body behind it. Thomas went down.

Onto his back he fell, his eyes closing shut and his arms outspread. Now he tried to recover from the terrible impact. . . .

By HBO's original plan, Tyson was not to have fought an optional title defense on May 30. That date had been set aside for the climactic heavyweight match in the series, Tyson vs. Michael Spinks.

Spinks was no longer a member in good standing in HBO's unification sequence, because promoter Butch Lewis had signed his man to a fight against Gerry Cooney, the emotionally conflicted left-hooker from Long Island. Fighting Cooney had always been an option Spinks had had, contractually, in the deal Lewis had made to bring him into the series. But exactly what the parties had agreed to—well, that eventually would be subject to differing interpretations.

On only this much would both sides concur: by the deal he had cut with HBO, Lewis was not restricted to the home TV screen for Spinks-Cooney. He had the right to take the fight the potentially more profitable route of closed-circuit television. In that event, HBO would produce the closed-circuit show and get the delayed telecast rights, and Lewis and HBO would live happily ever after.

That was the fairy-tale version of the contract. But within the deal, there was a sticky provision that appeared to present a formidable obstacle to making a Spinks-Cooney match: a contractual clause by which HBO insisted Cooney must guarantee to remain in the HBO series in the event he beat Spinks. That was crucial to HBO, as its stake in seeing the series through to its conclusion was considerable. To pull the plug before an undisputed champion was determined was to risk the wrath, and disillusionment, of millions of viewers who had started watching the heavyweight bouts with the expectation of a payoff.

But the attitude of Cooney's comanager, Dennis Rappaport, had always been that fighting on HBO was, for Gentleman Gerry, the equivalent of working cheap. Cooney as a white champion would be big business—bigger for sure, Rappaport believed, than what HBO could afford.

With HBO and Rappaport at an apparent impasse, it seemed Spinks-Cooney was grounded in the fine print. Yet whenever Sly would say as much to Lewis, Lewis would demur. "I'm tellin' ya, we can fight Cooney!" Ask him how—given the stipulation that Cooney must guarantee his continued participation in the series—and Lewis would just reiterate in his resolute way, "I'm tellin' ya. We can fight Gerry Cooney."

It wasn't until after the Spinks-Cooney bout was signed, on

February 20, 1987, that Lewis's rationale for superseding HBO's provision about Cooney emerged. It went like this:

During the negotiations to induce Spinks to become part of the series, Lewis said he and his attorney, Milt Chwasky, had been assured by Abraham that HBO would never stand in the way of a Spinks-Cooney bout, no matter what the language in the contract said.

Abraham, however, claimed that no such promise had been made, and in December 1986, HBO began a court action to stop the fight. When HBO was granted an injunction against the fight, the IBF, whose heavyweight title Spinks held, now insisted Spinks fight its number-one challenger, an undefeated (34-0, with one "no contest") boxer from Grand Rapids, Michigan, Tony Tucker. Tucker had built that flawless record of his against a series of anonymous lugs and accordingly had no marquee value to speak of. If Spinks fought him, he would be taking a cut in pay—by several million dollars. Spinks declined such vows of poverty, and by February 26, 1987, the IBF had stripped him of his title and declared that Tucker would fight James (Buster) Douglas for the vacated crown.

By doing that, the IBF unwittingly gave Spinks the legal grounds to fight Cooney. For without his title, Spinks's connection to the HBO series was severed and he was free to look for other job opportunities. So it was the court ruled in overturning the injunction against Spinks-Cooney in March 1987.

While the fight was not sanctioned as a title match by any of boxing's governing bodies, Rappaport and Lewis would say that various state commissions had endorsed it as a "People's Championship" fight. At a time when boxing titles were as plentiful as monopoly money—besides the WBA, WBC and IBF world titles, there were North American Boxing Federation champions, United States Boxing Association champions, Continental Americas champions, ESPN champions, even Stroh's Beer champions—what was one more claimant for titular distinction?

Spinks-Cooney was scheduled then for June 15, 1987, at the Convention Hall in Atlantic City. With HBO's series winding down, there would be a heavyweight life beyond unification—and the winner of Spinks-Cooney figured to be a big player in it.

Cayton and Jacobs were banking on Cooney to beat Spinks.

Months earlier, they had tried to dissuade Rappaport from going forward with the match against Spinks by offering him a Tyson-Cooney bout in which both fighters would have parity. Their objective was to keep Spinks in the series so that if Tyson became undisputed champion, there would be no carping about the quality of his accomplishment. With his historian's perspective on boxing, Jacobs regarded Spinks as a link in the heavyweight line of succession that dated back to John L. Sullivan. In beating Holmes, Spinks had whupped the reigning and recognized best man in the division, and Jacobs wanted Tyson tied in to that historic primacy. But Rappaport claimed that for all the fervor of their pitch, Cayton and Jacobs could not or would not fix a date for Tyson-Cooney that fell within his working definition of "foreseeable future." Cooney would fight Spinks.

In nudging the fight through the maze of legal and political constraints, Lewis had maneuvered Spinks out of Time Inc.'s grasp and, skeptics said, a sane distance from the fearsome Tyson. Of course, if Spinks were to beat Cooney on a free market, and out of HBO's contractual grip, a Tyson-Spinks bout would be a closed-circuit attraction that might make the $4 million Spinks was to get for fighting Cooney seem penny ante. While the oddsmakers did not think a Spinks victory was likely, Lewis had done all he could to position his fighter for fortune and glory.

As a promoter, Lewis was something of an anomaly. In contrast to Arum and King, who dealt in volume, moving from fighter to fighter and staging whatever bouts made fiscal sense, Lewis behaved more like a show-business manager with a limited clientele. In that role, he was not nearly as detached about his fighters as Arum or King.

While there was speculation about the financial arrangements between Michael and promoter—did they divvy up 33⅓–66⅔, or 50-50, or 30-70, with Spinks due a lifetime 30 percent share of Butch Lewis Productions, whatever that might amount to?—neither Lewis nor M. Spinks had ever gone on record as to how the fighter and promoter split their earnings.

In the documents promoters file routinely with the Nevada Athletic Commission for each bout, Michael Spinks listed no manager of record. So while Lewis might provide him with the personalized service that a manager did, going so far as to look into the adequacy of the school at which the fighter's seven-year-old daughter, Michelle, was enrolled, he was, for the record, Spinks's promoter.

Whatever. Together, the two constituted a rarity—a long-standing boxing relationship, one that dated back to 1977. Never mind that the pairing of Lewis, a talky man given to glittering rings and bracelets and his fight-night finery of tuxedo, bow tie, and no shirt, and Spinks, a far more quiet and conservative sort, was an incongruous one. By mutual trust, Lewis and Spinks not only endured, they were succeeding. But as they awaited the fight against Cooney, they stood as boxing men who knew what it was to travel the hard road.

Leon Spinks, right, partied as intensely as he fought, earning a grander reputation as a good-time Charlie than as a fighter. But through the complicated politics of boxing, by the 1980s he stood as a curious footnote to his sport—the last undisputed heavyweight champion. Spinks, shown with his trainer, Sam Solomon, had won the title from Muhammad Ali in February 1978.

TOP RANK INC.

With the exception of Larry Holmes, the heavyweight division in the early 1980s was the domain of mediocre titleholders, whose reigns lasted about as long as the fragrance of the cheapest perfume. But even Holmes eventually came crashing down: In September 1985 he lost his title to Michael Spinks.

HBO/WILL HART

The constant turnover in heavyweight champions cheapened boxing's most prestigious title. But late in 1985, Seth G. Abraham of Home Box Office proposed an idea to break the cycle: a heavyweight unification series.
HBO

As HBO launched its quest to find an undisputed heavyweight champion, nineteen-year-old Mike Tyson, shown here with his mentor, Cus D'Amato, right, was stealing toward the heavyweight spotlight.
HBO

Tyson, in shorts, had been paroled from a juvenile corrections facility in upstate New York to D'Amato, left, who was living in Catskill, New York. D'Amato had trained and managed two champions, heavyweight champion Floyd Patterson, second from left, and light heavyweight champion Jose Torres, right. When Tyson was only fourteen, D'Amato predicted the kid from Brooklyn would be the youngest-ever heavyweight champion.   THE BIG FIGHTS, INC.

Tyson, right, fought with a forward-march aggression and sprang at opponents like the great cats of a *National Geographic* TV special. When he beat Mitch Green, left, in May 1986 for his twenty-first straight victory, he blasted a piece of dental work, complete with a strand of wire, from Green's mouth.   HBO/KEN REGAN

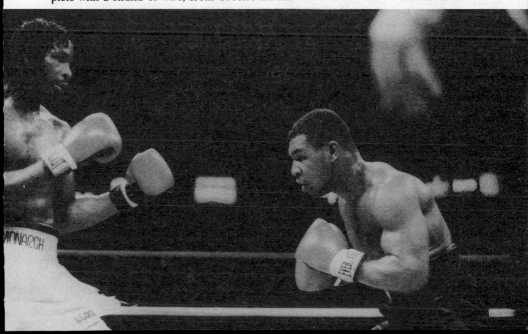

Michael Spinks's promoter, the fast-talking Butch Lewis, matched him against Gerry Cooney, the psychologically conflicted left hooker from Long Island. That move triggered a chain of events that resulted in Spinks's departure from the HBO series. Lewis, a man given to glittering rings and fight-night finery of tuxedo, bow tie, and no shirt, was a sharp contrast to the more quiet and conservative Spinks. Odd couple though they were, the two men had proven a successful boxing tandem.
BUTCH LEWIS PROMOTIONS

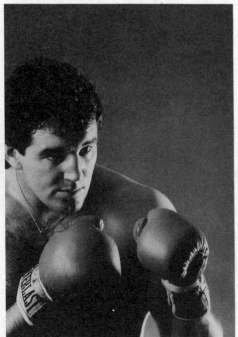

From the time he lost to Larry Holmes in 1982, Gerry Cooney had more false starts than a jittery sprinter as he tried to get his boxing career going.
HBO/JOE DIMAGGIO

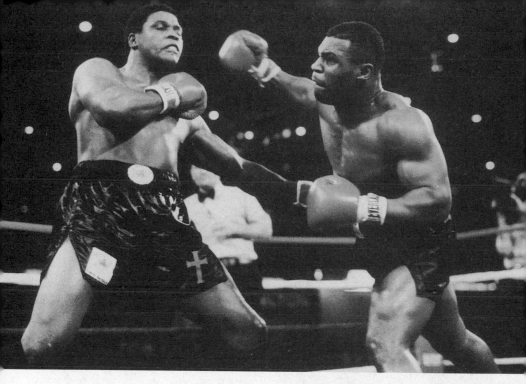

Trevor Berbick, left, was the WBC heavyweight champion when Tyson fought him in
November 1986. From the moment Tyson,
right, began landing punches on him, Berbick's face registered alarm. Tyson knocked
Berbick out in two rounds, fulfilling Cus
D'Amato's prophesy that Tyson would be the
youngest heavyweight champion in boxing
history.

As the HBO series unfolded, the opponent
Tyson seemed fated to meet in the unification
finals was the IBF champion, Michael Spinks.
In contrast to the confident Tyson, Spinks was
so unassuming that he referred to himself as
"Mr. Pitiful." Yet when Spinks fought, somehow he managed to figure the tactics to beat
the other man.

Wealthy realtor Dennis Rappaport, as Cooney's manager, had worked hard to get his fighter another shot at the heavyweight title. Rappaport was so eager to make a deal that when a lawyer representing then-champion Trevor Berbick raised an obstacle to a title bout, Rappaport leaped from his chair and choked the other man. But his efforts to make Cooney a champion ended in June 1987 when Michael Spinks stopped Cooney in five rounds.

JOHN P. GALLAGHER, JR.

The fighter who ended up in the HBO finals against "Iron Mike" Tyson was Tony Tucker, who succeeded Spinks as the IBF champion. In August 1987 Tyson became the first undisputed heavyweight champion since Leon Spinks when he won a unanimous decision from Tucker.

HBO/WILL HART

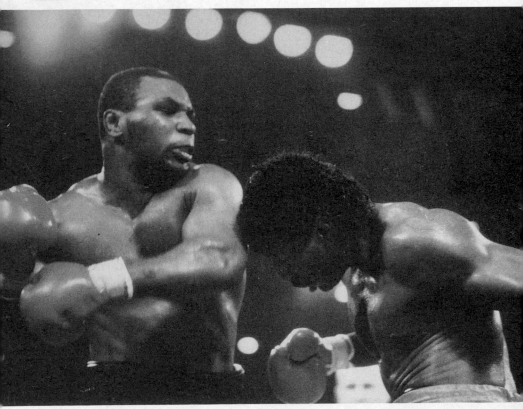

After he beat Tucker, Tyson was honored by promoter Don King at a coronation ceremony that had lots of glitter and more than a bit of gall. Tyson, right, wore a chinchilla robe, a jeweled crown and necklace, and a scepter from Felix the jeweler, Las Vegas. His date for the night was Robin Givens, a television actress.

As undisputed heavyweight champion, Tyson could afford to be pleased: He'd won $6.7 million in purses in 1987 and felt his career was proceeding without a hitch. "My life is so simple," Tyson said. "You wouldn't believe how simple it is."

When Cus D'Amato died in November 1985, it was co-manager Jim Jacobs, left, who provided the stability in Tyson's life. Jacobs was a national handball champion, a fight-film collector, and a dogged defender of Tyson. To the press, though, Jacobs sometimes seemed pompous, as when he told one reporter, "Allow me to add one more tasty tidbit to your already vast storehouse of knowledge because I might know a little more about this than you do."

THE BIG FIGHTS, INC.

In February 1988 Tyson married Robin Givens, right, who was a featured actress in a TV sitcom called *Head of the Class*. Givens, on the prospect of her first date with Tyson: "It seemed grotesque. A fighter." Tyson: "Until she met me. Then I took her off her feet. I suaved her."

BOXING ILLUSTRATED/HY SIMON

Jim Jacobs died in March 1988, and his death set off a power struggle for control of Tyson. Jacobs's friend fighter manager Shelly Finkel charged that the day of Jacobs's funeral Tyson told him that Don King, right, had offered him five easy bouts for $5 million apiece if he would back out of a previously arranged June 1988 match against Michael Spinks. Tyson was expected to earn $20 million from the Spinks bout.

In August 1986 Tyson had inscribed a photo of himself to his other manager, Bill Cayton, right, like this: "To Bill/From your boy Mike 8-22-86/To my dear friend and the man I love greatly." Prodded by his wife, Robin Givens; her mother, Ruth Roper; and promoter Don King, Tyson had an attitude change about Cayton. Suddenly, Cayton became an object of Iron Mike's disaffection.

As the controversy around Tyson escalated, what remained constant was his position in the boxing business: He was larger-than-life, Rambo in short pants.
HBO/WILL HART

Not since Muhammad Ali, left, had a heavyweight attracted the attention that Tyson did.
HBO/WILL HART

How big was Tyson's June 27 (1988) match against Michael Spinks? Big enough to prompt real-estate developer and casino magnate Donald Trump to shell out $11 million for the live-site rights, the largest such fee paid in boxing history.
TOM CASINO

At the weigh-in for Tyson vs. Spinks: Tyson, in jockey briefs, and his trainer, Kevin Rooney.
HBO/WILL HART

Tyson knocked out Spinks in the first round: "Twenty million dollars in 91 seconds and a reaction as emotional as sherbert."

BOXING ILLUSTRATED/FRED ROE

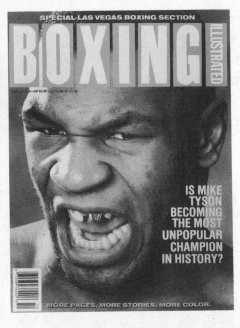

Success brought its own trick freight for Tyson. Not long after he beat Spinks, Tyson got into a street brawl with Mitch Green, crashed his car against a tree—purposely, it was alleged—was labeled a manic-depressive, was accused of being a wife beater, went on a dish-throwing rampage at his Bernardsville, New Jersey, mansion—the last provocative act that led Robin Givens to file for divorce early in October 1988. The result? A swift change in the public's perception of Tyson, as typified by this cover of *Boxing Illustrated*.

BOXING ILLUSTRATED/JOE DIMAGGIO

11

In 1976, right after he and his brother Leon had won gold medals in boxing at the Montreal Olympics, Michael Spinks declined to turn professional.

What kept him from taking the step was his fear that he might end, as many fighters before him had, with none of the spoils of his labors.

"That bothered me more than anything," he said. "I couldn't stand to see another person living comfortably by jerking me out of my money. Treating me like a horse or cow. It was too vicious."

Leon's troubled career also shaded Michael's reactions to his business. "What Leon went through," said Lewis, "was like a rush through the Twilight Zone. Being so close to it, Michael's reaction was: 'You mean, this is what I have to look forward to? If that's it, I don't want it.' He had questions about whether he wanted to continue fighting. He wasn't in love with boxing after the Olympics and he still isn't. Michael Spinks doesn't like to fight. It's just his profession."

How different the brothers were. Where Leon was impulsive and given to the moment's pleasure, Michael was thoughtful and, in the upkeep of his career, farsighted. There were no all-points bulletins needed to track Michael: between fights he did the roadwork and requisite gym hours on his own, so that when a fight was in hailing distance, he had an athlete's keenness. What a luxury for his Mr. Lewis, who had needed the bounty hunter's stealth and persistence to keep Leon within his sight. With his "other" Spinks, there was no muss or fuss. Michael was a professional, and for his attentions had eluded the fiscal ruin he feared.

In June 1985, in his ninth year as a wage-earning boxer, Spinks and Michelle moved into a six-bedroom house on a five-acre estate in Greenville, Delaware. The house had a swimming pool in the backyard, and when Spinks pulled into his driveway, he did so in a gray 1984 Mercedes.

But these material assets were not the only measures of the security the fighter had gained. According to Lewis, Spinks had enough savings that he could have lived off the yearly interest alone—$106,000.

Fighters as a group tend to be less farsighted with their money. But Spinks, who grew up in the hard and violent setting of the Pruitt-Igoe housing project in St. Louis and was raised on the family's welfare checks, was cautious about his finances, to the point of nearly comic frugality. "If he lends somebody a five or ten, he'll remember it," said Lewis. "This guy never forgets."

When Spinks fought Dwight Braxton—now known as Dwight Muhammad Qawi—to unify the light heavyweight title in 1983, he could not overlook a loan he had made to Braxton in the days when Braxton worked as a sparring partner for him. Though a couple of years had passed since the money had been advanced, Spinks referred to it in a news conference before the bout, when he told Braxton, "One of the reasons I'm going to beat you is you didn't pay back the hundred and forty-five dollars."

The picture of Michael as a fiscal conservative contrasted sharply with that of free-spending Leon, who was never up to the demands and pressures of holding the sport's most celebrated title. Success consumed Leon, as well as the millions of dollars he earned in purses.

"Money?" Leon told Sly in March 1986, as he trained for a title bout against Qawi, the WBA junior heavyweight champion at the time. "You have it and then you don't have it. You learn from your mistakes."

Leon's mistakes had come back to haunt him. By March 1986, he had been evicted from his $125,000 home in the Rosedale section of Detroit, for failing to keep up the mortgage payments; his possessions had been auctioned off after he missed payment on a storage fee; and he was being pursued by the Internal Revenue Service.

Although Michael remained close to his brother and rued the troubles Leon had seen, he was more detached about them come 1986 than he had been in the past. As Michael saw it, the troubles had started when Leon grew tired of the very active role that Lewis played in his career while Butch was a vice-president at Top Rank, Inc. The switch to the Detroit lawyers, Bell and Hudson, came soon after Spinks beat Ali for the title.

"They had 'em," said Lewis, "where the brothers were not speaking to one another. They'd tell Michael: 'You got a message? We'll give it to him.' And Michael, 'You don't tell him anything. That's my brother.' And they'd hang up on him."

Michael became so convinced that Leon's ways were wrongheaded that one day he kicked Leon in the shins. "He said to me, 'Michael, you kick me again, I'm gonna knock you on your butt,'" Michael recalled. "I told him, 'Whatever it takes not to let those people put their names on your checks.'"

For his part, Bell claimed that his firm had no role in turning brother against brother. "That never happened," he said. He dismissed charges that the blame for Leon's financial comedown could be put on anybody other than the fighter. "The Light Brigade and all the king's men couldn't stop Leon from spending," Bell said. "We put money in a trust fund for him. In excess of one million. In the National Bank of Detroit. He took the money out. It was there for a little while. But it was his money. And when he got ready to take the money out, he could. And did."

Michael Spinks came to the boxing profession when life after the Olympics proved disappointing. Following his gold-medal triumph, he found work as a maintenance man on a midnight shift at a St. Louis chemical plant. "One day," said Spinks, "I'd empty ashtrays. The next day I was cleaning out latrines."

Caught napping on the job one night, Spinks was scolded by a supervisor, in language that troubled the fighter. "He cursed me out and talked as if I was trying to be a privileged character," Spinks said. "And told me, 'You ain't nobody.' I told him I deserved punishment, but he didn't have to talk to me like a dog. He talked to me so bad I broke down and cried. That day I decided I'd leave. Everything was pushing me to turning pro. I saw the signs. Breathing chemicals every day, I figured I'd die quicker here than in the ring. Told myself, 'Take your chances, brother.' When that man cursed me out, that was my cue."

In 1977, his first year as a pro, Michael Spinks won all six of his fights while signed to Top Rank. And on the February night that Leon captured the heavyweight title in 1978, Michael earned a decision over Tom Bethea for his seventh straight victory.

But after beating Bethea, Michael put his career on hold while he tried to help straighten out his brother Leon, who was having trouble coping with the complexities of holding the heavyweight title. Then Leon lost the title, and Lewis left Top Rank.

By 1978, when Lewis went on his own as a boxing promoter, he had a New York office, a secretary, a fighter named Michael Spinks, and no idea how long he could afford them.

Those were the days when his attorney, Chwasky, declined to bill him for his time on the premise that a man who counted as a blazing success a boxing promotion that showed only a $200 loss might need a little help from his friends.

Those were the days when Lewis, promoting in places like White Plains, New York, and Louisville, Kentucky, filled out his undercards with midget wrestlers like Ed (Too Small) Jones and tattooed female boxers. Back then a crucial issue might have the Lewis organization, such as it was, fending off the local politicians or county gendarmes who wanted to see its fights for free, taking up seats for which real money might be had.

"In Louisville one time," recalled Chwasky, "we were told that all deputy county police had to be comped. We found out there were about five hundred of these deputies—everybody who contributed to the political party in power got a badge. Well, they got away with it the first time. But the next show, what I did was, the night of the fight, I got a roster sheet and when the freeloaders came around, I asked them to sign their name, write who assigned them to duty and what time they checked in and out. It was a subterfuge and it worked. All these potential comps executed an abrupt about-face."

Lewis had problems too at the TV networks, which resisted his proposed fights as a matter of course. Without his affiliation to Arum, he found himself a bit player in the fight game.

"I'd get headaches," Lewis said. "Tension headaches every day. But I remember Mike—he'd see I was depressed—he'd put his arm around me and say, 'We're gonna do it, and do it together. I ain't gonna let us down.'"

Spinks fought his first fight for Lewis on December 15, 1978, in White Plains, where he knocked out Eddie Phillips in four rounds. But soon afterward he incurred a knee injury that would keep him inactive for almost a year. While Spinks did leg extensions with a sand-filled bucket to strengthen the knee and its adjoining muscles, Lewis struggled in the promotion business and awaited his fighter's return.

On November 24, 1979, in Spinks's first fight in eleven months, he knocked out Marc Hans in one round in Bloomington, Minnesota. The victory signaled a Spinks ready to challenge the top contenders, enough to bring rival promoters around to test Spinks's allegiance to Lewis.

"The fight was over," said Lewis. "I'm in my suite. Here comes Mike, knocking on the door. Couldn't have been two hours after the Hans fight. He says to me, 'What's going on here?' And he tells me about Harold Smith. Harold Smith took him a briefcase with two hundred and fifty thousand dollars in cash with a contract sitting on top. We go look for Smith. Smith's in the lobby. Grinning. With a cowboy hat on."

By Lewis's account, Smith's grin disappeared when he was told, in no uncertain terms, to take his business and his loaded case elsewhere.

As promoter of Muhammad Ali Professional Sports, Smith later was convicted of embezzling $21.3 million from the Wells Fargo National Bank and received a sentence of ten years in prison, a $30,000 fine, and three thousand hours of community service.

With Lewis and only Lewis promoting him, Spinks fought his way up the rankings.

1980

February 1	— John Wilburn, Louisville, Ky.	W 8
February 24	— Ramón Ronquillo, Atlantic City, N.J.	TKO 6
May 4	— Murray Sutherland, Kiamesha Lake, N.Y.	W 10
August 2	— David Conteh, Baton Rouge, La.	KO 9
October 18	— Yaqui Lopez, Atlantic City, N.J.	KO 7

1981

| January 24 | — Willie Taylor, Philadelphia, Pa. | KO 8 |
| March 28 | — Marvin Johnson, Atlantic City, N.J. | KO 4 |

On July 18, Spinks fought Eddie Mustafa Muhammad for the WBA light heavyweight title, and won a fifteen-round decision to begin a four-year reign as champion.

As champion, Spinks turned out to be one of those athletes who appear to get results almost in spite of themselves. There were a few like him, competitors who might not have the picture-perfect moves their peers did, yet managed to excel anyway. Billy Kilmer, the quarterback, threw passes that did not spiral and were jokingly referred to as "wounded ducks." Yet he could do what quarterbacks are supposed to: make a team win. As the baseball executive Branch Rickey once said of Eddie Stanky, the second baseman: "He can't run. He can't throw. He can't hit. All he can do is beat you."

Spinks's style lacked the balletic grace of Ali's or Leonard's. Where those men boxed as though on divine instruction, Spinks was stiff-gaited, and his herky-jerky movements were accentuated by the knee wraps he sometimes wore. But just as the stand-up comic understands the unique way he is wired to make others laugh, so did Spinks know what to activate to make a winning fight. In short, he could adapt, while most fighters were constitutionally inflexible.

Against pedestrian light heavyweights, such as Mustapha Wasajja and Oscar Rivadeneyra, he would size up his man and then finish him, usually with the lightning-strike right hand that he referred to as "the Spinks Jinx." But against big punchers, Spinks was not the stalking slugger. Rather, he was a survivalist, mixing strangely syncopated feints and retreats with often off-balance volleys of punches. He could improvise, or he could follow a detailed fight plan. Either way, his skill was in neutralizing the other man.

Take Dwight Braxton. In 1983, Braxton was a small-scale version of Tyson—a perpetual-motion aggressor who tracked opponents with PacMan relentlessness. But Spinks beat him by not letting Braxton stay in character.

"Braxton," said Eddie Futch, Spinks's trainer, "had a habit. As the opponent jabbed, he would force him to the ropes and to his left, making him walk right into the looping right hand he threw. He did it expertly. He cut you off so you had to move to the left. He'd run the man into his right hand. The other thing he'd do, in the center of the ring, was drop his left hand to draw your right hand. As the man threw the right, Braxton would roll and take the right on his shoulder and fire back. He did that real well."

Spinks was advised to move to his right, away from the looping right, when he jabbed. Then, in center ring, he was to jab and use the left hook. "I told Michael," said Futch, "'Don't show your right till he shows his.'"

The brawl that everybody expected never materialized. "And after, everybody said, 'Braxton didn't do much,'" recalled Futch. "But that was because Spinks didn't let him do much."

There was a moment that night, before Spinks went out to fight, when Futch worried whether Spinks would be able to perform. It occurred when Spinks's sister-in-law, Sibby, suddenly appeared in the dressing room, holding in her arms Michelle, then a baby. The mother of the child, Spinks's common-law wife, Sandra Massey, had been killed weeks before in an auto accident.

"I remember," said Futch, "his sister handed the child to Michael, he turned his back to me and started to cry. It brought back the memory of that tragedy.

"I thought, 'This is the worst thing that could happen. I'll never be able to get him back to where he should be!'"

But Spinks managed. Whatever it took to carry on, he did it. So how was it that a man about to make $4 million for fighting Cooney could labor so skillfully for so many years without gaining wide public acceptance? Well, Spinks's relative obscurity could be put to the curious lines along which his career had

run—not to mention a style of fighting that never quite had the
visceral impact that, say, Tyson's did.

As light heavyweight champion for four years, Spinks
reigned over a division that historically had been the Liechten-
stein of weight classifications. Then in bouts that drew him to
the limelight and conceivably could have won him a greater following—those against Braxton and Holmes—Spinks fought
with a cunning that earned him the judges' decision but not the
hearts and minds of the populace.

Lurching and twisting and sometimes actually running
from a punch, Spinks made a mild case for winning ugly. Even
the boxing hard-cores, who should have known better, tended
to lowball him. Futch, who worked with Holmes too, would re-
call how Holmes had underestimated Spinks before he fought
him: "'He can't do this, he can't do that.' Or, 'He can't jab. He's
awkward, off-balance.' But they find out it's a lot different
when you're in the ring with him than when you're looking at
Michael from outside the ring."

Taking Spinks for granted was a knee-jerk response, and
the fighter did little to dispel the notion, often acting as though
he hadn't a clue as to what he meant to do against his foe. He
often sounded perplexed, even overwhelmed, by the very prospect of fighting. In fact, that tack of giving the opponent more
credit than he might deserve was part of Spinks's prefight prep-
aration. Where most fighters rely on the brandished fist and
bold talk to prime themselves for battle, the bravado approach
didn't cut it for Spinks, who even referred to himself as "Mr.
Pitiful."

"I don't need to feel invincible," the thirty-year-old Spinks
said. "My approach works for me. I couldn't handle it any other
way."

Sometimes, as Michael Spinks moved through the lobby of
the Catskill Mountain resort at which he trained, he would be
called by another name. Leon.

If this bothered him, it did not show. Michael, who was
taller and not as muscular as his brother, might quietly offer a
correction—I'm Michael; Leon's my brother—or just sign the
autograph or exchange the pleasantry that the particular trans-
action seemed to require.

He was ever-gracious as this celebrity Spinks, Christian

name Michael, not Leon. He would, for instance, look directly at the civilian, and smile, or speak the few words that would simulate a conversation. There were Big Names who put their signatures to a scrap of paper and never bothered to glance at the individual to whom they were handing it. Spinks had more sensitivity than that. He understood what others wanted from the moment and patiently, cordially, tried to provide the personal touch.

For all that, he did not really covet the attention—not as, say, Cooney did. Cooney equated these moments with love, affirmation. For Spinks they were duty. As personable as he might be, there was always the sense that he held the real Michael in reserve.

While his brother's missteps may have offered cues, it was Michael's own caution and detachment that kept him from the snares that accompany success. Sociability in a fighter left him open to all the two-bit hustlers who saw him as a touch. Michael might be easygoing and, in company, given to laughter, but there was a loner's reserve that discouraged scheming hearts.

In training he would hole up in his room and read—he carried a huge dictionary to camp—or listen to music. Back in Delaware, he kept to his bedroom in a house that two years after move-in remained largely unfurnished. His were hardly the habits of a man seeking costly excitement or conniving comrades.

"I don't fall for drugs," he said. "I fight all this junk—the no-nos. I don't have a lot of unnecessary friends. I don't need no friends. Once I started rising, there were lots of new friends. It wasn't no shock."

Unlike Leon, who dwelt on the humiliations of his childhood, Michael's recollections were of what a curious world he had come into, and the care that need be taken to negotiate it.

"As I grew up," he said, "I learned. I put a few things together. How strange things were. Like they had this project called the Fun Boat. White people came to play with the black kids, teach us games, kid games—volleyball, four-square, can in the middle—games we didn't know how to play. Same time, as I went back and forth to the store, shopping, I'd hear other white folks, under their breath, say 'nigger.' I was young then. Ten, eleven. I wondered. Just a question. I wondered why I was called these names. Putting it all together. Hell, this world is messed up. I'm walking around on a hope and prayer. Ten years old. Thinking, I should be very careful with my life.

"I don't know why I thought this way. I think it's good I did. It helped me develop a way of being. It helped me remain pretty sane. I took on the belief that there was something out there strictly meant for me. Sum it all up: I had to be careful with my life. Which I try to do. Be careful. You don't want to live life on no humbug or on general principles."

What guiding precepts moved Cooney these days was harder to say.

After Sly had written a lengthy *Times* profile on Cooney in January 1986, he had not seen the fighter again until a few days before Cooney was to fight Gregg five months later. Cooney was training in a gym in San Francisco. A sunny day, a borderline street. In the doorway of the gym, pedestrians passing by stepped carefully past drunks sleeping off yesterday's bottle before they peered in at Cooney. The famous Cooney. He was there just to break a sweat, no sparring. At one point during his workout, as he saw Sly penciling notes, Cooney sidled up and asked reproachfully: "Did you get a degree in psychology?"

Later, when the two of them sat and talked in a dressing room, Cooney's answers to Sly's questions were clipped, intentionally so, it seemed. And while that fell short of what the Ayatollah might have exacted for revenge, Cooney's intention was clear enough. After a few minutes of this perfunctory talk, Sly flipped his notebook shut and let Cooney shower.

With the demolition of Gregg in the Cow Palace a few days later had come war cries conjuring up a Cooney who would be more active than a high-powered detergent. But by year's end, 1986, it was business as usual: Cooney had yet to fight again, and when a December 26 fight against one Bill Thomas of Newellton, Louisiana—aka the Bayou Moose—was postponed, Sly would write:

> As ever with Cooney, there are explanations that yield twists and turns as serpentine as William Faulkner's prose. Did the Moose's asking price turn unreasonable? Are there Arab sheiks hovering in the wings with a big-money offer for Cooney to fight abroad? And so on.
> The more pertinent question is—What gives with

Cooney? Why is life apparently so perplexing for him? And what was the Bayou Moose doing on his calendar when there were Buster Douglases and Bonecrushers out there for a real heavyweight man to fight?

Questions, questions; with Cooney there always seemed to be questions.

Two months later, in February 1987, Cooney signed to fight Spinks for a $2.5 million guarantee. In April, he made his entrance at a press conference by stepping through a mechanically created cloud of smoke—the pugilist as demigod. The question was whether the Spinks fight would reduce him to merely mortal dimensions.

In May, a month before the Spinks fight, the big fellow was hunkered down at his training camp in New Jersey, in no mood, really, to sort through those sticky puzzlements about his motives and intentions—and why he could never follow a simple through-line in what career he had salvaged after fighting Holmes. "I sometimes get tired of answering questions," he said. "I've always had it in my heart to fight."

The Cooney camp had expected Spinks to resort to the kind of arrhythmic hit-and-run tactics he had used against Holmes. But on fight night Spinks came forth as a willing, though not reckless, combatant. The moves were economical and, by Spinks's standards, conventional—a step to the side here, a feint there. To protect against potential damage from Cooney's left hook, Spinks moved clockwise, away from the hook, and he held his right-hand glove high at the side of his head, as if he were mimicking a phone conversation. But while he was probing and measuring Cooney, Spinks was showing more authority than he had against Holmes. Early on, he made good use of a stiff jab, and before long he was linking the jab with right hands that rattled Cooney's head. Cooney, it was clear, was a very accessible target.

Not that Cooney appeared ruffled by the punches. His nearly drowsy expression suggested he was prepared to absorb Spinks's punches to get in his own presumably heavier blows. It was not quite so simple, though. Gripped by some species of anxiety, Cooney was struggling to catch his breath, and from the occasional glance he sneaked toward his corner, he seemed troubled by Spinks's unexpected aggression.

Spinks had his concerns, too. Toward the end of the second round, he incurred a cut over his right eye, near the bridge of his nose. Returning to his corner, he shook his glove in annoyance, or anger, for letting himself get cut. A wound like that, if aggravated as the bout went on, could be cause to stop the fight.

Yet he did not let the cut impede him, continuing to do as he had before—and beat Cooney to the punch. Not once, but repeatedly, the jab snaked through Cooney's defenses, bringing the bad news that Spinks's hands were quicker. At one point in the third round, Cooney swung his left arm back, and then started his money punch, the hook, forward, only to find that his target was no longer there. He froze the punch in midair and immediately walked smack into a right hand of Spinks's.

Yet a round later, here was Cooney moving forward and rapping Spinks with left hooks, showing that his power just might be the resource to neutralize the other man's superior hand speed. Pain was the element that could make a quick hand diminish. But whether Cooney had it in him to discourage Spinks remained to be seen.

Watching films of Cooney's fights, Butch Lewis had noticed that whenever the big man was made to retreat he ceased to punch. Moving backward, Cooney was stricken impotent. A seductive thought was planted: at the opportune time, Spinks could slay the giant.

With 1:28 remaining in the fifth round, Cooney missed a left uppercut, and Spinks slammed a right off the side of Cooney's head. Another right to the head, a left uppercut flush on his chin: Cooney's head snapped back, and his face went sour. Spinks read his weakness and pounced. He hammered three right hands off Cooney's head, each blow thrown with his whole upper torso turning into it.

Cooney stood in place, absorbing the punches. Then he was in retreat, his upraised gloves trying to ward off the punches that came at him, in volume too great for that pattycake defense. A right, a wicked left uppercut to the chin, and another right put Cooney onto the seat of his trunks. There, leaning on his right elbow, he looked to his corner and struggled to his feet.

"You all right, man?" Frank Cappuccino, the referee, asked.

Cooney nodded, and then stood waiting for Spinks to mis-treat him. Six foot five inches upright he was, with his hands out in front of him, rolling in little circles to intersect or deflect Mr. Michael's incoming. These were hardly the evasion tactics that boxers in deep shit are taught. When under siege, as Cooney was, a fighter is advised to move what will move—legs, head, and shoulders—so the target is a shifting and, with any luck, an elusive one. As an acceptable Plan B, he is told to drop any pretense of pride and grab the other man like last dance at the Senior Prom—hold him as tightly and for as protracted a period of time as the referee permits. Then repeat this pro-cedure until the bell brings a reprieve, and the hurly-burly of ice shocks, and a trainer's logic.

Cooney did not bend his knees or roll his head and shoul-ders. He did not reach those long arms out for the smaller man to hold him fast while the clock wound down. The poor bastard was performing the hotcha flourishes of a chorus girl with his gloves.

Not surprisingly, Spinks popped him—and good. Whap whap whap: big noisy shots that raised the beastroar from the crowd in Convention Hall and, under the bright lights, had Cooney looking like Alka-Seltzer commercial material. His face went slack and oafish. Spinks hit him and hit him, and Cooney took a seat, slowly flexing down, his weight on his right elbow.

Cappuccino was on one knee now, shouting numbers into the noisy night. "Five . . . six . . . seven. . . ." Cooney had raised himself to his feet by the time the count got to eight.

"You all right?" Cappuccino asked. "You know who I am, huh?"

Cooney mumbled he did.

"Okay," said Cappuccino.

Now came Spinks's final assault. At the end, at close quar-ters, he crouched slightly and drove three right uppercuts, one after the other, through the bleary-eyed Cooney's guard until merciful Cappuccino stepped between the fighters and, nine seconds before the end of the fifth round, made Gerald An-thony Paul Cooney an ex-fighter.

"That's all, Gerry," he said. "You're taking too many shots."

As Cappuccino ended the bout, Lewis rushed in and jubi-lantly carried Spinks across the ring, high-stepping like a drum majorette as he did.

According to a computer punch count, Spinks had landed 84 of his 101 punches in the final round. Cooney's face registered the damage: it was puffy and his eyes were glassy and bewildered. By contrast, Cooney landed only five of twenty-six punches in the final round.

In his dressing room afterward, Cooney held ice to his face—there was swelling beneath the right eye—and wailed, "How can I fucking lose like that?"

12

All that stood now, in June 1987, between Mike Tyson's chances of becoming the undisputed heavyweight champion was a stout man with a bushy mustache who figured it was time to cash in.

His name was Cedric Kushner, and he was the promoter of Tony Tucker. On May 30, Tucker had won the IBF title that was declared vacant when Spinks had insisted on fighting Cooncy.

The night Tucker got the IBF title, Kushner, of Easthampton, Long Island, had good reason to be pleased.

Kushner, who had promoted Tucker since 1982, not only gained a promotional share of a heavyweight champion but also a chance to recoup at least some of the money he had sunk into Tucker's career during harder times. Kushner's investment in Tucker was not a niggling one. The night Tucker beat James (Buster) Douglas for the IBF title, Kushner was down $450,000.

How does a promoter get himself into that sort of a bind?

The story goes back to December 1970, when Kushner, a sixth-grade dropout, left South Africa to make his fortune. He sailed on a cargo ship that was transporting rhinoceroses to Europe. Kushner's job was to clean the animals' cages. From Europe, he made his way to the United States, arriving on his twenty-second birthday, in July 1971.

Through a contact he had made while in Europe, Kushner found a job unloading automobile springs at a warehouse in Dorchester, Massachusetts. He was there until Thanksgiving 1971, when he awoke to the first snowfall of his life. "I phoned up the next morning to give notice," he said. "And hitched to Miami Beach."

He applied for a job at the swank Fontainebleau Hotel but was turned down.

"They didn't need anybody," he said. "But the guys working at the pool earned so much money in season that they were looking to have somebody do their dirty work. That was me. I used to pick up all the towels and clean the pool and sweep the deck and 'neath the lounges. And they'd pay me, depending on how much they earned. When I lived in Miami Beach, I lived in a room which at the time cost almost everything I was earning. I was really struggling. I never had any money, I never had any friends. In the evenings I used to go and stand outside the Fontainebleau and watch the wealthy people get in cars and go out. That was my pastime."

Leaving Miami Beach, Kushner worked as a messenger in New York and then for a Ferris wheel operator in Asbury Park, New Jersey. At the 1972 Olympics in Munich, Germany, he scalped tickets, his bilingualism earning him a $5,000 profit and the attention of a wealthy Austin, Texas, businessman.

"He was impressed," said Kushner, "with my entrepreneurial display as he heard me negotiating outside the Olympic stadium in both English and German. Anyway, he gave me his card and invited me to have lunch. We chatted. He told me if I ever came to America and wanted to start a business to call him."

Eighteen months later, Kushner phoned. "I got past the secretary, and, to my amazement, when I told him what I wanted to do—promote concerts—he asked me a few questions and simply said: 'What is your address?' And proceeded to send a check for five thousand dollars. Five grand for a fifty percent share of my business. Well, I lost forty-four hundred, though the concert—in Plymouth, New Hampshire, and featuring the group Steppenwolf—was a logistical success. That is, everybody was happy, everybody was paid. My Austin, Texas, friend even sent me twenty-five hundred more—for survival: I was tapped out.

"About a week or so later, I was at a bar in Greenwich Village. A guy came back from the men's room and asked me to step outside because he was somewhat offended that I was trying to put the make on his girlfriend at the bar. What I proceeded to tell him was that I wasn't interested in fighting over a girl, there were more important things on my mind. We shook hands and struck up a conversation. I told him about my adventures in rock promotion. At which point he said to me he could help. 'The financial part wouldn't be a problem,' he said, and he asked could he invest seventy-five. I said I had somebody who'd invested seventy-five and he was a fifty percent shareholder and if I took him in I'd be running a business with no margin for Ced Kushner. He then proceeded to say that he meant seventy-five thousand.

"I said, 'Well, I'm sure we can get together as soon as you like.' I pulled out my diary, which didn't have an appointment till the year 2040, and said, 'Uh, let's see. I think I can push my nine-o'clock . . . how would eight-o'clock breakfast tomorrow be?' By nine-thirty the next morning we had agreed to a fifty-fifty deal with the understanding there would be some arrangement with my associate from Texas. That then did give me a certain security and provided me with the impetus to go on."

In the years that followed, Kushner became a major rock promoter, but in 1980 ran his career aground when he was indicted for antitrust violations for collusion with another promoter over territorial rights.

"I was given two years' probation and fined ten thousand dollars," Kushner said.

A year later, he had become the manager of a welterweight named Teddy Mann, whose contract Kushner acquired for an investment of $2,500. In six months, Kushner reported, the $2,500 expenditure grew to $20,000. "He can't get to the gym. His car is broken. His wife is going to have a baby—all of a sudden the responsibilities become mine."

Kushner decided to switch to the promotional side of boxing. When Tucker severed his relationship with his managers, Lou Duva and Shelly Finkel, and with his promoter, Bob

Arum, Kushner signèd him to a three-year contract for a $100,000 signing bonus, money he was reluctant to spend.

But because Kushner was, as he put it, "a South African and novice in boxing," he decided that he had to make a play to establish himself.

There was no speedy return on the investment, because the fighter's career was jinxed. A knee injury in August 1982 kept Tucker out of the ring for the next fifteen months. A broken hand in November 1984 cost him another eight months.

Even though Kushner's promotional contract with Tucker had a clause that lengthened its term for such contingencies, the promoter found himself being asked to help support the fighter during his period of inactivity.

"There was no question that the need was legitimate," said Kushner. "But I was a little reluctant and a little concerned, for obvious reasons. Was I in over my head? I'd spent more than three hundred thousand dollars after two years to keep Tucker going."

During this time, Kushner had promotional interests in other fighters, including Gerrie Coetzee, who became the heavyweight champion, and John Collins, a middleweight. But while the promoter says he showed a marginal profit on his other boxing ventures, these funds did not absorb the spiraling cost of keeping Tucker's career afloat.

Why didn't Kushner simply bail out?

"You analyze how much you've already invested," he said. "At the thought of losing that, you say, 'I'll give it another ten grand.' You're sure the fighter's shot will come."

By 1986, with his contractual obligations to Tucker escalating, Kushner was forced to get financial infusions from others—from the promoter Jeff Levine and from Cooney's manager, Dennis Rappaport—or risk "blowing the four hundred thousand plus."

"Had I taken the four-hundred-and-fifty-thousand outlay over five years and put it in a bank or mutual funds, I'd have six hundred and fifty thousand," Kushner said. "But then being an entrepreneur in a business of risk—that was truly my nature."

Kushner had stretched his risk to the breaking point, and now that Tucker was the IBF champion he meant to make back as much of his $450,000 as he could. The promoter's dilemma was that while Tucker had said he would fight Tyson for $1.2 million, Kushner needed to cut his own separate deal that would wipe away the tab he had run up on Tucker's account. Don King, who would promote Tyson-Tucker, was offering only $1.5 million to accommodate the fighter *and* his promoter. However, Kushner was obliged to split half of his $300,000 with Jeff Levine, who a year earlier had provided some of the capital Kushner needed to keep him from losing his contractual hold on Tucker. Kushner knew that if Tucker lost to Tyson he would have few immediate prospects for earning his money back off his fighter.

In early June, he told King the $1.5 million offer was not satisfactory. He would need, he claimed, $2 million.

The number was a stretch, but Tyson's camp, he believed, had a stake in having its fighter become the undisputed heavyweight champion, and he guessed there might be some "give" in the $1.5 million offer King had made. Cayton told him just how much give there was.

"I met with Bill," said Kushner, "in King's office. Cayton gave me an ultimatum. 'Take one point seven million or there won't be any fight.' That's when I brought in Mickey Duff."

A close acquaintance of Jacobs's, Duff was to serve as a kind of *amicus curiae,* using his influence to convey the facts of Kushner's red-ink situation. This he did, over a series of meetings, making it clear to Jacobs that he was acting as a paid consultant so there would be no confusion later if word got out that Mickey Duff made a few bob—$30,000, as it turned out—speaking up for his friend Kushner.

Duff's lobbying helped. Toward the end of June, Kushner was patched into a conference call emanating from Seth Abraham's HBO office. With King and Jacobs also in on the call, Abraham asked what would it take to close a Tyson-Tucker deal. "Two million dollars," was Kushner's reply.

"I'll close it at one point eight," said Abraham.

"That's unacceptable," said Kushner. "If you want to close, and you're looking for a compromise, and want to do it right here and now, I'll take one point nine million. Call me back."

The one point nine stuck. Kushner got a call from King asking him to meet that day to finalize the contract. Kushner told him he was tied up until later that night, but agreed to meet at 1:00 A.M. at the Westbury Hotel, near King's East 69th Street office.

"I wanted him to be tired," Kushner said. "Because it makes sense to do business that way. I was fresh. Certain elements of the deal had not been discussed. Air fares, the number of hotel rooms, the number of comp tickets. I remember King nodding out while I was reviewing the contracts with [the fighter's father and comanager] Robert Tucker and his attorney, Greg Reed. Don King fell asleep."

A few days later, Kushner got a call from Jim Jacobs. It turned out that King had forgotten a detail—he hadn't discussed future options on Tucker's fights—that could be crucial in the unlikely event that Tucker beat Tyson. For the three options that King routinely got with opponents of Tyson specified an eventual rematch with Iron Mike.

"Jim was so aggravated," said Kushner. "I said to him, 'Jim, do you think it right to come to me now, after the deal's been signed?' He said, 'I don't blame you, Cedric. Don was supposed to get these things done beforehand.'"

With Mickey Duff now intervening on Jacobs's behalf, Kushner agreed, eventually, to go along with Jacobs's request. *If* he could get Robert Tucker to agree. But Tucker wouldn't hear of it. A deal was a deal, and too bad about Don King's little oversight.

FOR IMMEDIATE RELEASE:

GLORY HALLELUJAH!
THE UNIFICATION:
UNDISPUTED WORLD HEAVYWEIGHT CHAMPION
MIKE TYSON, WBC, WBA CHAMPION
VS.
TONY TUCKER, IBF CHAMPION
FIFTEEN ROUNDS
LAS VEGAS HILTON, LAS VEGAS, NEVADA
SATURDAY, AUGUST 1, 1987

Glory Hallelujah!
Those are the words Promoter Don King used, and it couldn't have been spoken better, with the signing of the contracts for a Mike Tyson–Tony Tucker battle for the undisputed heavyweight championship of the world—at the

Las Vegas Hilton, Las Vegas, Nevada, on Saturday, August 1st, 1987.

It marks the culmination of the "Hard Road to Glory—The Ultimate." It spells the end in sight of what could easily be called "Mission Impossible" for Don King, HBO, and the Las Vegas Hilton. It will be the fantastic finish of the World Series of Boxing, the Unification of the Heavyweight Championship and produce the first undisputed world heavyweight champion since Leon Spinks stunned the boxing world by defeating Muhammad Ali on February 15, 1978, to win the titles.

"Nobody believed that it could be done," declared King. "But here we are ready for the Coronation. The obstacles were incredible and too numerous to relate but we never gave up and come August 1st, we will have the first undisputed world heavyweight champion in almost ten years. It will be a glorious moment, a time for pageantry."

So came the word from Murray Goodman, King's PR man. In *his* prefight story, Sly was somewhat less rapturous. The fight itself was neither so rousing as Goodman predicted nor as dreary as Sly expected; Tyson emerged the victor by unanimous decision but found it difficult to land more than a single punch at a time. For his part, Tucker lifted Tyson off his feet with a left uppercut in the first round and nailed him with straight right leads early in the match. Then, as he lost the snap in his punches after the fourth round, he fought just to last the twelve-round distance.

Tucker would say afterward that he broke his hand in the second round, and the Los Angeles physician who examined him, Dr. Anthony Daly, would find "what looked like a fresh fracture" to the third metacarpal bone of the right hand.

Even so it remained an interesting fight for the survivalist tactics Tucker deployed with some effect against Tyson. He circled and grabbed. He sidestepped Tyson's charges or deflected them by pushing Tyson with his gloves. Sometimes he neutralized his opponent by pressing Tyson's head down as he came forward.

To his credit, Tyson showed more patience than he had in the past, this time even using his jab to set up his heavier blows. A computer punch count had him landing more jabs than Tucker. Afterward, in the dressing room, Tyson exulted: "I found I could outjab him."

"Oh, he was excited," said Jacobs. "It was like a new tool."

In the end, the words "Glory Hallelujah" seemed less a reflection of the bout itself than of a promoter's joy in the fact that Home Box Office's unification series at last had an ending. It was a miracle that an undefeated heavyweight champion had emerged—given what the "naysayers and doomsayers" King liked to conjure had predicted when the series had been announced eighteen months earlier. What had started out as a seven-fight series for which HBO had planned to pay $16 million had ended up as a ten-fight series for which the pay cable service paid out $22 million.

The Tyson era had begun.

A few hours later, in a chandeliered ballroom of the Las Vegas Hilton, as six trumpeters in Elizabethan blue velvet costumes of feathered caps, knickers, and sequined tunics sounded their instruments, the ring announcer, Chuck Hull, stepped forward.

Now outfitted in a Beefeater getup, right down to the knee socks, he intoned: "Hear ye! Hear ye! By order of the people of the world of boxing, in this glorious year of nineteen hundred and eighty-seven, it is hereby proclaimed that in lands near and far, one man above all others shall stand triumphant in the four-corner-square ring of battle, hereby trumpeted as the ultimate world heavyweight champion."

So began a Don King–designed "coronation" ceremony. The "thronization," as he called it, had pizzazz and more than a bit of gall. It was Florenz Ziegfeld meets Crazy Eddie.

Several of the major players in the Home Box Office heavyweight unification series were trumpeted down a red-carpeted pathway to the stage, introduced as Sir this and Sir that; Tyson sat in street clothes on an elevated red velvet throne. There were songs from the Little Angels, a children's choir out of Chicago, and from Janet Lynn Shinner, a gospel singer from Cleveland.

Then, with entertainment stars such as Eddie Murphy, Robert Guillaume, Heather Thomas, Dennis Hopper, and Philip Michael Thomas to do the honors, trophies were handed out to, it seemed, every boxing official remotely connected with the series.

As Murphy, pointing to Tyson, joked: "The man whipped everybody's butt and he ain't got a trophy. All the white men with trophies. I don't understand."

In time, Tyson—who reportedly was a reluctant party to the pageantry—came forward adorned in a chinchilla robe and a jeweled crown that Muhammad Ali had set on Tyson's head (after feigning to put it on his own), a jeweled necklace, and a scepter from Felix the jeweler, Las Vegas.

As King blared, "Long live the heavyweight king, long live the king," Tyson showed a sheepish smile and, responding to the cries of "Speech" from the crowd, asked: "Does this mean I'm going to get paid bigger purses?"

Then he said: "Pleasure to be here. I came a long way. I look forward to defending the title as long as I can."

From the two-page outline for the ceremony:

—Don Announces "Long Live the King"
—Everyone Returns to Their Seats
—Beefeater Introduces Al Green to Sing "Precious Lord"
—At End of Song, Don Brings Forward Rev. Williams to Bless the Food
—Don Says Let the Festivities Begin.
            The End

The end for Cedric Kushner came a bit earlier in the evening. After the fight he asked King for his tickets to the party, only to be told the promoter had none for him.

"He wouldn't give me any tickets," said Kushner, "even though my fighter had just fought for the unification title."

It reminded Sly of the story a Hollywood guy had told him about the comedian Mel Brooks. Brooks had gone from making films under others' auspices to creating and producing them himself—at a cost of diminished humor, it seemed to an acquaintance of his.

"You were funnier when you weren't the producer," the man insisted.

"Ah," said Brooks, "but it's good to be king."

"Can I tell you something?" asked Tyson. "I really never hated anybody. I think I hate Tyrell Biggs."

Tyrell Biggs was not an obvious choice as an object of disaffection—Tyson's or anybody else's. He was a big, smooth-featured kid from Philadelphia who spoke well and was not averse to having a laugh or two. Without much promoting, he would launch into his impression of the comic Rodney Dangerfield, fussing with his collar, as Dangerfield did, and wiping imaginary perspiration from his face. "I tell ya. No respect. I went to the dentist, asked him what I should do about my yellow teeth. He told me, 'Wear a brown tie.'"

As an impressionist, Biggs was a better fighter, hardly cause to revile him, as the heavyweight champion did, all the same. Weeks before their October 16 bout in Atlantic City, Tyson confided that he wanted to hurt Biggs, to punish him— words that had an extreme and rather personal edge.

The problem went deeper than Biggs, really.

More than most fighters, Tyson's identity was tied to his boxing prowess. The amateur phase of his career was a bad memory; Tyson felt he had been treated like an outsider. While Tyson had won titles as an amateur, without an Olympic medal that success seemed hollow—somewhat like being an actor in a Broadway show that had closed out of town. In part, he said, he missed out on Olympic glory because his boxing style was not geared for the amateurs; the rest, he insisted, had to do with politics. Not the least of that, he said, could be put to the resentment amateur officials bore D'Amato, a pro boxing man.

Biggs, a gold medalist in the super heavyweight class at the 1984 Olympics, represented the epitome of the "funny style," as Tyson called the hit-and-run approach that often succeeds in the amateur ranks. Tyson believed Biggs symbolized the fighters who, unlike himself, had the backing of the potentates of the amateur sport. Not only did Tyson openly resent Biggs's success, but when he was an amateur he had even tried to bait him, unsuccessfully, into fights outside the ring, bumping against him or giving him a hard look.

His problem with Biggs dated back to those amateur days

and what Tyson perceived as a superior attitude on Biggs's part.

"That was his style," said Tyson. "To make fun of you."

Tyson said that as an alternate on the United States Olympic team in 1984, he was in an airport with Biggs, headed for Los Angeles, when a woman wished him good luck.

"Biggs made some comment indicating I didn't have to be wished good luck," said Tyson. "He said, 'She must mean good luck on the flight.' That one thing stuck to my mind a long time."

Whatever.

By this time in his career, Biggs was growing accustomed to failed expectations. From the beginning he had struck Sly as that species of gifted pro who lacked the stiff-backed element in his nature—call it purpose, fury, ambition—that stretches a fighter's skills and animates his career.

Though early in their pro boxing lives Biggs and Tyson were often spoken of as natural future rivals—the Ali and Frazier of the '80s—the notion fizzled as time went on. Oh, there were occasions when Biggs could bounce about the ring on the balls of his feet and pop-pop-pop the jab, as Ali used to. He had done it with just one functioning hand, after breaking his right collarbone in the second round against Jeff Sims in March 1986. With a left jab and a lot of legs, he outboxed Sims and won the decision in a nationally televised ten-round fight that raised expectations of a new, transcendent Biggs.

But that Biggs now resided in the video archives, stuck in time with the thickly muscled, glowering Sims. The "other" Biggs—the one who would succumb to cocaine at the start of his career and, when clinically rehabilitated, to mental drowsiness in his fights—sometimes looked uninterested in the ring.

On occasion it seemed that the shadow of Tyson, the big puncher, loomed, coaxing Biggs to show the world he could also slug. Against David Bey in March 1987, for example, Biggs turned puncher and found himself the victim of overhand rights that opened a cut over his left eye that only thirty-two stitches would close. Referee Richard Steele was on the verge of halting the fight and awarding it to Bey when Biggs suddenly rallied and stopped Bey in the sixth round.

"I don't know why I do it," Biggs said afterward, "but

sometimes I have to get myself in trouble before the best comes out in me."

It was after the Bey fight that Sly would write that he wondered why Biggs's managers, Shelly Finkel and Lou Duva, had agreed to fight Tyson when Biggs appeared to need more seasoning. Never mind the seven-figure payday. As a gold medalist at the 1984 Olympics, Biggs was regarded as a fighter who merited careful handling for long-term gains.

Sly continued:

> Yet last Saturday, when he fought David Bey, Biggs's inability to avoid Bey's punches was shocking to see for a fighter who had been noted for his skill at avoiding punches when he came into the pros. And it underscored the suspicion that in their decision to go for the May 30 date with Tyson, Duva and Finkel may have decided that Biggs's future was not as rosy as once thought. In that case, a managerial philosophy of take-the-money-and-run served the fighter, too.
>
> The speculation became academic Saturday when Biggs suffered a deep gash over his left eye against Bey, an injury that precluded his fighting Tyson on May 30.

Part of what a boxing writer did was to assess the talent and shoot down the pretenders. Biggs had come in for his share of the barbed prose, and was aware of Sly's views, facetiously greeting him as "my main man" when Sly turned up at the fighter's Lancaster, Pennsylvania, training camp.

But while Biggs disagreed with the thrust of what had been written about him—that he lacked the focus and fire to succeed—his coffee-shop conversation with Sly proceeded in a mostly congenial way. On those occasions when Biggs's brother, Xavier, tried to interject a more querulous note, the fighter backed him off.

Their dialogue was far more orderly than that of the final prefight news conference, just days before the bout, where there was, it was noted, "namecalling and even some nastiness . . . a rhetorical club fight, so to speak," involving Tyson and Biggs's camps.

In the months leading up to a bout Tyson seemed to have

no interest in the psyching that other fighters practiced. At press conferences, when his opponents made wild-eyed declarations about what they intended to do to him—one boxer, Alfonso Ratliff, even promised: "Boy, I'm gonna use you like a government mule"—Tyson would sit impassively, apparently indifferent to these attempts to unnerve him, as though he recognized them for what they were: the comedy legacy of Muhammad Ali, who had made talking trash an art form.

Ali's impetus for monkeying with his opponents had come from that upright citizen Gorgeous George, a pro wrestler whose fanciful boasts were a masterwork of promotion. Ali had met George and seen what a sales tool those incantations of braggadocio could be: they were to a sports page what the neon sign is to the commercial establishment. And "getting ink," as Ali understood, had a direct bearing on the final count at the box office. Tyson's style resisted such rhetorical flourishes. Fighting was, he knew, a form of show business—D'Amato had told him as much. But his role in it was confined to being the beast that walked the night.

As for the match against Biggs, the fighters were pushed to the background of a dispute that featured their managers. It started with Lou Duva telling Tyson that Biggs would teach him a thing or two about boxing "that you've never been taught or been concerned about."

That apparently broke an understanding Jim Jacobs thought he had with Finkel and with Dan Duva, Lou's son and Biggs's promoter. The understanding was that Lou would say what he wanted at the press conference but would not address any remarks to Tyson, as he had in the past.

When, by Jacobs's view, Duva crossed the boundaries of good taste, Jacobs let Finkel know that, in effect, all bets were off.

When his turn came to speak, Jacobs let go. He said that eight months before, the Biggs managerial team had come to Cayton and him and said that in Biggs they had a "mental case" on their hands, a fighter who on occasion just disappeared from sight. Jacobs said that Biggs's managerial team had asked his help in getting HBO to approve first Renaldo Snipes and then Bey—"fighters of relatively no merit," Jacobs called them—as opponents for Biggs.

"Because," said Jacobs, "in their scrutiny of things, the

management of Biggs felt that those two were the only heavy-weights in the division he was capable of beating."

Jacobs said that he and Cayton had, in fact, used their "good offices" with HBO to get Snipes and Bey as HBO-approved opponents for Biggs and that Biggs had barely beaten both men.

"I hope your mental case is as good as your team thinks he is," concluded Jacobs, before he sat down.

At that, both Duvas rushed to the microphone, inviting Jacobs to spell out his allegations.

"Come on, Jim," said Lou Duva. "Let's talk about this here."

Jacobs declined to rejoin the fray.

Tyson, the final speaker, summed things up this way: "I found the press conference entertaining and distasteful."

Afterward, both Duvas and Finkel denied ever calling Biggs a mental case in their dealings with Jacobs and Cayton.

"When you're negotiating to make a fight," said Dan Duva, "you don't say, 'My guy will kill yours.' You say, 'My guy's nothing.'"

Jacobs, however, insisted that both of the Duvas and Finkel—whom Jacobs called a friend—had used the term "mental case."

"What can they do but deny that with their fighter sitting there?" said Jacobs.

Jacobs also said that members of the Biggs team had referred to the fighter as "fragile."

Lou Duva said Jacobs's allegations were lies, and Dan Duva remarked dryly, "His name's not Emily Post, it's Jimmy Jacobs."

Biggs went into the bout with strategy.

A few weeks earlier in Lancaster, George Benton had walked him through a fight plan calculated to unravel Mike Tyson.

By Benton's scheme, Biggs, a nimble heavyweight, would circle Tyson and knock him off balance with a stiff jab that would set up his heavier arsenal—left hooks and straight rights.

By this prefight plan, the six-foot-four-and-three-quarters Biggs would rap Tyson, then use his superior footwork to glide out of range to avoid engaging Tyson in a full-scale brawl.

Bang, bang, and be gone: that was the plan. The notion was to confuse and frustrate Tyson.

Benton pointed out, for example, that when Tyson prepared to shoot his vicious left hook, he tended to rock from side to side, as if winding up the coiled machinery of the punch.

"When you see that," said Benton to Biggs, "what do you do?"

On cue, Biggs nonchalantly stepped away, a movement calculated to leave Tyson grounded.

The key, as Benton saw it, was for Biggs to keep out of the corners of the ring and off the ropes, where Tyson could dig in his heels and unleash his powerful punches. For those occasions when Tyson did close on Biggs, Benton had an unorthodox strategy for his fighter to regain his space: he instructed Biggs to lower his head and drive his shoulders into Tyson's chest—moving him just enough to regain the operating distance Biggs needed to implement his battle plan.

Benton had even calculated the referee's reaction to what constituted a borderline tactic. He told Biggs not to try to punch Tyson after he had shouldered him across the ring. The trainer's belief was that if his fighter did not gain an advantage when he backed Tyson off, the referee would probably allow it.

So went the theory: the reality was otherwise.

As he had before—with Bonecrusher Smith, who had talked war and then suffered an instant case of terminal timidity when Tyson began to hit him—Tyson made a changed man of his opponent. After Tyson belted him a few times, Biggs was virtually unrecognizable.

Tyson was in Biggs's face from the opening bell, and, working methodically, he pummeled Biggs without letup. By round two, Biggs was down off his toes and there was a look of utter resignation on his face that this was not to be his night. The Ali-like gliding movement with which Biggs planned to circle Tyson and the long-armed piston jab with which he planned to orchestrate his offense were quickly nullified as Tyson did what Tyson does: he imposed his will.

As for the Biggs jab that had dominated the best super heavyweights in the amateur ranks, well, that jab disappeared over the course of the fight. By the computer punch count, Biggs threw thirty-seven jabs in the first round. After that, he had seventeen jabs in round two, eighteen in round three, twelve in round four, ten in round five, seven in round six.

By the seventh round, it was no longer a question of whether Iron Mike would finish Biggs, only of when, as Tyson continued landing booming lefts and rights with hardly a combative response from Biggs.

A left hook and a right uppercut by Tyson knocked Biggs onto the canvas and through the ropes toward the end of the seventh. As referee Tony Orlando counted, Lou Duva leaned through the ropes and screamed: "Get up, get up!"

Biggs got up, just in time to run into yet another of the vicious left hooks that Tyson had been landing with impunity. This one sent Biggs reeling backward several steps and finally onto the seat of his shorts. And this time, Duva had seen enough. He climbed into the ring just as Orlando was waving an end to the bout one second before the round expired.

Tyson seemed to savor the destructive beauty of the job he had done on Biggs. "I could have knocked him out in the third round," he told the scribes afterward. "But I did it very slowly. I wanted him to remember it for a long time. He didn't show any class as a professional boxer, so I made him pay for his actions with his health."

At the end, Biggs was hardly the picture of health. Blood streamed down the left side of his face from a cut over his eye, his lower lip bled, his right cheekbone swelled.

"By the third round, I knew I had him," Tyson said, "because when I was hitting him to the body, he was making noises. I knew I was affecting him a great deal."

Asked what type of sounds Biggs had made, Tyson said: "Like a woman screaming."

In beating up on Biggs, Tyson indulged in the sort of nasty flourishes he had more or less hinted at in his prefight grumbling about Biggs. In the Atlantic City ring, he elbowed Biggs, butted him, and on occasion hit him after the bell. Nor was there any rote praise afterward for Biggs—the sort of conciliatory gibber-jabber that bitter enemies typically exchange after punching on each other under the hot lights of an arena or ballpark.

In another fighter that malice might have brought outraged public reaction. In 1965, for instance, when Ali taunted Floyd Patterson while punching him at his whim, he was criticized loudly for his cruelty. Yet no outcry arose over Tyson's mean-spirited excess. Patterson was a respected ex-champion and Biggs a fighter with no devoted following, but the reasons for the differing reactions appeared to lie with the victors.

Ali was a fighter of flash; Tyson a destroyer. Their artistic cores were contrary. When Tyson insulted the rules, he was doing what he was wired to do and, like the eccentric old coot who uses chronic foul language, was accepted for what he was.

What he was on the night he beat Biggs was America's gladiator, Rambo in short pants. His unswerving commitment to action was a spectacle—rock-'em-sock-'em that flirted with extremes and excited the souls of civilians otherwise sunk in the humdrum. For however long it took him to punch holes into another man's will, he was a hero.

That image must have struck Tyson as odd, for neither in his demeanor nor in his rowdy approach did he appear to curry the favor of the crowd. As he prowled from one corner of the ring to the other in his hightop black shoes, he evoked the same whoo-boy that all those hooded and simian hulks who acted the villain in wrestling's acrobatic cartoon did. The difference was that the sight of Tyson cued applause rather than hoots and imprecations. That acceptance, Tyson admitted, sometimes threw him: deep down he felt more the villain than hero when he went to work.

As a boxing type, his elemental *shtarke* was not new. Of modern times, Sonny Liston, who had been heavyweight champion between 1962 and 1964, had brought the same foreboding air to the job. But Liston, an ex-con out of St. Louis, never had the public approval that Tyson did. When Liston knocked out Floyd Patterson in September 1962 to become champion, he was thirty years old, according to the record books. Thirty years old with the personality of a sweaty sock. Tyson was another story. In private he hadn't Liston's baleful stare or intimidator's air. But as he slipped in and out of faces, he made that question—what's Mike Tyson really like?—a slithery exercise, like *Rashomon*'s shifting answers.

The soft voice seemed a trick of lip-synching, and even then the words suggested Tysons within Tyson. After a fight he was sure of himself as he recounted the action—from the crucial punches right down to the vital organ—the liver, the kidney—that he was seeking to disturb. At those moments he had the rhetorical precision of D'Amato or Jacobs, and seemed mature beyond his years.

There was another, more boyish side. Two weeks after he had knocked out Pinklon Thomas, to Sly's Mrs. he had said after not having seen Leslie Brooks Berger for months, "I'm in love." He was referring to his relationship with a TV actress named Robin Givens; and he blushed accordingly. Charming in its way.

But there were skeptics who insisted Tyson's was an ingenuity that cons had for ingratiating, and that the real Tyson was an even slicker reprobate than Liston ever knew how to be. On occasion Tyson would tell a reporter that without boxing he'd have ended up out on the streets, doing crime. He offered this not for some larger view of life's radical possibilities—it wasn't irony he was intending—but rather to indicate what a joy jumping-thy-neighbor could be. The romance of outlaw life.

In a man who walked and talked violence and was subject to changing moods, what did the mix make for? Was his a personality so combustible that the yellow brick road that D'Amato had started him on was bound to get bumpy? Was there a detour to calamity in his future?

The theory that Tyson was wired to undo his success was not new. With his first national exposure, certain boxing men would say of Tyson that he was a "time bomb" waiting to go off. That was back in late '85, early '86, and the underlying premise was that Tyson's intense fight itinerary—he was boxing about once a month then—was so pressurized that eventually he would have to bust out. And when he did, the theory was, he would hark back to the impulses that had ruled his life prior to his hooking up with D'Amato. In fact, before Tyson had turned pro, Torres had occasionally been dispatched to find the fighter when he bolted Catskill. The path, said Torres, invariably wound back to Brownsville and, from what Tyson told him, to "old tricks" of street crime.

"The same things he was doing when he was a kid," said Torres. "I assume it was a matter of habit."

One night over dinner Tyson spoke of two fighters, Tony Ayala and Roberto Duran, whose willful excesses he openly admired.

Ayala was one of four Chicano brothers out of San Antonio, Texas, who had been raised to be fighters by their father.

In the early 1980s, Ayala had landed on the boxing scene and fought with an anger, and abandon, that accelerated him in practically no time up the junior middleweight rankings. Like Tyson, Torito, as Ayala was known, had an anything-goes attitude in the ring. He shared Tyson's indifference for the bell that ended a round, and often continued belaboring his opponent after it sounded.

On January 16, 1981, when he had fought José Luis Baltazar, who had had the temerity to insult Ayala's mother before the fight, Ayala knocked Baltazar down and then spat on the fallen man.

As for Duran, he had enraged Ray Leonard before their first fight with his boorish behavior, the ultimate insult occurring when Duran threw the middle finger to Leonard's wife, Juanita.

That sort of wretched excess was no put-on with Duran. He was an authentic yahoo. In the ring, it made him a sneering attack dog of a fighter in whose dark eyes the rage was positively luminous. Out of the ring, he was not so dashing a figure: between fights he blew up like a Macy's balloon on a Thanksgiving Day float. As he took on weight—fifty, sixty, seventy pounds beyond his fighting trim—he squandered his personal fortune in what seemed inverse proportion to his caloric intake. Eventually he made it to a first-name basis with the Internal Revenue Service.

Ayala was not so talented with real life either. In April 1983, just months before he was to have fought for the world junior middleweight title, he was found guilty of a sexual assault on a woman in New Jersey, for which he was sentenced to a prison term of thirty-five years, and ordered to serve a minimum of fifteen years before he was eligible for parole.

Sly supposed that Tyson could not be faulted for his attraction to these hard-boiled characters. For all the civilizing touches that D'Amato and Camille Ewald had wrought, the champion lived best when he was punching the bejesus out of an oversized adult. In the prize ring, he had not only marauder's privileges, but the civilized world's approval. A lovely paradox that was—and it did not discourage his pleasure. His passage from Brownsville hood to admired pugilist was not so radical a shift in one man's orientation. The rewards still came from abusing others; he was now an officially sanctioned lord of chaos.

To Tyson, sport was what running jumping fools like Magic Johnson and Michael Jordan and Larry Bird did. What *he* did was beyond sport. It was gladiatorial, and for Tyson it had a code that invited the darkest impulses—the rage of the deprived. It was a quality he accepted and, more, welcomed in himself and in others.

He was the unapologetic warrior.

14

There was a market for Tyson's brutality. Big money he was making—money that, like the pottery shards of an ancient civilization, offered clues to daily activity. In Tyson's case, it didn't take an expedition to faraway places. Kaufman Greenhut Lebowitz & Forman, the fighter's accountants, were at One Madison Avenue in New York, and their balance sheets showed a prizefighting man's progress.

On January 1, 1987, the CPAs had listed his assets as:

Cash

Marine Midland Bank	14,022
Irving Trust Co.	22,212
Irving Trust Co.	1,461,967
Reserve Account—Berbick	10,000
Investment in tax exempt securities	315,762
	$1,823,963

By the end of calendar year 1987, the picture from Kaufman Greenhut was more complex.

MIKE TYSON
BALANCE SHEET
DECEMBER 31, 1987
A S S E T S

Cash—Forman Account	$ 79,526
Cash—Marine Midland Bank	25,551
Cash—Irving Trust Co.	113,063
Cash—Irving Trust Co. Money Market Account	15,860
Cash—Apartment Account	31,886
Merrill Lynch Cash Management Account	1,213,552
Investments—Tax Exempt Securities	1,466,652
Investments—Single Premium Life Insurance Policies	2,000,000
Automobiles	241,007
Net worth	$5,187,097

MIKE TYSON
STATEMENT OF RECEIPTS AND DISBURSEMENTS
AND CHANGES IN NET WORTH
FOR THE YEAR ENDED DECEMBER 31, 1987

Receipts	
Income—Fights	$6,737,686
—Reel Sports*	191,015
—Interest and Dividends	127,381
	7,056,082
Disbursements (Schedule)	1,430,412
	5,625,670
Taxes paid	2,262,536
Excess of Receipts over Disbursements	3,363,134
Assets—January 1, 1987	1,823,963
Net worth—December 31, 1987	$5,187,097

MIKE TYSON
DISBURSEMENTS
FOR THE YEAR ENDED DECEMBER 31, 1987

Expenses	
Cash drawings	$ 332,545
Medical	1,051

*The company set up to receive income from subsidiary activities like commercials and endorsements.

Equipment	445
Luggage	704
Food	55
Cablevision	807
Apartment—equipment and furniture	228,627
Rent—New York City	18,150
Telephone—New York City	2,863
Electricity—New York City	563
Records and tapes	157
Telephone—Catskill	1,227
Telephone—Albany	2,522
Electricity—Albany	1,160
Rent—Albany	7,150
House Repair—Catskill	20,000
Miscellaneous	704
Limousine and car rental	71,078
Travel	19,315
Hotels	35,480
Messengers	49
Photos	136
Bank charges	88
Accounting	19,055
Legal	13,244
Insurance	2,022
Sharpei (Dog)	864
Settlement—Law Suit	105,000
Keogh and IRA plans	62,000
Sister's rent and drawing	9,150
Jewelry	219,819
Rory*	17,330
Clothes	178,314
Dry cleaning	1,070
Gifts and guest expenses	2,223
R. Givens	7,560
Camille Ewald	15,370
Christmas expenses	1,334
Moving expenses	103
Air fares	22,222
Contributions	8,226
	$1,430,412

*Rory Holloway, a friend from Albany.

For Sly and his boxing brethren, Tyson's financial records offered a picture of a champion who had eased out into the fast lane. Tyson had money, and he was not averse to spending it, as the numbers showed. $178,314 for clothes—he had graduated to Gucci sportswear and tailor-made suits. $219,819 for jewelry—his gold Piaget watch was diamond-studded, and worth at least $65,000. At one point he owned four cars—a Mercedes, a Corvette, a Jaguar, and a Rolls-Royce.

By land or by air, he was getting around.

Sly ran into him from time to time in Vegas, at bouts Tyson attended as a spectator. In the early morning after one of those big fights, Sly came across Tyson sitting at an unmanned black-jack table, attempting to interest the pretty dealer at the adjoining table in meeting him later. Judging by her expression, he was a long way from convincing her. Spying Sly, Tyson waved him over and tried to enlist him to his cause. "Tell her," he said. "Tell her I'm a good guy."

To his friends, he was a right guy. Rock Newman, who worked as a spokesman for Butch Lewis, had wandered into the Gucci shop at Caesars Atlantic City on the morning after Tyson had knocked out Tyrell Biggs and noted the doors were locked so that a group of young people could go on a shopping spree.

"I counted twelve people," said Newman, "and they were: 'Give me two of these, two of those.' I said to a salesperson, 'What's going on?' She said, 'These people are guests of Mike Tyson. We're taking care of them, giving them what they want.' I watched. One person rang up twenty-seven hundred dollars in ten minutes. And the saleslady said they were charging it to Mike Tyson."

The changing contours of this man, the heavyweight champion, concerned the boxing press to an inordinate degree. The assignment was to know Tyson, and assess him. Every small shift in the status quo was looked at, inquired about, and interpreted.

When he turned up in Vegas before the Bonecrusher Smith fight, it was with a bald patch on his scalp that he said a doctor had diagnosed as being from "nerves." But "nerves" was not a word with the harmonious associations his managers preferred. Cayton and Jacobs circulated the amended view that it was just a medical quirk unrelated to nerves. Then Sly bumped into José Torres, who, in the course of conversation, would say: "It happened to me when I was fighting. I lost my hair, and the doctor told me the same thing he did to Tyson: it's from nerves."

Jacobs was the archdefender; he conceded no flaw, no problem, where Tyson was concerned. While the scribes knew this about Jacobs, certain of them baited him anyway, enjoying—perhaps perversely—his carefully enunciated dicta concerning Tyson. Others sought out Cayton, who, though a staunch Tyson man too, let gradations into his conversation that got a man a little closer to the facts.

The situation was complicated by Tyson, who kept himself at a distance from the newsgathering process. Even when he did his turn with the press, there was no telling if he would be subject to those moods of his that reduced his answers to non-answers.

There were usually signs:

Sly was "sir" or "Mr. Berger" when the fighter was out of sorts or in a quiet mood; "Phil" when he was in good spirits. And the moods could shift. Once, on a day he was shooting a TV commercial, Tyson was stone-faced when he greeted Sly as "sir." An hour or so later he slapped a friendly bear hug on him, backstage.

Tyson patrol was not the lonely vigil that following L. Spinks had been ten years earlier. Where Spinks was a novelty item of a champion, Tyson was the real thing, and the coverage of him drew a crowd. With the boyo himself growing scarce, a newsman had to tap into sources to develop the latest about the heavyweight champion.

In time, a fellow on Tyson patrol came into possession of facts, rumors,* all brands of Tyson miscellanea, some of it useful, some not. He came to know, for instance, that Tyson:

—liked Chinese food and Häagen Dazs vanilla Swiss almond ice cream.
—had named a white pigeon of his Gerry Cooney.
—occasionally saw a hypnotist.
—cried when his friend Mark Breland lost his WBA welterweight title to Marlon Starling in August 1987.

*An article in London's Sunday *People*, by Frankie Taylor, a former fighter, had hinted that Tyson was gay.

—would tell his cut man, Matt Baranski, just before heading to the ring: "I'm going to fuck this guy up," referring to his opponent.

—carried big wads of money, which he liked to flash.

—favored kung fu and horror films.

—often prefaced remarks by saying, "Can I tell you something?"

—was knocked out in the amateurs by one Al Evans.

—had his picture on a billboard on Main Street in Catskill.

—owned more than a thousand fight films.

—subscribed to pigeon-fancier magazines, through Jacobs and Cayton, who arranged it.

—had the following quotation affixed to the wall when he went to training camp: "You are a poor specimen if you can't stand the pressure of adversity."

—had a sister, Denise, who lived in Brooklyn, and a brother, Rodney, who was in Japan. And had he used his father's name he would have been Mike Kirkpatrick.

—ate thirty-six steamed clams for dinner every night while in training for Tucker.

—did boxing's best imitation of Leon Muhammad, a hefty corner man regarded as something of a character.

—had told a UPI writer, Dave Raffo, that a truck from Raffo's company had run over his dog—only to be advised that the vehicle was in the service of UPS.

—had in his New York apartment on Second Avenue in the 40s a black Hefty bag full of autographed apparel from pro basketball players he admired.

Such odd bits of detected and recollected material were stored in memory, and eventually, as a fight of Tyson's neared and Sly got a quota of words to use, he would draw on what pieces seemed relevant to advance his print portrait of Tyson. The stories often caught the contradictory streaks in Tyson— the gentle and vulnerable coexisting with the street-vulgar and violent. The only time Tyson had shown anger toward him, Holloway said, was when he had inadvertently mishandled one of Tyson's pigeons.

For Rory Holloway, a close friend from Albany, the Tyson he knew was the fellow who regularly sat in front of Holloway's, the family grocery store in Albany, eating two or three dozen chicken wings and "talking and laughing and joking." Or the

Tyson who from time to time would leave $200, $300 in the hands he shook of old cronies back in Brownsville.

But a degree of the wild abandon with which Mike Tyson fought stuck to his private life. Before he took his own apartment in New York, he would often show up unannounced at the door of Steve Lott. Show up and expect Lott to scare up a diversion or two for him. There were even occasions when Tyson would materialize at Lott's apartment accompanied by a woman, and Lott, catching that "pretty please" in Tyson's eyes, would surrender the apartment—clear the hell out—so Tyson could be alone with his latest.

In June, there was a problem in Los Angeles with a woman. A spokesman for the city attorney told the press that following a Run-DMC concert, Tyson had bear-hugged a female parking attendant and demanded a kiss. Then, when a male parking supervisor asked the woman if she was all right, Tyson allegedly struck the man three open-handed blows. Misdemeanor charges of assault with a deadly weapon (hands) and battery were filed. Tyson was to have been arraigned that August, but the case was settled out of court for $105,000.

The incident prompted more questions about Tyson's self-destructive side. In September, Sly wondered in print if Tyson was under control:

Last week, Mike Tyson, the undisputed heavyweight champion, did not show up for a scheduled interview in Catskill, New York.

When asked later what had happened to Tyson, the fighter's comanager, Bill Cayton, said he wasn't sure.

Tyson's missed appointment brought to mind an incident in July when Tyson was training in Las Vegas, Nevada, for his August 1 match against Tony Tucker and there were reports that he was becoming uncontrollable.

On July 17, three reporters who were scheduled to watch Tyson work out at Johnny Tocco's Ringside Gym in Las Vegas, and interview him afterward, were advised by Don King's aide, Murray Goodman, that Tyson had to bow out because he had laryngitis.

Not long after, at a news conference in Las Vegas for the Tyson-Tucker match, Jim Jacobs, the fighter's other manager, was responding to a story that Tyson had bolted training camp and had flown to Los Angeles to patch up his relationship with his girlfriend, Robin Givens, the television actress.

Jacobs said that Tyson had not flown to Los Angeles on the weekend in question but had gone to Albany to be with Camille Ewald, the woman in whose Catskill home Tyson was raised from the age of fourteen by his boxing mentor, Cus D'Amato. Ewald, said Jacobs, had been ill and Tyson, who regards her as his "mother," was concerned enough to want to see her. Tyson, Jacobs said, had sought and received permission to leave training camp.

While the story Jacobs told sounded reasonable enough, it made a man wonder about the earlier version, concerning laryngitis, that had been given as Tyson's reason for not appearing at Tocco's. Tyson's departure from Las Vegas to New York—by Jacobs's account—happened to coincide with the three reporters' being stood up by the fighter.

What made things even more curious was that as Jacobs was giving his account of Tyson's leave-taking, a well-placed Las Vegas boxing source was dismissing it, insisting at the same news conference that the fighter had indeed gone to Los Angeles.*

Even to reporters assigned to him, the microscopic attention accorded Tyson sometimes seemed excessive. Yet was there a choice? Boxing was marquee business, and in 1987 Tyson constituted the sport. The light was on.

But that light occasionally caught shadows of a Tyson no longer the broad sweet hammer in the Cus story. The wheel turned and, turning, left that eager acolyte in a receding past. Nothing stayed the same.

For now the light shone; eventually it would dim. That was the smirking promise time held for all fighters, even for Larry Holmes, who thought maybe, maybe he could connive against inevitability.

---

*Tyson later would say he was "psychologically not prepared" for the Tucker fight because of problems with Givens. While Tyson said that the relationship with Givens had improved since then, he conceded that if a similar problem arose in the future, "I'd probably react the same way." "Maybe I'm immature," he said. "These things happen. I do my best to deal with them."

On a Wednesday night in November 1987, at the Larry Holmes Commodore Inn on U.S. 22 in Phillipsburg, New Jersey, friends and relatives of the proprietor gathered in a ballroom for a surprise birthday party.

Holmes, who had turned thirty-eight, had come straight from his workout at the Larry Holmes Training Center in nearby Easton, Pennsylvania, thinking he was about to deliver an antidrug speech to a local youth group.

When the former heavyweight champion, dressed in a black Stetson, black satin jacket, and denims, stepped through the dimly lighted ballroom doorway, he heard the cry of "Surprise!" Momentarily transfixed, he tried to cover his sheepish smile with his hand.

While the motel at which the approximately 150 invited guests had gathered was part of Holmes's expanding business portfolio, the crowd—which included Holmes's wife, Diane, and his four children, Misty, nineteen, Lisa, eighteen, Kandy, seven, and Larry Jr., five—had come to honor not the young entrepreneur but the old fighter of the same name.

At each table a single pink rose blossomed from the grip of

an Everlast boxing glove. The large birthday cake on a table at the rear of the room had a pair of boxing mitts sculpted from frosting. And then there was the boxing T-shirt which Diane Holmes presented to her husband, a gift that may have proved the best of all. For what Holmes read, when he held up the white shirt to examine its red block letters, was this: MIKE TYSON/32-1.

The "32-1" referred to the record that Holmes's partisans expected Tyson, undefeated in thirty-two fights, to hold after Holmes got through with him on January 22 at the Convention Hall in Atlantic City.

Tyson was, of course, twenty-one years old, and, to paraphrase the comedian Chevy Chase, Holmes was not. In fact, Holmes had become a grandfather in August, when Misty had given birth to six-pound-seven-ounce Jeffrey Allen Dorsey, Jr.

Yet in Phillipsburg on this winter night, Larry Holmes did not sound like a man who believed he would be laboring under a handicap come January 22. Never mind that Tyson had knocked out twenty-eight of his thirty-two opponents. Or that he was unrelenting in his need to impair. Or that he habitually forced prefight boasts of opponents into sober reassessments with practically the first lick he hit them.

None of that seemed to faze Holmes, who told friends and family in Phillipsburg that Mike Tyson didn't scare him one bit.

"This guy," said Holmes, "is made for me."

When he quit the boxing business in April 1986, after losing a rematch to Spinks, Larry Holmes did not go gently into the night.

In that postfight interview before the HBO television audience, he invited judges, referees, and promoters to "kiss me where the sun don't shine."

That indelicate moment followed a controversy that took place seven months earlier, centering on Rocky Marciano, who had retired as heavyweight champion undefeated in forty-nine bouts. In September 1985, when Holmes fought Spinks for the first time, he was attempting to tie Marciano's all-time undefeated record for heavyweight champions.

Marciano's brothers attended the Holmes-Spinks match and made plain to all their hopes that Holmes would lose so that Marciano's record would survive. This galled Holmes, and after losing to Spinks, he told newsmen, "Marciano couldn't carry my jock." It was a tasteless remark about a widely admired champion who had died in an airplane accident in 1969. Holmes's public image was dealt a serious blow.

The long-respected champion was suddenly viewed by many as an embittered soul, a crank lacking the good sense to take his leave with a modicum of dignity.

But to hear it from Holmes the backlash rolled straight over his broad shoulders, leaving the president and chief executive officer of Larry Holmes Enterprises, Inc., quite intact.

"After that [second] loss to Spinks," said Holmes, "people thought I'd go hide. Or I'd get a gun and blow my brains out. But the Monday morning after the fight I was back in Easton, seeing where I was going to invest the one million they paid me."

From his corporate offices in Easton, Holmes tended to his businesses: a disco, a restaurant and lounge, the motel on U.S. 22, the training and recreation center, and his investments. He began promoting boxing matches and broke ground on a five-story professional office building on 3.2 acres on Larry Holmes Drive in Easton.

"I sit in Easton," Holmes said, "and take care of our little business. People shake my hand. I'm a happy guy doing it."

Maybe so. But in the ever-so-casual note of such pronouncements was there just a bit of artifice? Was business success simply a buffer for him against his ring disappointments? It sometimes seemed so. In June 1987, for instance, during the week preceding the Spinks-Cooney fight, Holmes had appeared in the show room of an Atlantic City casino, cofeatured with another former heavyweight champion, Joe Frazier, and performed a medley of songs. His most memorable lyrics were rap-song lines delivered by a man who sounded as though he believed what he sang:

> *I trained real hard to do the job.*
> *Then beat the man and I got robbed.*
> *Yeah, won that fight.*
> *[Pause]*
> *Everybody knows I beat Spinks,*
> *That's okay.*
> *Politics stink.*

In June, Holmes was, to all appearances, holding to his retirement. There had been attempts to lure him back into the
ring, against Cooney, Tyson, even Tyrell Biggs. But nothing
came of the offers.

While Holmes worked out from time to time, and even
joined the Easton YMCA so he could run on its overhanging
oval track (nineteen laps to the mile), it was not until he sat
ringside with his trainer, Richie Giachetti, at Tyson's August 1
bout against Tony Tucker that the former champion got serious about being back in boxing.

"He turned to me during Tyson-Tucker," recalls Giachetti,
"and said, 'Richie, I can knock this guy out.'"

In October, Holmes signed for a reported $3.1 million to
fight Tyson. According to the promoter, Don King, the negotiations began with Holmes giving him the grand tour of his business holdings.

"Then," said King, "he pulls out a fifty-thousand-dollar interest check and says, 'See this, Don? I ain't fighting for the
money.'"

Why, then, at his age, was Holmes coming back?

Well, the answer to that question lay in Holmes's difficult
nature. Here was a man engaging and antagonistic by turns—
one moment joking, the next fuming, here professing indifference to the opinions of others, there currying their kind
words.

"Did you ever meet a fighter like me?" he asked Sly. "Tell
me what impresses you about me."

And moments later: "What don't you like about me?"

The world according to Larry was an adversarial one, full
of people refusing him his due.

"How do *you* feel about yourself?" he asked. "Do you like
yourself? Okay. Do I have the same right to feel good about
myself? How come when I say I love me, someone puts me
down? How come when I say I'm greater than Rocky Marciano,
I should apologize?"

And in practically the next breath, he did apologize, for
having said that Marciano couldn't carry his jock. "It was a poor
choice of words at the time. But it was too late. I said it. They
didn't let me take it back."

On the afternoon of his surprise party, Holmes worked out
for about forty-five minutes—mostly shadowboxing and aero-

bic movements—and then, in private dressing quarters, did sit-ups on a slant board to tighten his somewhat thickening waist-line. After he weighed himself (232 pounds), he began to speak.

Here was his stream-of-consciousness projection of Tyson vs. Holmes:

"He'll be throwing forty-five to fifty punches a round—forty-eight blocked, two will graze me but look like they landed. And I'll be jabbing, thirty, thirty-five punches a round. Landing. All of a sudden a right hand out of nowhere. Bam bam! Uh oh. I changed up."

Then the Holmes monologue took a left turn, as the fighter recalled various men who had worked with him, in one capacity or another, and had gone on to enjoy success else-where. Why their success? he asked, rhetorically. The answer, in Holmes's own singsong crooning words: "Be-cause of Lar-ry Holmes."

One after another he traced the greening of these people who, as Holmes saw it, would never had made it but for the start he gave them. Soon he was asking Giachetti and the others in the room why these men had prospered.

Grinning and laughing, they took the cue and chanted along with him in the singsong answer: "Be-cause of Lar-ry Holmes."

The party was over when, some time later that evening, Holmes wandered into the bar of his Phillipsburg motel.

Spying Giachetti, he asked, "Do you love me, Richie?"

The same question for Sly.

And, looking to a handful of drinkers along the bar, one more time: "Do you-all love me?"

From the bar came a halfhearted murmur of assent, enough to send the former heavyweight champion of the world out the door and into the night, for the moment at least a happy man.

One after the other, Tyson hit his opponents hard enough to leave knuckle prints on their psyches. Yet in time each of them would step back into this world of longitudes and latitudes, of zip codes and area codes, with a version of what had befallen them that sanitized the facts.

Biggs believed that his first-round stick-and-move tactics had "exposed" the real Tyson, and regarded the lack of liveliness that struck his legs afterward as a quirk of nature separate and apart from the thudding punches Tyson landed on him. By Biggs's account, the strange business with those legs became a kind of Bermuda Triangle mystery: his underpinnings just vanished into the night.

Tyson's other victims—Berbick, Thomas, Tucker, Bonecrusher Smith—had elaborate tales of could-have and should-have and injuries to speak of, white lies and bald-faced lies necessary for their staying in business.

Poverty made fighters; illusion kept them going.

In November, at the Larry Holmes Training Center in Easton, the eponymous owner was standing before the speed bag, talking—riffing, really—as his hands beat a steady rhythm on the small bag.

"I ain't going to do nothing to hurt me," Larry Holmes intoned. "I love me. Thank you, Jesus. Lord, have mercy. Thank you for giving me the power to be strong."

Rat-a-tat, rat-a-tat was the sound of the speed bag. Holmes took a deep breath, and continued:

"This old man is gonna shock the world! They going to say, '*And the neewww chaaamm-pi-oooooon. . . !*'"

Meanwhile, in his bedroom at the Ocean Club, by the boardwalk in Atlantic City, the lord king heavyweight, Tyson, was studying history.

Years of watching old fight films had proved a *Clockwork Orange* reinforcement of his visceral approach to boxing and had given him much affection for early-twentieth-century boxers and respect for the rigors they had known—bouts that were scheduled for twenty, forty, fifty rounds and that were fought with gloves that hadn't the attached thumbs to prevent retinal injuries or the volume of horsehair padding to cushion blows that the modern mitts have. That fight game was the legalized version of a sport only a step removed from its underground origins, when bouts were staged on barges and at secret rendezvous to keep a step ahead of the gendarmes.

For Tyson, the flickering images from those grainy films he watched in his upstairs bedroom in the Victorian house were the equivalent of the romance that most boys see in the Old West of Saturday matinees. In place of Hopalong and Hoot he had Joe Gans, Sam Langford, Jack Johnson—the primordial mugs of a boxing ice age.

To Tyson they were heroes, and he consciously emulated them. As those old-timers sometimes wore whitewall haircuts, so on occasion did he. And the tapered trouser legs that the fighters from long ago favored were part of his fashion statement too.

Nor was it simply a case of taking on a few superficial touches. Tyson believed in the spartan feeling the old fighters had toward their sport. He thought they had fought as much for love of sport as money, and he admired that compulsion. When Tyson arrived in Atlantic City in late December to begin training for Holmes, Steve Lott had taped black-and-white photographs of old-time fighters to the walls of the apartment.

Among the photos was one of the lightweight champion Battling Nelson, standing across the ring from a fallen opponent, Dick Hyland. Hyland had just been knocked out in the twenty-third round of a 1909 fight. Nelson held his arms akimbo, and his expression intrigued Tyson.

"I laughed when I saw it," said Tyson. "It was just such a great shot. There he was with an attitude like 'Who's next?' I wanted to do this myself."

While fighters like Holmes and Tyson had their ways to rouse their appetites for combat, Donald Trump looked to his numbers to give him his caffeine jolt.

A few weeks before the Tyson-Holmes fight—to which he had bought the live rights—Trump pointed to a model of Trump Parc, a thirty-seven-floor condominium he owned on Central Park South, and matter-of-factly told an office visitor it was "virtually sold out."

In that day's newspaper, the small print of a full-page ad for the "sparkling new Trump Parc" had this notation: "Trump Parc homes presently priced from $220,000 to $4,000,000."

Those kinds of numbers went with the forty-one-year-old real estate developer's name as neatly as mustard went with a ballpark frank.

"I study numbers," Trump said. "I know numbers."

For a long time, those numbers dealt mostly with the grand buildings that the billionaire had raised or renovated for fat and steady profits. But in 1987, Trump had suddenly become a force in the world of boxing in Atlantic City, buying the live rights to prime-time bouts that once were almost exclusive to Las Vegas casinos.

He had secured the rights to Spinks-Cooney in June and Tyson-Biggs in October, and staged both bouts in the Convention Center, adjoining Trump Plaza, one of the two casinos he owned in the boardwalk city. (Trump Castle was the other.) The Convention Center, which could seat up to sixteen thousand spectators for boxing, opened in 1929. But it was not until Trump's arrival in the city that the arena was regularly deployed for big-time fights. In using the Convention Center, Trump had the benefit of a walkway he built that ran from his casino to the arena. This did not happen by chance. Trump got permission for the walkway even before he became involved with Trump Plaza. With it, he had what no other casino operator did—an arena that was, in effect, an extension of his casino. He did not want to move potential gamblers too far from their gaming tables, and with the walkway he did not have to.

Before Trump came onto the scene, boxing in Atlantic City had been restricted mostly to casino showrooms built for seven hundred to a thousand patrons, or to ballrooms only slightly roomier. The best of these fights landed on network television on weekend afternoons, and frequently their live audiences consisted of the casinos' preferred guests, who often seemed to have a negligible interest in or knowledge of the sport.

Occasionally, a fight with more marquee value would materialize and end up in the 2,500-seat ballroom of the Convention Center. Since taking complete control of Trump Plaza in May 1986, Trump had staged a few of these ballroom fights himself.

But the notion that Trump had seen boxing all along as a profit-maker for his casino was, by his own admission, false. Trump more or less stumbled into the fight business—the walkway that he built had been intended for other events, including concerts.

Trump began to think of boxing for the Convention Center when in his review of the Trump Plaza pit drop—defined as the cash and/or markers put into circulation, exclusive of slot machines—he saw what he referred to as "blips." The blips were the disproportionately high numbers the casino did on the days it staged fights in the 2,500-seat ballroom next door or on its own premises.

"What I began to see over a fairly short period of time," Trump said, "was that there is a direct relation between a high roller in the gaming sense and a boxing fan. If we have world gymnastic championships in the Convention Center, nobody cares. Well, a few people care. And those that do are not competitive types.

"A boxing fan is competitive. He likes to gamble. Now the Miss America Pageant is a fabulous event. Convention Center is packed. Thousands of people. But those people aren't instinctively people who gamble. They're from Ohio, and it's a big event if they lose twenty-five cents at my tables. Boxing more than any other sport brings out the highly competitive person."

For Trump Plaza, the more high rollers the merrier. The

figures—Trump's instructive blips—went into orbit after the Spinks-Cooney and Tyson-Biggs matches.

For Spinks-Cooney, Trump reportedly paid $3.5 million for the live rights to a fight that drew a crowd of 15,732 and, according to Mark Etess, an executive at Trump Plaza, a gate of "just about three point five million."

That meant the live event was roughly a break-even proposition for Trump. Where he profited was in the casino's pit drop.

"Normally on a Monday in June, our pit drop would be one point two million," Etess said. "But that night, June 15, we did seven point two million. For the Saturday and Sunday preceding the fight and the Tuesday after it, we did four million above the norm for a Saturday, Sunday, Tuesday in June. That's a roughly ten million incremental increase in the four days' drop.

"If the casino wins fifteen percent of the incremental increase of ten million, that means one point five million in casino win, or profit, that it otherwise would not have experienced. As it turned out, we played a little luckier during Spinks-Cooney. We are like actuaries. All casinos win fifteen to seventeen percent of the table drop. So we're in the business of positively impacting the drop."

Beyond the immediate pleasure of making money, Trump appeared to relish his role as the hard charger in Atlantic City's boxing war with Las Vegas. In conversation, he had the pitchman's reflex for elevating Atlantic City at the expense of the other gambling town. In the typical Trump spiel, Las Vegas was depicted as a long camel ride away for the average American, in contrast to the rapid-transit access of Atlantic City.

And to Trump's mind the Las Vegas boxing facilities paled against the architecturally rich Convention Center ("Those big rounded arches—you couldn't build a building like that today"). The Las Vegas Hilton's indoor arena, where Trump had watched Tyson become the undisputed heavyweight champion in August, had "a crummy tile ceiling." He impugned Caesars Palace's permanent outdoor stadium as nothing more than "a parking lot."

Of course, Las Vegas casino potentates had their own version of the comparative pleasures of the two cities. By their account, Atlantic City was a cold claustrophobic sliver of a boardwalk resort, flanked by a sea on one side and a ghetto on the other.

Whatever.

With this latest Trump show the night lit up.

> *. . . cordially invite you*
> *to attend a*
> *Sumptuous Celebrity Buffet*
> *preceding*
> *The Undisputed Heavyweight*
> *Championship of the World*
> *Friday, January 22, 1988*
> *6:30 P.M. to 8:00 P.M.*
> *Imperial Ballroom*
> *Admit One*

That was what it said, in fancy script, on the invitation that got a man into the Tyson-Holmes prefight soirée at Trump Plaza.

On this night, Trump was boxing's Gatsby—not so much for the Haut Buffet touches, the ice-carved figures of Tyson and Holmes, the chocolate confection prize ring, but for the celebrity A-list he commanded. It was led by Jack Nicholson and boasted Kirk Douglas, Cheryl Tiegs, Tatum O'Neal, John McEnroe, Dennis Hopper, Joe DiMaggio, Muhammad Ali, and Norman Mailer. Somewhere in this night, Sly would encounter Barbra Streisand and Don Johnson, in a holding pattern, waiting for their big-shouldered retainers to whisk them along a carpeted stretch of the casino. Johnson/Streisand eventually landed ringside, next to Trump and his wife, Ivana, and Ali.

Ali, in a dark suit and wide-lens sunglasses, looked as though he were receiving the night on a tape delay. His movements, his reactions, had the dreamy self-absorption of the underwater swimmer; once the boy beauty of movement and ring wit, Ali was now the haunting man. But what regret there might be for Ali was a flickering candle. The night was a green light to the beastpleasure of action, the hurly-burly of heavyweight men taking their big whacks.

Though Ali might rate only a passing thought, his presence at ringside bore on the proceedings. Like Holmes, Ali had fought until an advanced boxing age—he was thirty-nine years old in 1981, when Berbick beat him in what would be Ali's last fight. His impaired physical state now was widely thought to be connected to the damage that he suffered late in his career, when he was more inclined to stand and take punches that earlier on he had ducked.

By that time, he could have been out of boxing, and living without financial pressure. But Br'er Ego had him by the throat and wouldn't let go. No mystery there: the voice of an approving crowd was, as a comedienne friend of Sly's once put it, "such an affirmation. It's attention, love, it's everything but food and rent."

Not long after Ali retired, Sly had spent an afternoon with the former champion at his home in the Hancock Park section of Los Angeles. Ali's was a sprawling dwelling three floors high. Outside were cypress trees and prune bushes, a swimming pool. Inside, an atmosphere of restrained elegance—Ali's wife was a collector of antiques.

Ali sat at a table, making notes from religious tracts and displaying only a mild interest in Sly's questions, which concerned Ali's experiences with his trainer, Angelo Dundee.

So limited was Ali's attention—and so unresponsive his answers—that sooner than he expected the visitor was phoning for a taxi to carry him from Hancock Park. While he waited, Ali got up from the table and began performing magic tricks, running his patter in his new muted voice, that parched whisper.

The cab arrived, and Sly headed for the door.

"Wait," Ali said. "Wanna show you this one."

"This one" led to another trick, and another. Sly had the taxi driver start his meter. With sponge props and scarfs and playing cards, Ali carried on, gauging his audience out of the corner of his eye, a muted smile on his face. At what seemed the opportune moment, Sly expressed his pleasure at Ali's legerdemain and told him *adiós*.

Riding into the balmy Los Angeles day, he could not lose the image of that sideways glance of Ali's by which the world's most recognizable man, as Ali was known in his prime, was assessing his impact. Weird, very weird it was, and a bit sad. Ali off-off-Broadway. So naked.

Not so hard to understand, really. Without the kilowatt

pleasure of a crowdroar, life was far more ordinary. What was being the chief Babbitt of Easton, PA, against the allure of king-of-combat? The nighthowl coming down on the spotlit ring in a casino town—that wall of sound rising from the Bo Derek VIP seats to the john doe last row—on what street in Easton, PA, was a man going to find a match to that?

Tyson came crashing forward. And as before, the best-laid schemes and dreams of the opponents of Mike Tyson went awry.

In Holmes's case, they also went crashingly horizontal. In the fourth round of a scheduled twelve-round bout, Tyson hit Holmes a thudding right hand to the jaw and confirmed what Holmes appeared to know from the moment he stepped—tentatively, as it were—from his corner for the opening bell: there was no way, at his age, that he was going to withstand Iron Mike.

Three times in the fourth round, beginning with that persuasive right that Tyson uncorked, Holmes went down.

After the first knockdown, Tyson did what he does best: he went after his man with a fury. Occasionally, Holmes, in his prime known as the Easton Assassin, shot back a punch. But mostly he was leaning this way and that, trying to do with his upper body what his old-guy legs couldn't—get out of harm's way.

The third time Tyson knocked him down, Holmes hit the deck hard. There was no question in the mind of the referee, Joe Cortez, that the Easton assassination was over. Not bothering to count, Cortez waved an end to the bout at two minutes and fifty-five seconds of the fourth round.

As Holmes's handlers clambered through the ropes, obviously fearful their fallen fighter was badly damaged, Tyson stood across the ring, arms akimbo, staring at the fallen opponent with a look that appeared to say, "Well, that takes care of that."

It was the body language of a conqueror, and more: it was Tyson's way of recognizing his gladiatorial legacy. For in that moment of victory, with Holmes flat on his back, he was linking himself to that continuum of fighting men. His stance was an homage, really, to another tough son of a bitch, Oscar Matthew Nielsen, better known to turn-of-the-century fight regulars as Battling Nelson.

If silence really had been golden, then civilized society might have been treated to the rare case of a Butch Lewis with nothing to say.

But from the earliest days of his wage-earning adulthood, as a used-car salesman, Lewis had recognized that for him the mother tongue was an economic ally. In trying to hustle up a fight against Tyson for Spinks, Lewis's lobbying went beyond talk, however. When Tyson had fought Tucker in August, Mr. Pitiful watched the fight from the cheap seats.

While Tyson was beating Tucker, Michael Spinks was among the 7,024 spectators at the Hilton's indoor arena. He sat with Lewis in the last row of the bleachers, the only seats, they claimed, they were able to secure.

Maybe.

It was possible that for all his connections in the fight business, Lewis couldn't scare up a pair of ringside tickets.

For the sake of argument, let us assume a more skeptical view and figure the bind that Ronald-Butch was in. Here he was with brother Spinks—the shockmaster blaster of Cooney, and the logical foe now for broad-beamed Tyson. In routine times, a Tyson-Spinks match would have been made like *that*.

But with his fighter's defection from the HBO series, Lewis had made problems, and created enemies. HBO and the Hilton were about to sue him for breach of contract, and Cayton and Jacobs were speaking of "commitments" for other fights they were honor-bound to keep.

A digression. British fight manager and promoter Mickey Duff once had spoken to Sly of the guidance a veteran boxing man gave him when he was just starting out. What his colleague told Duff was that at the outset of a manager's career his energies had to be directed toward finding and signing fighters. But there would come a time, the other man said, when Duff would have all the boxers he could handle, and that was when the agenda would shift.

"From then on," Duff recalled, "he told me, 'You spend your time getting even.'"

In the summer of '87, if there was anybody who could appreciate that quirky little tale, it was Lewis. For though he had the fighter the public most wanted to see against Tyson, he had wholesale enmity as well.

Lewis was feeling increasingly like the object lesson of Duff's story.

Hence the cheap seats.

Lewis understood that he was playing by boxing's Golden Rule—he who has the gold makes the rules. Cayton and Jacobs had Tyson. All Lewis had was a long-range view.

The heavyweight division in 1987 was a lot like that trick circus coupe from which a multitude of clowns emerge. The question was how long the public, and the press, would put up with watching Tyson go against the bozos.

Spinks was thirty-one years old, not a bad reason for Lewis to want to accelerate the public clamor for Tyson-Spinks, and bulldoze Cayton/Jacobs from their philosopher-prince talk of commitments and principles. Up there in bleacher heaven, Spinks was, like Chaplin's Little Tramp, the archetypal underdog. It was the picture worth a thousand words. And it was Lewis's fighting chance. Keep the pressure up in the media and maybe—a big maybe—it would affect Tyson and/or Cayton and Jacobs. If Lewis could inflame popular opinion he might be able to amend the Golden Rule.

So when Cayton and Jacobs continued to insist Tyson was "committed" to other opponents through the next twelve to eighteen months, and possibly longer, Lewis sought to undercut their position by noisy opposition.

By October, the measure of his impact was in Jacobs's rare solicitation of reporters to spell out his position on Spinks, which he said was being distorted by the press. The issue to which Jacobs repeatedly returned was the defection of Lewis and Spinks from the HBO series and the absence of denunciations of them by the very same reporters who were now being so hard on Tyson for not fighting Spinks.

The problem the press had with Cayton-Jacobs was that those "commitments" they insisted they had for Tyson were no more binding than New Year's resolutions. They existed as tacit understandings between boxing friends; sooner or later Cayton/Jacobs would see to it that their heavyweights got in for a payday with Iron Mike, so good buddies could prosper right along with them.

No problem there. That was a prerogative reserved to the managers of the heavyweight champion. It was when Cayton and Jacobs insisted on depicting what was merely a vague future arrangement as devolving from high-minded principle that the scribes, who knew how these things worked, began to lay into them. Had the managers announced that what they meant to do was punish a business enemy—stick it to him good—it would have sat better with the boxing press, which recognized that hardball tactics were not entirely out of order for the bind Lewis had left Cayton/Jacobs in when he had slid deftly past the contractual barriers to get his man in against the best friend Michael Spinks ever had, the left-hooker Gerry Cooney.

For whatever reasons, Cayton and Jacobs insisted on making themselves out as the Albert Schweitzers of their business—doing so with a debating student's earnestness that made the scribes more than a little ornery. "The Self-Righteous Brothers," one reporter called them. Failing to rouse the support they hoped to, by New Year's Day 1988 Cayton and Jacobs recognized that they had better adjust their timetable. What's more, their own fighter was beginning to get stir-crazy. Even though in public Tyson mouthed the party line, in private he let Cayton and Jacobs know that musical question "When ya fightin' Spinks, man?" he heard whenever he stepped out in public was beginning to grate on him.

Jacobs was sympathetic. Not only because he appreciated his fighter's perpetual combat-readiness, but because as a historian he understood how great fights built immortal reputations. Ali without Liston, Frazier, or Foreman would not have occupied the same high station in boxing history. Louis without Schmeling, or Conn, was diminished too.

Beyond that, Jacobs had his own reasons for not wanting to put off the fight much longer. In January, he had undergone an operation to have his spleen removed. It had left him pale, twenty pounds below his normal weight, and keenly aware of his own mortality. Nine years earlier he had been diagnosed as having lymphocytic cancer and told he was not likely to survive more than seven and a half years.

On Thursday, January 21, in their suite in Trump Plaza, Cayton and Jacobs made Lewis an offer: a $10.8 million "guarantee" for Spinks and him to split as they saw fit. The sum was based on projected minimum net revenues of $30 million. Minus $3 million for King's promotional fee, that would leave Tyson $16 million plus. An equitable split, they believed, and one that could be enhanced if Lewis agreed to take a third of net profits above $30 million. Lewis asked for and got time to assess the figures.

On Saturday, a day after Tyson had flattened Holmes, Lewis was back, with numbers that anticipated optimistic net revenues which, he felt, obliged fair-thinking men to raise Spinks's ante. Lewis's projected net was $36.1 million, and from that Spinks's asking price became a guaranteed $13 million. As it turned out, that was not Lewis's final word. Ronald-Butch came at them with this curve: he wanted a guarantee of $15 million for Spinks.

"But that's two million above your own figures," Cayton said. "How do you propose we do that?"

"I don't care," said Lewis. "Take it out of the promoter's advance."

The promoter was Don King.

"You mean if you don't get fifteen million, two million above your own figures, it's not a deal?" Cayton asked.

"Yes."

Lewis started toward the door.

"If you walk out," said Cayton, "don't come back."

Lewis walked out.

In absentia, Don King was the sticking point.

Lewis hated him.

Not on an exclusive basis, necessarily; Butch Lewis was not, for instance, real crazy about his old boss, Arum, either.

"I could see him lying on the sidewalk, just hit by a train, and I'd walk over him," he once had said.

Nor was he any more kindly disposed to Cayton and Jacobs, whom he had called "vicious sons of bitches."

Yet for now at least, King roused his deepest animosity. As the Dynamic Duo, Inc., King and Lewis had been partners in HBO's heavyweight unification series until Lewis came to believe that King was playing fast and loose with the money that was due them in equal shares as copromoters of the series. Rather than siccing accountants on him or engaging in rough-and-tumble rhetoric, Lewis did what fight guys do when enough was enough: he sued.

Lawsuits in boxing were as common as doorstops, and the animosities they circumscribed were not rare either. What was unusual in this instance was that Lewis appeared ready to blow off a $13 million deal for a mere grudge, which, by the rigid standards of that fictional arbiter of business mores, Don Vito Corleone, was bad form.

Yet it was that idiosyncratic glimmer in Lewis that had incited him to get radical with the HBO series and noodle his man into a prize ring with the hyperventilating hulk Cooney. He was obstinate, but creatively so. Now here he was, staring at $13 million, and he couldn't resist fiddlefucking with it.

To Cayton, Lewis lacked the plain sense that businessmen are supposed to have. Who needed to fight Spinks when there was a muscular Brit named Frank Bruno, a black man modest in demeanor (and skills) but beloved by the English populace, who would fill Wembley Stadium's fifty thousand to sixty thousand seats if Tyson was transported there in the nearly sunny clime of London in June? With Bruno, they could make a fair sum—not as much as for fighting Spinks, but a good dollar anyway—and teach Lewis his p's and q's.

That was Cayton's notion of how to go. But Jacobs, well, Jacobs differed. He wanted Tyson-Spinks and was willing to put up with the raggedy extremes of Lewis's behavior, recognizing that Butch was bound to act up after having been jerked around as he had been since June. Besides, the fight would give Tyson unequivocal standing as *the* heavyweight of his time.

While not indifferent to his partner's desires, Cayton had reached a point where he could no longer abide Lewis and was not about to initiate contact with those in the Spinks camp whom he considered more reasonable.

It was at that impasse that Shelly Finkel appeared.

In 1965, Finkel, then an NYU student, was moonlighting as a salesman, working hard at moving a line of copy machines to corporations all over Manhattan.

One day, though, Finkel got the sinking feeling that the product might not be up to the level of his sales genius. That was the afternoon he took an emergency phone call from the mail room of a high-powered Manhattan advertising agency.

"What's wrong?" Finkel asked the caller.

"Come over," the mail-room guy said. "See for yourself."

What he saw when he arrived was a copy machine that had

exploded, sending a geyser of black toner up to the ceiling in Vesuvian fury.

"There had been complaints about the machine," said Finkel. "But that was the last straw. I concluded that this particular copy machine was not as good as the competition's."

The incident led Finkel to shift his attention to the computer-dating business—a venture that in turn would precipitate other opportunities.

"My partner and I," said Finkel, "were standing in the parking lot of a club called the Action House in Island Park, Long Island, giving out fliers for our computer-dating service. The owner of the club had guards grab us. 'You two, come inside.' This owner had other business interests he needed to look after. He thought I was an enterprising young kid. He asked me to run his club."

Finkel transferred from NYU to Hofstra so he could manage the club. The job gave him an inside view of how the pop music business operated. By the time he was twenty-three, Finkel was promoting concerts and managing a music group. In 1971, he and Jim Koplik became partners in Cross Country Concert Corp., which would stage more than two thousand concerts over the next seventeen years. Among them was the 1973 Watkins Glen, New York, event that drew more than 600,000 spectators, the largest such gathering until then, according to *The Guinness Book of World Records*.

Finkel's association with boxing was as unplanned as his career in pop music. In 1977, in his building on New York's Upper East Side, a next-door neighbor died, leaving a wife and son behind. Finkel began to spend time with the boy, trying to help him recover from the blow of losing his father.

One night, he took the youngster to see Golden Gloves boxing at the Felt Forum. As it happened, that night a fighter named Alex Ramos fought and won, and made an impression on Finkel. Finkel began following Ramos's amateur career and developed a friendship with the fighter that led, eventually, to his managing Ramos when he turned pro in 1980.

That same year Finkel became comanager with Lou Duva of Johnny Bumphus, Tony Ayala, Tony Tucker, and Mitch Green, and established himself as a managerial force.

As fight guys went, Finkel ran against type. At forty-three, with his clear-rimmed eyeglasses and balding head, he had the owlish look of an economics professor and a demeanor that deepened the impression. He spoke softly and favored under-statement.

Finkel didn't appear to possess the boxing world's tin-man urgency. He was unassuming, and his halting Woody Allen rhythms didn't play all that well in public. On daises, Finkel was a hello-goodbye kind of guy, leaving the rah-rah, and laughs, to his managerial partner, that raging bulldog Duva.

But the voice seemed to work in private. In 1984, it was Finkel who recruited the Olympic fighters at the Los Angeles games. With that calm and reasoned manner he induced Meldrick Taylor, Pernell Whitaker, and Tyrell Biggs to sign on with Lou Duva and him as managers and Duva's son, Dan, as promoter. With Breland, Finkel had had a long relationship, and he went it alone as manager, though both of the Duvas would be involved in Breland's career. Finally, with Evander Holyfield, he came aboard as a consultant to his manager, Ken Sanders, and arranged for the Duvas again to participate.

In January 1988, Finkel, a close friend of Jacobs's, was well aware of the bad blood that existed between Lewis and Tyson's managers. He thought it a pity that a fight as compelling as Tyson-Spinks should get bogged down in personal dif-ferences—and wondered whether a neutral party like himself could set the negotiations straight. Finkel asked Jacobs if he could try to mediate and was given permission to proceed. The talks resumed, with Finkel and Lewis's attorney, Chwasky, at-tempting to refine the positions of both sides.

The fifty-seven-year-old Chwasky, like Finkel, hadn't the rowdy temperament that many a fight guy did, but he could, if necessary, adapt, and meet the enemy on his own terms. There was the time, for instance, when King and Lewis were attempt-ing to finalize a contract as Dynamic Duo, Inc.

"And King," recalled Chwasky, "said to Butch, 'Every time we got a contract, Chwasky fucks it up. I'm sick and tired of white people keeping us apart. We could be the biggest thing in boxing.'

"I told King, 'You're a no-good racist motherfucker. You're insulting to Butch's intelligence. Your game's not going to work. Go fuck yourself.' And Don told Butch later: 'I didn't know he was crazy. He's a crazy motherfucker.'"

Without such theatrics, Chwasky and Finkel went to work,

in pursuit of the contours of a deal. Their progress was un-
even; a few days into the negotiations, the headlines blared:

SPINKS-TYSON CALLED UNLIKELY
"TOO FAR APART,"
MEDIATOR SAYS

Then, quickly, the parties began to narrow their differences. Lewis lowered his $15 million asking price and de-
cided that rather than seek a guaranteed advance against
percentages he would take a buyout. That way he could avoid
speculation about Don King's arithmetic.

By February 3, Lewis had agreed to a flat guarantee of
$13.5 million. That left the rest—minus expenses* and Don
King's promotional fee—to Tyson. Tyson now stood to earn a
purse of some $20 million—the most any fighter had made in
boxing history. While that bonanza depended on his first defeating Tony Tubbs in Tokyo in March, a victory over Tubbs
seemed guaranteed. In fact, since Tyson had turned professional, his life in and out of the ring had appeared failure-
proof and largely free of problems. Most of the complications
involved business intrigues, and somehow or other those complex situations—the HBO deal, the Berbick fight, Kushner's
red ink, the Spinks negotiations—had been solved by others,
without involving him. His career moved apace, the rewards
beyond what any heavyweight champion before him had
known: $4 million for fighting Holmes, an anticipated $6 to $7
million for Tubbs, and now, at that crook in the road where
Spinks would climb into the ring with him, $20 million.

Even when that parking-lot incident in Los Angeles came
up, it had been smoothed over with a generous provision of
cash and without requiring Tyson to trouble himself.

Tyson was free to do what he had to—to fight for a living—without feeling he had to concern himself with those myr-
iad details for which the good Lord, in his infinite wisdom, had
created CPAs, lawyers, and managers. "My life is so simple," he
had told Sly just before he beat Berbick for the title. "You
wouldn't believe how simple it is."

Then one day life wasn't simple anymore: the heavyweight
champion of the world took himself a bride.

---

*Among the expenses: $1.5 million for Finkel to run the closed-circuit/pay-per-view
operation for the fight.

17

Down a narrow corridor they went, with photographers and TV cameramen jockeying for position.

The champion's wife wore a simple black dress; when the bright TV lights came on and the microphones were raised toward her, she displayed the five-carat diamond ring Tyson had given her and, smiling, said she was very much in love.

At the end of the corridor they turned and took seats inside a TV studio, where a satellite news conference linking New York and Tokyo was soon to begin. Under ordinary circumstances Tony Tubbs and Tyson would have been the focus of attention for the reporters in both cities. For it was their fight, scheduled for March 21, that had occasioned the transcontinental hookup.

But on this night early in February, Tyson and his wife, Robin Givens, who was featured in the ABC-TV situation comedy *Head of the Class*, were the bigger story. And that story, which Givens related before the news conference started, went like this:

While Tyson had broached the subject of marriage before, their wedding had been a spur-of-the-moment thing. The couple had gone to Chicago to watch the National Basketball Association All-Star Game, and while there Tyson had said, "Come on, let's get married."

"So we went off and got married," she said. "Michael, to say the least, is very spontaneous."

The ceremony, she reported, was performed by the Rev. George Clements, who had been portrayed not long before by Louis Gossett, Jr., in a television movie about his life. From Chicago they had flown to New York, where they had been married again in a civil ceremony performed earlier the same day.

Givens was no stranger to the press. Over the past year she had turned up with Tyson at fights and boxing-related functions; the relationship had occasionally found its way into print, usually in tales of lovers' pique.

Months before, after the two of them had argued, she had driven his 560-SL Mercedes into the rear of the '87 Rolls-Royce Silver Spirit he was driving. There was damage to both cars, and rather than keep imperfect machines, Tyson had traded them both for a white Rolls Corniche convertible.

It was in this sort of context or merely in passing that Givens had usually been noticed by the boxing press. For all her visibility as a prime-time actress, and for all her fine-boned elegance, she was not under constant scrutiny by those writers, who regarded her as one in a cast of many Tyson women.

In fact, as recently as November '87, Tyson had told the savvy British sportswriter Colin Hart that he was resisting Givens's desire to marry—"I ain't ready to settle down"—and at the same time reiterating how stormy their relationship was. The *Sun*, the tabloid for which Hart worked, put it this way:

MIKE TYSON EXCLUSIVE
MY STORMY LOVE LIFE!
"She kicks me where it hurts" "She smashes up my Rolls so I banned her" "She reckons she's better than me"

When I asked Tyson [wrote Hart] what Robin did when she flew into a rage at him he gave me a sheepish grin and said, "Well, she knows she can't hurt me if she kicks me in the head so she tries to kick me in another place."

Once the marriage was announced, Sly and his colleagues were charged with making the sort of inquiries that seemed more properly the mandate of prowlers on the society beat. There was a lovers' story, and it began sometime after Tyson won the title from Berbick. That was when he had caught a glimpse of the brown-haired, brown-eyed Givens on the television screen and . . .

SHE: I was in Washington, D.C., giving an anti-smoking speech when I got a phone call saying that Mike Tyson wanted to meet me. I knew the name and my reaction was, "Oh, my God, Mike Tyson!"

HE: *(wryly)* You had a problem with that?

SHE: I did at the time. Mike Tyson—it seemed grotesque. A fighter.

HE: Until she met me. Then I took her off her feet. I suaved her.

Not quite. The first meeting was at Le Dome, a Los Angeles restaurant. Tyson arrived an hour late because his flight from New York was delayed. Givens said that her mother, Ruth, who was part of the large group dining that night, at one point suggested they leave, thinking Tyson would not arrive.

SHE: My sister Stephanie said, "He called. To say he'd be late. How can you leave?"

HE: I was kind of nervous. I never met somebody with her mother, her publicist, her sister. I couldn't make no smooth moves. Everybody was focused on me. I couldn't manipulate. There were witnesses.

SHE: He was very handsy with my sister, who was on his left. I told him: "Maybe you two should get together."

HE: *(joking)* She was in love with me.

SHE: *(needling)* I didn't even like you. . . . *(Seriously)* While it was romantic for him initially, it happened at a different pace for me. I'm almost rational to a fault.

Tyson did his best to overcome Givens's detachment. "He was very persistent," she said. "I never met anybody who could be so persistent. One night we were standing outside the Improvisation in L.A. He wanted to kiss me. I said no. I started running. He was chasing me. We were running around cars."

During that first week, Givens recalled, Tyson appeared at the door of her Beverly Hills home at 3:00 in the morning. When she answered, Tyson told her, "I want you to be my girlfriend."

It led to another chase on the street outside her home. Tyson slipped and fell but wound up posing, hand to chin, like a dancer putting a final flourish on a move.

"Persistent," she said. "In every way. Flowers. Seeing you all day long. My mother said, 'He's crazy.' Initially, it was like a game to him. He came to L.A. to 'get me.' It was a game. The conquest.

"In the beginning he'd try to be tough, macho. 'Hey, baby.' 'Ciao, baby.' That bugged me. Oh, I hated that. Being in love was hard for Michael. You have these sensitive feelings. You want to touch, kiss. It goes against what being heavyweight champion is. He got mad because he loved me. He used to get mad. It'd cause arguments."

"All the time," said Tyson.

On a vacation in Colorado, as a joke Tyson locked Givens in the bathroom, causing her to cry.

"He was teasing me," she said. "And he went too far. After I cried, he felt so sad. I looked over. He was sitting on the bed—he's in tears. Things like that surprised me."

There were other stories, and, one morning shortly after the couple were married, Sly entered them onto the lined pages of his note pad while sitting in the living room of Tyson's East Side apartment. The fighter was moving about in black trousers with tapered legs and white pinstripes. He wore no shirt. Robin, in a house dress, appeared to have just awakened. Her mother, Ruth Roper, was in the kitchen, making coffee.

As Robin tidied a bit, Tyson joked: "My wife likes to clean. She's domestic. Her mother raised her right. Right, Ma?"

Roper smiled.

The following day, Tyson left for Tokyo to begin five weeks of training for Tubbs, and in that ebb and flow by which events got prioritized as news and not-so-news, Givens became of less consequence to Sly, who felt he had met the public's momentary interest in the new Mrs. Tyson. He expected that she and her mother would slip to the fringes of a story that had to do, after all, with business, and with sport.

Just the same, in the event that he was wrong, he started a Givens file. With a phone call to Capital Cities/ABC, Inc., he secured her official biography—a single page that appeared on corporate letterhead.

From the satellite conference and the later interview at Tyson's apartment, Sly's impression was of a new-breed woman who, articulate and self-assured, was, as the self-help magazines like to say, "having it all."

In that passing glimpse of her, she had impressed him with the skill by which she navigated a reporter's questions, and for the occasional intellectual twist with which she enlivened a notion. Speaking of the chaotic nature of her relationship with Tyson, she invoked the "law of entropy," which she said held that "a stable state is the most confused state."

"If molecules are all in a line, that's when they are most unstable," she said.

Sly, a science/math knucklehead, hadn't a clue if any of what she said coincided with what existed in those science texts his schoolboy mind had recoiled from years before, or whether she was fabricating it wholesale right in front of his snout. But he liked the agility of the mind that could come up with the thought, even if her manner held a glibness that left a lingering doubt. But what the hell, he thought, she's young and she's an actress.

What do you think of her? became a topic of conversation where boxing men met, at least for a few weeks. Among the fight crowd there was wholesale skepticism about what a college-educated beauty would want with a tenth-grade dropout.

While Tyson trained in Japan, Givens faded somewhat into the background.* But soon, very soon after Tyson knocked out Tubbs in two rounds in Tokyo, events would unravel that would put Givens, and her mother, at the center of a convoluted scenario in which the heavyweight champion would begin to say and do things that seemed out of whack with past behavior.

---

*She did make news, though, when Tyson revealed for the first time to newsmen in Japan that he was an expectant father.

CAPITAL CITIES/ABC, INC. **TELEVISION NETWORK GROUP**
BIOGRAPHY

ROBIN GIVENS
Darlene in the ABC Television Network's "Head of the Class"

Robin Givens, who portrays Darlene, a speech and debate dynamo, has accomplished much in her 21 years.

The actress was born in New York, where she and younger sister Stephanie—now studying at Boston's Northeastern University—grew up. At age 15, Robin enrolled in Sarah Lawrence College in New York as one of the youngest students to ever attend that prestigious school. Robin graduated at 19, and was accepted to Harvard University's Graduate School of Medicine.

Robin's academic excellence was almost surpassed by her love for the theater. She began studying dramatic arts at the American Academy in New York when she was 10, and subsequently appeared in such films as "Fort Apache: The Bronx," starring Paul Newman, and "The Wiz," which starred Diana Ross and Michael Jackson.

While studying at Sarah Lawrence, Robin landed regular roles in the daytime soap dramas, "The Guiding Light," and "Loving."

She also became one of the top young models at New York's Ford Agency, and was featured in such publications as "Seventeen" and "Mademoiselle."

When Robin began medical school, she thought that her acting career would take a back seat to her academic studies. However, during a trip home to New York, she read for a guest role on "The Cosby Show." The series' star, Bill Cosby, was so impressed with her talent that he became her mentor. Cosby encouraged Robin to pursue a full-time acting career and gave her mother a unique proposal: If Robin was not a successful actress in just two years, he would not only make sure that she returned to school, but he'd also pay for the remainder of her education.

Robin recently moved to Los Angeles, with acting as her sole career and desire. She appeared with Powers Boothe in the HBO series "Philip Marlow: Private Eye," and she co-starred in the motion picture for television, "Beverly Hills Madam," starring Faye Dunaway.

Her hobbies include swimming, working out, and viewing movies.

VITAL STATISTICS

BIRTHPLACE: . New York, N.Y.	BIRTHDATE: .... Nov. 27
HEIGHT: .... 5'6"	HAIR: .... Brown
EYES: .... Brown	

— 1987-88 —

The Tubbs fight was televised back to the States on Sunday, March 20; in Japan it was already Monday. On Tuesday, Tyson and his wife and Cayton and his wife, Doris, flew back to New York. Jacobs was not with them.

In mid-February, the press was told Jacobs was in Texas on business matters. In fact, he was in New York's Mt. Sinai Hospital, receiving chemotherapy treatment. But in late February, Jacobs came down with infectious pneumonia, and on the night Tyson fought Tubbs he lay gravely ill.

On March 23, as Tyson drove to Mt. Sinai to pay a visit, a call came over on his car phone. It was Givens, who gave him the news: Jim Jacobs had died.

Jacobs had not been an easy man.

Like Tyson, he was a private person, not wont to reveal himself or the particulars of his business. When, for instance, he returned to his Los Angeles home from the Korean War, he hid from his sister, Dorothy Zeil, and his mother, also named Dorothy, the fact that he had won a Purple Heart.

"My mother," said Ms. Zeil, "found out by accident. She was putting away things of Jim's and saw it. I remember when he came home, he had scars on his face and on the back of his head. I asked, 'What happened?' This I remember vividly. Jim told me he had some moles removed. But I had seen many shrapnel wounds, having been in the service, and told him so. Well, he looked at me very intensely, 'As far as you know,' he said, 'these are moles. Don't mention them to Mother.' Was he close-to-the-vest? Yes, he was."

Zeil said that Jacobs never let on to the family that he had cancer. Only a few people—Loraine Jacobs, Cayton, and Steve Lott—knew from early on. Some others, like his boyhood friend Nick Beck, found out later.

"At Christmas 1985, he came to see his mother in Los Angeles," said Beck. "I met him there, and in the course of things he said, 'I have to let you know. I have lymphocytic cancer. The prognosis on this is seven and a half years. I was diagnosed seven years ago. I'm telling you this because I'd like to know if anything happened to me, you and my mother will continue to have contact. I'll never mention this again. And you won't either.' He was afraid she was going to outlive him. As it turned out she died at Christmas 1986."

From D'Amato he took a distrust of journalists that led Jacobs—with his own private streak—to speak with a caution that found expression in a stilted language ridiculed by the press.

"It was not the way he was with friends," said Beck. "With friends he never lectured or talked down. I remember once in Vegas, there were a bunch of his old handball buddies and myself, and we were all laughing it up in his suite. All of a sudden a writer walked in and Jim started to stiffen. He did that very thoughtful pose."

Because of his close-mouthed nature, certain rumors about Jacobs over the years took on the weight of fact. Those rumors, for instance, had it that Jacobs was born rich and, through his father, Phil, sometimes referred to as a real estate millionaire, had gotten the money to start his comic-book and fight-film collections.

"My father," said Zeil, "was a salesman for Alfred Hart Distilleries, a liquor salesman. Before we came to L.A., he had been in ladies' ready-to-wear in St. Louis. When my father was old and retired and had nothing, Jim sent him a check every month, and that was before Jim was as well known as he became."

For whatever reasons, Jacobs was uneasy about what his father did for a living. Once when Sly asked what his father's occupation had been, Jacobs became argumentative, disproportionately so, it struck the writer, to the subject. Twenty minutes after the phone conversation ended, Jacobs called back to apologize. Asked again what line of work his father had been in, Jacobs said he had had a business machine and supplies company.

"I know Jim said that," said Cayton, "but it wasn't so. Jim loved his father. He was very proud of him. But he wasn't proud of his father's profession. He just didn't like people to know that."

Enemies of Jacobs depicted him as a man who lived far beneath his means, implying that he accumulated money the way he did his fight films and the more than 800,000 comic books he kept in storage in Los Angeles. But others told of a Jacobs who was a generous man.

Before they managed Tyson, Jacobs and Cayton managed another world champion, Wilfred Benitez. "And for one fight of Benitez's in Las Vegas," said Beck, "Jim invited all his friends out. Everybody from both coasts stopped in his suite, where Loraine handed each of us an envelope in which was a check reimbursing us for air fare and for room."

In their youth, both Jacobs and Beck had collected fight films. While Jacobs's 16mm movies were adaptable later for commercial use, Beck's 8mm were not; all the same, when Jacobs became successful in business with his fight films he wanted Beck to have copies from The Big Fights, Inc., archives.

"But," said Beck, "I just had a home movie projector. Jim said, 'Why don't you get a sixteen-millimeter projector?' Well, that cost four hundred, five hundred dollars and was a strain on my budget. . . . Anyway, at Christmastime that year—this is more than twenty years ago—Jim called and told me to come over to his mother's place. I went over. He had a brand-new projector for me. 'Now you can collect sixteen-millimeter,' he said. And he started shipping me literally hundreds of fight films."

"He told me a story once," said Shelly Finkel, "that he used to go up to Green Haven prison every Thanksgiving and play a handball exhibition against the best black inmates and the best white inmates. He'd play up to the competition rather than demolish them. Why take away their pride? The first year he drove back from Green Haven he had a car accident. So in the years to follow, he'd sleep in a prison cell that night. Thanksgiving night."

In 1987, when Jacobs learned that ABC-TV boxing analyst Alex Wallau had cancer, he arranged to have dinner with Wallau.

"At dinner, I was telling Jim how self-absorbed I was with the cancer, how bothered I was because of radiation to have lost my hair and my beard," said Wallau. "Well, Jim took my hand and put it to his chin. I could feel he had no beard. A chill ran down my spine. It was his way of giving strength and support without asking for support back. One thing that was important for my wife, Martha, and me was to have the support of friends. His way was very secretive in dealing with his illness."

"This past February," said Ms. Zeil, "Jim called me four times, which was unusual. He didn't usually call that much. He told me, 'I'll be home soon. It's not a matter of choice, but I have to come home. I have to.' It didn't mean much to me. I didn't know he was ill."

Jacobs was a man whom Tyson had depended on and trusted. Their closeness was rooted in their regard for D'Amato and a shared passion for boxing. As Jacobs once told a friend: "I'm a rich man doing what I'd do for nothing." In company, he and Tyson would play boxing trivia, with Jacobs showing off the fighter as a protégé.

When D'Amato died, Jacobs was the natural successor as a surrogate father to Tyson. And with the death of Jacobs, Cayton stood ready to aid and abet a fighter with whom he had had a cordial relationship. In August 1986, on a photo that showed him landing an uppercut to the jaw of Marvis Frazier, Tyson had written: "To Bill/From your boy Mike 8-22-86/To my dear friend and the man I love greatly."

The photo hung on Cayton's office wall, and the inscription seemed to suggest a strong personal relationship. But compared to the one that Jacobs had had with Tyson, Cayton could not claim, nor did he try to, as binding a hold. That left him, it turned out, susceptible. No sooner was Jacobs laid to rest on March 25 in Los Angeles than Cayton's control of Tyson was challenged. In an affidavit that Cayton gave months later, he stated:

> Jim's funeral was held in Los Angeles, California. José Torres and I delivered eulogies. Mike cried at the funeral. . . . The morning of Jim's funeral, in the lobby of the Beverly Hilton Hotel, Mike told Shelly Finkel,* who is also a boxing manager, that he was told by Don King that he did not have to go through with the Spinks fight and that Mr. King had offered him a deal of five fights for $5 million a fight. Since Jim's funeral, indeed, immediately thereafter, Mr. King began courting Mike.

When he had gone after Butch Lewis's heavyweight, Greg Page, a few years before, King had managed in a very brief time to ingratiate himself with the Page family so that when the fighter's father passed away, King was a pallbearer and an inconsolable mourner—emotion that struck Lewis's attorney, Chwasky, as being disproportionate to the relationship King and the deceased had had.

"We were the last two," recalled Chwasky, "to leave the gravesite. As we walked away, our eyes met. And I just laughed. But Don, Don looked at me and said: 'This boxing is a bitch.'"

To enfranchised managers, King was the lurking body-snatcher, but in the case of Tyson the promoter denied having any

---

*Finkel confirmed the conversation.

designs on the fighter, protesting: "At an hour of crisis when one of my beloved friends dies, I'm gonna rush in?" But after a couple of disagreeable incidents over money, Cayton had already begun to reassess the promoter.

In October 1987, Tyson had gone to Chicago to fight an exhibition bout against James (Quick) Tillis to raise funds for the Rev. George Clements's Holy Angels Church, which had burned to the ground on June 9, 1986. "The understanding was all of us would pay our expenses," said Cayton, "except for Tillis, who got five thousand dollars. What happened was, without saying a word to us, King deducted fifty thousand for expenses for that exhibition in a later financial accounting on a fight of Mike's. Well, when Jim saw that fifty-thousand-dollar item, he hit the ceiling." When objections were raised, Cayton said that King promised to look into the matter and soon after wrote a check to The Big Fights, Inc., for $34,000, insisting he was entitled to the remaining $16,000. While Cayton and Jacobs disagreed, they chose to let the matter lie.

King said that the money he held back was not for him but for others who had been involved in the exhibition. From a deposition:

KING: The workers got to be paid, not me. "But when we get everything, when the bills come in, Jim [Jacobs], I will make a reconciliation and give you the difference of the money." All right, unfortunately for me, Jim was gone. But I took back $35- or $36,000 to Bill Cayton and I gave it to Bill Cayton, left $14,000 of expenses.

Q: $15,400.

KING: Whatever it is. This man wouldn't pay the $15,000 to go to the people that was out there, poor people out there trying to do a job and Jim and him both agreed to it.

Q: One of those people was who? Mr. [Al] Sharpton and who else?

KING: Whoever was out there. That's what their expenses was. I'm not going to reply on Mr. Sharpton. Whatever you want to do to Mr. Sharpton, you do it. Don't make no derogatory inferences or intonation about Mr. Sharpton. I like Mr. Sharpton. Whether you do or not is immaterial to me.

Q:	I don't know Mr. Sharpton.
KING:	What we did is one good job for Jim Jacobs and Father Clements. My allegiance was to Jim Jacobs and that's what I did. His partner leaves a lot to be desired.
Q:	You kept back $15,491?
KING:	Whatever.

Later, when Tyson fought Tubbs in Tokyo, the on-site promoter there was Akihiko Honda, who was Japanese. King's role was limited to producing Tyson's opponent. "And for that," said Cayton, "he was to keep the difference between the one point two million the deal provided for the opponent and the price that Tubbs was getting, which was nine hundred thousand. With added expenses, King was looking at five hundred thousand. Well, when that was offered, the man went berserk, and said, 'I was promised by Jim I'd be paid and paid in full.' When we offered a million, he rejected that. I was astonished.

"King left the office. Jim said to me: 'I did tell him he'd be paid. And I thought this would be more than adequate. But I want peace.' Jim knew he was going in for intensive chemotherapy. So I said to Jim: 'Whatever you want to give is okay with me.' King came in the next day. Jim said, 'Is two million satisfactory?' King said yes indeed. I was surprised by the amount. But Jim said it, and I backed him up. I felt it was outrageous. King reached into Mike Tyson and took two million dollars."

King would confirm the $2 million figure but under deposition he depicted Cayton as the problem.

KING:	Bill was very obstinate. "Don didn't do nothing. Why should he get paid? I did this. I. I. I. I." So—
Q:	Who said that?
KING:	Bill Cayton. When you hear *I* it's Mr. Cayton. He said, "The Japanese don't want Don and I got to do this great public relation job for Don to get him into Japan because the Japanese don't want him in Japan and I'm going to work to get it in. Like I do with the press. I got control of the press. Look at this good press you're getting, Don. You never get this good press until I say good things about you. You look at your reputation when you come in to me and work with me and Jim, now,

since you have been working with me and Jim I got the press doing what I want them to do. Aren't you getting good press?" I said, "Yes, Bill, I'm getting good·press. Understand that if you ain't working with us you wouldn't get this kind of press because I'm the one that's doing it. Yes, Bill, you're doing it. Bill, you got to pay me. You can't get me no press and no press release and don't pay me. You gotta deal with me and the deal with me is the deal you-all gave me and you got to live up to this deal."

Q: Go ahead.

KING: I said, "You got to live up to this deal." He said, "I don't think you should be paid. You ain't did no work and I don't care." . . . He said, "You are getting paid for doing noth-ing." He said, "I did all the work, you know, and you just supplied the opponent and I got to pay you and I don't like it." And he said a remark I will never forget. He said, "You blackjacked a sick man," he told me in this meeting about Jim. As if I had blackjacked Jim into paying me when Jim was just more man than he was and he didn't understand that.

On the day Jacobs was buried, there was another develop-ment that would concern Cayton. An attorney named Michael R. Winston, who stated he represented Tyson and Givens, wrote Cayton asking for copies of contracts, tax returns, and information and other documents related to Tyson's finances.

Like Cayton's revised opinion of King, this letter had a his-tory behind it. On February 14, following a wedding reception for the Tysons at the Helmsley Palace, Cayton had fallen ill and had been taken by ambulance to New Rochelle Hospital, where he was placed in the intensive care unit for two days and treated for endocarditis, inflammation of the heart lining and valves. Once he was well enough to be moved to a private room, Cayton began conducting business from his hospital bed.

Among the phone calls he would receive while hospitalized was one from Givens, which, he told acquaintances, opened with these words: "I'm Mrs. Mike Tyson, and I'm taking over." Disturbed by the tone and content of the call, Cayton chose not to respond to the request she made at that time for her husband's financial records.

Roper's version of the origins of the problem with Cayton differed: "Michael wanted a home before he decided to be married. There was a house up near the Catskills, and he'd talk about it with me. He'd say, 'I'm jealous. Robin has a house [in California] and I don't.'"

In March, Tyson became interested in buying a castlelike gray stone home he found on fifteen acres in Bernardsville, New Jersey. The estate, called Kenilwood, had been built in 1897 and was patterned after an English manor. For Tyson it was the "dream" house for which he was willing to part with just over $4 million to call his own.

"I talked to him about getting a mortgage," said Roper. "But Michael wanted to pay cash, and he thought he'd be able to pay cash. But when it came down to it, he couldn't. And he was surprised. He didn't know where his money was. That was when Michael Winston suggested we get an audit to figure where the money is. We had asked Bill Cayton before, and he didn't want to discuss it. It was: 'None of your business. We've taken good care of Mike since he was fifteen. Why do you want to know?' He was a man offended by two women, two black women, asking questions. But it was motivated by Michael not knowing where his money was. He wanted to pay cash, and was shocked by the fact he didn't have it. Where is it?"

Before Tyson had left New York for Jacobs's funeral, he had given his wife short-term power of attorney to close on the Bernardsville house. When Givens and Roper turned up at the Merrill Lynch branch where Tyson had an account, they encountered problems in the signatory process by which money was freed up.

"What happened," said Roper, "was when it was time to close on the house, Michael went to Merrill Lynch and told them that Robin was going to close. He wanted the house set up by the time he came back. He spent forty-five minutes explaining to them, and they said, 'Fine.' Michael's attorney [Winston] said, 'You understand, Robin is going to write a check on the account, or maybe transfer money?' They said, 'Fine.'"

The next day there were problems, Roper said, when she, Givens, and Winston turned up at Merrill Lynch, reportedly to switch $1.9 million from the Tysons' joint account to one solely in Givens's name.

"They told us," said Roper, "'Can't do it.' And this was after we spent time the day before going over it and being told it was okay. They went on and on about it not being able to be done. Robin was livid."

By chance, Bert Sugar, the editor-publisher of *Boxing Illustrated,* happened to be in the anteroom at Merrill Lynch's Pan Am Building office at the very moment Givens and Roper were asking for the money. From his seat there, he was privy to the unfolding scene:

"I heard the commotion—women's voices saying 'Bullshit' and so forth. And here came all these Merrill Lynch guys, trying to creep out the back and get away from a nasty scene. They were like people jumping off the *Titanic.* There was an attitude of the-hell-with-this. Jesus, they were running out. Like, 'Let me outta here.' Robin Givens and company were in with a Merrill Lynch manager type. You could hear him speaking *sotto voce* about signatory this and signatory that. And then women's voices: 'We don't need that shit. It's our money.' Murmur murmur murmur: the Merrill Lynch guy speaking. And then the women: 'Give us our money!' A lot of shouting."

Roper: "We were a little stern. And emphatic. 'Do it!'"

The money eventually was moved, but when the press learned of the incident it was reported that Givens and Roper had raised a clamor, stomping through a great financial institution, demanding "their" money. For the first time the public was afforded an unflattering view of Tyson's women. This occurred at nearly the same time that news reports appeared about King's funeral-day move on Tyson.

A tableau that Sly stumbled onto by chance gave him his first intimation of what pressure Tyson might be feeling. On Tuesday, March 29, a press conference was scheduled at the Plaza Hotel in New York to announce Tyson-Spinks for June 27 in Atlantic City. Sly went there by cab, disembarking on Fifth Avenue before the small park directly in front of the hotel.

On one of those park benches sat Tyson, speaking with Shelly Finkel. Sly went over to say hello, but soon he sensed he had caught the two men in the midst of a conversation weighted with trouble. So he quickly cut away.

The uneasiness that lay like a cloud over that conversation concerned the developing conflict between Cayton and Givens/Roper. At sixty-nine, Cayton was an established business success and accustomed to dealing from strength. Even in conversations with newsmen, he sometimes struck an autocratic tone, trying to lead them to preferred conclusions: "You *must* say that Mike Tyson . . ." Or "As I'm sure you're aware . . ." He had a certainty that came from forty-odd years of making deals with the monoliths of the business, advertising, and communications industries.

Givens had been raised to be bright and sassy, and by twenty-three she was as assertive in her way as Cayton in his. While she hadn't his long *curriculum vitae,* she possessed the conviction of youth, beauty, and a determined mother's fine-tuning. In her words and in her manner, there was the presumption of privilege.

One can imagine what Cayton's reaction was when out of the wild blue came this Terry & the Pirates sleek beauty with a mouth on her that must have made Cayton long for pre-lib America. Did she fail to give the respect that Cayton felt he deserved? Or was it a case of Cayton's misreading a legitimate need to know? Cayton would tell Sly: "I'm sure Mike's marriage and career will be well managed if Mike takes care of his career and Robin takes care of her career." But as Roper told an ally of Cayton's: "If he thinks he has a couple of dumb niggers here, he's got another think coming."

The pressure from his wife and mother-in-law to shake things up was compounded by the daily business of being the heavyweight champion. The morning of the press conference Tyson had been up early to appear on *Good Morning America,* the ABC-TV show, and then had returned to the Plaza Hotel, where cubicles had been set up for photographers in a back room. Tyson went from one cubicle to the next, posing for each photographer in turn. As he was finishing, Michael Spinks appeared, and Tyson's mood, not cheery to begin with, turned foul.

Back up in his room he was restless and wanted to get away from the hotel. Finkel volunteered to go with him, and the two had ended up on the park bench, where Sly had found them.

A little peace of mind was all Tyson sought. "He just wanted to relax there," said Finkel. "All of a sudden a couple of people see him and ask for autographs. They don't speak English but they recognize him and point to him. Turns out they're from Spain and Italy. In ten seconds, there's a line for autographs. Mike said, 'Shel, Shel, can you stop it?' He just wanted breathing room.

"Another guy comes by, says, 'I'm homeless. Can you spare some change?' Mike starts reaching into his pocket, saying, 'I don't know if I have change.' He pulls out a bill and, without looking at it, gives it to the man. A hundred-dollar bill. The guy looks at it, looks at it, looks at it. A big grin. 'Thank you, champ.' And he skipped off. Actually skipped. Mike didn't focus on what the bill was. I don't think he cared. This was in his pocket: he gave it to him. We're sitting there. Mike says to me, 'I'm a great fighter, but I don't deserve all this attention.'"

Late on the afternoon of the press conference for his fight against Spinks, Tyson had gone to Cayton's office and to his accountant's office, where his financial records were shown to him, and, according to Cayton, Tyson said he had not authorized Winston's letter.

A day later, on March 31, when he answered the phone from his Bernardsville home, Tyson was crying. What could bring the heavyweight champion to tears? To judge from the events that would occur over the next week, it was the terrible conflict he felt—that fine line he was forced to tread between loyalty to a longtime manager and love of a woman. That love sometimes appeared double-edged. For he and Givens had constantly argued: on the day of the Spinks press conference, Tyson had told a friend, "This marriage can't last."

On April 1, Tyson flew to Los Angeles with his wife and mother-in-law. Following that weekend, on Monday, April 4, Don King, phoning his New York office from the airport in Cleveland, heard he had a message from Mike Tyson. But it wasn't until King made it to New York that he finally contacted Tyson.

"Tyson asked me to come out to L.A. to talk to him," said King. "I asked him, 'What do you want to talk about?' 'Me. My career. I need help.' He was angry. He said, 'I ain't gonna fight Spinks.' I told him, 'Okay, man. But I got to talk to Bill Cayton first.' He was infuriated because he felt Bill Cayton disrespected his wife and disrespected him. 'Tell Bill Cayton I'm angry and I ain't gonna fight.'"

King met with Cayton on Tuesday, April 5, and conveyed Tyson's sentiments. "Why did he call you?" Cayton asked.

King: "I said, 'Bill, I don't know why he called me. Ask him. He wants me to come out and talk to him. Bill, you're in a precarious position. At least I can go out and talk to him and tell him the truth.' Bill then told me about the letter that'd been sent through the lawyer and the full disclosure asked for, all the contracts. He said he felt offended by it. I told him, 'I don't know nothin' about it.' And Bill said, 'Why is Mike Tyson calling you?' I said I don't know, but you should be thankful it's me. Bill said, 'I just wonder what he wants.' Told him, 'I don't know. Ask and you'll find out.' Bill said, 'I'll call and tell him to come back to New York. That way you won't have to go.'"

Late that afternoon, as King waited for Cayton's call, Tyson phoned again. "He said to me, 'Man, what plane you on?' Told him, 'I'll be there tonight.' At seven-fifteen, I call Bill Cayton at home. And I told him: 'Nine-thirty is the last plane and the man done call again, and I done committed to see this man.' I told him, 'Bill, rest assured, I wouldn't do anything detrimental, or against your interests. Your interests are my interests.'"

King flew to L.A. Tuesday night, and when he got to his condo in Westwood he found another message from Tyson. But it was 2:30 on Wednesday morning, too late to contact the fighter.

When first reports of King's "moves" on Tyson at the funeral reached Cayton, he had let King know he viewed him with suspicion. But after that meeting in which Tyson's calls to King were discussed—a matter about which the press knew nothing at the time—Cayton told reporters inquiring about King's status: "Don will work with us on future promotions. We have no other promoter in mind."

That signaled a temporary truce to the boxing press, which, gathering now in Las Vegas for successive weekend fights—Evander Holyfield vs. Carlos DeLeon for the undisputed cruiserweight title on April 9 and Starling vs. Breland for the WBA welterweight title on April 16—shifted its attention to others in the business.

On Friday, April 8, Sly was working the phone from his

room at Caesars Palace, gathering material for a weekly "boxing notebook," when a fight guy told him: "King's in L.A.
wooing the kid."

"What's your source on that?"

"Look, I'm telling you as a friend. There's big problems
there."

Sly began tracking the rumor. In doing so, he would land
smack dab in the next phase of a Byzantine power struggle that
would go on for months before it settled into a courthouse in
Lower Manhattan to be adjudicated. While it lasted it would
prove as entertaining in its way as *Dallas* or *Dynasty;* in the
weeks preceding Tyson-Spinks, Mmes #1 and #1A, Bwana
Don, suit-and-tie Cayton, and the by then snarling champion
would jump from the sports page onto tabloid page one.

On April 9, the tensions and the drama were, like the common iceberg, seven-eighths removed from view; the press had
been diverted by Cayton's dispensation for King. But with the
cue his source had provided, Sly began phoning around, and
found that the platitudes and denials of earlier in the week
were gone, and in their place the battle cries of blatant conflict
were sounded.

Cayton: "Don King is making moves, I guess, to take over.
It's something a lot of people told me he would try—people
familiar with the history of Don King."

On April 9, under the headline "Cayton, King Fight for
Control of Tyson," Sly wrote:

> ' . . . When Cayton first heard from King [in L.A.], he
> said the promoter told him he was out there to protect
> Cayton's interests.
>
> Since then, King has reportedly informed Cayton that
> when Tyson returns to New York it will be to discuss
> changes in his business arrangements.
>
> "My feeling, with all the rumors that I had heard," said
> Cayton, "was that Don King was too smart to make a move
> like this. Because whatever you say about Don King, he is
> not stupid. Now I don't know what to think."
>
> Cayton said his contract with Tyson entitles both
> Loraine Jacobs, the widow of his late partner, Jim Jacobs,
> and him, to one-third of Tyson's boxing earnings and runs
> until 1992.
>
> King could not be reached for comment. He was re-

ported en route here with Tyson and his wife for tonight's cruiserweight unification bout between Evander Holyfield and Carlos DeLeon.

But Al Braverman, King's director of boxing, said that whatever moves King was making were to protect himself against Cayton. Braverman said that Cayton had recently discussed with other boxing people "dumping" King as Tyson's promoter.

"He is not looking to steal the fighter," said Braverman of King. "He's looking to retain his position."

Cayton denied he had met with others about dropping King. He said the subject of King's status was taken up with Tyson when Cayton and the fighter met March 30. But Cayton declined to say what particulars he had put forth to Tyson.

"It was a private conversation," said Cayton. "I told Mike that things were going on that I was not happy with."

However, Cayton did say that he and Jacobs were aware of a rumor that when Tyson beat Trevor Berbick for the World Boxing Council heavyweight title in November 1986 Carl King approached Tyson about defecting to him. Carl, son of the promoter, manages fighters.

"At that time," said Cayton, "Jim and I decided to disregard the rumor. It was something we thought the Kings were too smart to try."

The next logical step was to visit Tyson, who was due to land in Las Vegas that day. That was not the easiest meeting to arrange. Tyson was a moving target, and not often inclined of late to sit still for a one-on-one with a writer. But Richie Giachetti, the burly Holmes trainer, was encamped at the Las Vegas Hilton and was worth a try. Giachetti, a street-smart compatriot of King's from Cleveland, was now working with the promoter, and he promised to do what he could to put Tyson, and King, in earshot of the *New York Times* man.

It wasn't until the prelims for Holyfield vs. DeLeon were underway that Sly saw King, Tyson, Givens, and Roper settle into one row at ringside. That night, Holyfield pounded De-Leon without letup until, at one minute and eight seconds of the eighth round, the referee, Mills Lane, stopped the fight. As Sly wrote up his account of the bout, Giachetti called him to say he had arranged for Sly to join Tyson and King for dinner that night at the Barronshire Prime Rib back at the Hilton.

By now Sunday's paper was on the stands with the story of the Cayton/King conflict. An interview with Tyson would advance the Sunday article and keep the *Times* a step ahead of the competition. That accelerated Sly through his last paragraphs of Holyfield vs. DeLeon, out the back exit of Caesars, and into a rented Avis.

Tyson's group were dining in an isolated nook of the restaurant. Sly drew up a chair next to King and across from Tyson. The champion's wife and mother-in-law sat between the men, at the far end of the table. After a few minutes of small talk, Sly began questioning King, who had barely begun to respond when Roper leaned toward him and whispered in his ear.

"Ruth," said King, "would rather we wait until dinner is over."

Having eaten already, Sly left the table and, with Giachetti, adjourned to the restaurant bar. Some thirty minutes later, Givens and Roper walked past the bar and out of the restaurant. Sly returned to the table and got right to the point, asking Tyson why Cayton was saying Don King was "making moves" against him.

Tyson said Cayton's fears were misplaced. "There is no way I'm thinking of double-crossing Bill Cayton. Nothing's changed. I don't know why he feels threatened. Bill sounds like he's worried I'm going to leave. I'm not a rat fink or a traitor."

Then why had he summoned King to L.A.?

"Because I wanted to know what was going on with my money," Tyson said. "Bill Cayton showed me figures in the accountant's books. But I'm not that sophisticated to comprehend. So I said to myself: 'Don King knows what's going on.' But by no means do I trust Don King. It was just that in some things I thought I was being treated unjustly."

Tyson cited specifics. Spinks's money was guaranteed and his was not. Finkel, the closed-circuit coordinator, was co-manager of Biggs and a consultant to Holyfield—hardly a recommendation, Tyson seemed to imply, for making money off him. "If Evander Holyfield and I were drowning, who is Shelly gonna save?" asked Tyson. Finally, there was the deal that Mickey Duff, another close friend of Jacobs, had made for the closed-circuit rights in Florida for the Tyson-Spinks fight.

Tyson said that Duff was given the rights for $750,000 despite another offer of $1 million.*

"When you're dealing with this kind of money—it's astronomical money—you can't trust anybody," said Tyson. "It's bad to be like that. But then all of a sudden, you hear they want to make money and help friends of theirs make out too. I have a wife, a child on the way. It's my obligation to take control. If Bill and them love me, they should be proud of my taking care of business. If there's nothing wrong with what's going on, then why worry that I'm with Don. Cus D'Amato was like a father to me. He wanted me to be a champion. But he said he'd be successful when he made me independent of him. Deals can't go on without me knowing about them."

By now Givens and Roper were back at the table, and Tyson was saying that for the next two weeks, while Robin shot a made-for-TV movie, *The Women of Brewster Place,* he would be in L.A. When he returned to New York later in the month, he said, he expected to convene a meeting with Cayton, King, and Finkel. "We'll sit down and talk, and it shouldn't be a problem," he said.

It was soon after, without any cue from the conversation, that Givens cut in to say: "Don King's never approached me or my mother." It was a perfect non sequitur, meant to dispel re-

---

*Cayton's rebuttal: "The fact is we could right this minute guarantee Mike twenty million. In boxing the smartest business managers operate the way we are on the Tyson-Spinks fight. Ray Leonard's attorney, Mike Trainer, did the same thing for Leonard-Duran number one. They bought out Duran for a flat fee and kept the differential. That's smart business. Mike Tyson is essentially guaranteed well over twenty million. We have eleven million from Donald Trump for the live site fee, three point one million from HBO for the delayed rights, we'll have well over two million for foreign TV rights, at least half a million for promotional fees with major companies, and twenty million in closed-circuit and pay-per-view rights. That's about thirty-seven million. Thirteen point five million to Spinks. Don King gets three million, out of which he pays expenses. So that's sixteen point five million in costs, leaving twenty-one million for Mike."

Cayton said the choice of Finkel to run the closed-circuit operation was made by Jacobs, and he said that Jacobs had apprised Tyson of that well before he died on March 23.

"Jim had confidence in the honesty of Shelly Finkel," said Cayton. "Also, Butch Lewis didn't trust Don King to handle closed-circuit.

"As for Mickey Duff, if we pushed for more money we could have gotten it. But Mickey Duff has more than double the closed-circuit seats than there were for Hagler-Leonard. We figure him to realize well over one million in closed-circuit revenues. The one-million offer that Mike mentions was a buyout figure. With Mickey Duff, we should do well over a million."

cent speculation that she and her mother had allied with King to encourage Tyson to defect from Cayton.

Sly wrote her words down, studying Givens's expression for a clue as to what had prompted her to say them. As he did, Tyson said, "Oh, my wife is getting upset." With an elbow he nudged Sly in the ribs, saying, "Please leave. Please leave."

Sly looked over to Givens and did not think she appeared upset. In fact, suspecting it was a private joke, he hesitated to move, even as Tyson's elbow was prodding him. But when Tyson said, once again, "Please leave, Please leave," and as that persuasive elbow pressured his ribs, Sly began to realize that Tyson might be serious.

Still, he was hesitant to budge. He was on to a story that was taking an important turn, and like any reporter, he wanted to poke around it for as long as he could. Again, he eyed about the table, at Robin, who still did not register the anguish Tyson appeared to think she felt, and at the others to see if their expressions would let him in on the joke. But there was no such encouragement, and Tyson's own pained expression seemed genuine.

Sly got up and left.

But there were instructive echoes in dinner with the Tysons. As he exited, it dawned on him that Tyson had been most convincing, most believable, where his wife was concerned.

"I'm loyal to Bill Cayton," Tyson had said at one point. "But I love my wife more than anything. I hope I'm not being offensive, but other men want their wives in the shadows. I'm not working that way. Everybody's making a big issue about my wife asking me about what I've made. If my wife asks something, just give her what she wants. Look, if she asked for every dollar in my account I'd give it to her. No questions asked. Bill works for me. He's not in a position to say no. Just give her what she needs."

When talking about dollars and cents—those complaints about Duff, about Finkel, about Spinks's guarantees—he had seemed rehearsed. The irony was that as rational as he sounded talking money, he was not as credible as when he spoke about and reacted to his wife, irrational as he might seem then. The image that came to Sly, as he headed out to his rental auto, was of dogs that hear high-pitched whistles the human ears can't sense.

To put a fine point on it, Tyson was long gone on his Robin, and it was only now beginning to occur to Cayton that the reasoned arguments that might have succeeded with his fighter in ordinary circumstances were useless here, where obsession ruled. More than once over the next few months, he would refer to that "Please leave" dinner scene, which Sly had reported in the *Times,* and say: *"You* know what's going on. You know what it's like. You experienced it."

There were times, Cayton said, when he would be talking by phone to Tyson and would hear the champion's voice change in midsentence as Givens came into the same room. A meeker, more hesitant sound it became, and it told Cayton all he needed to know about what he was up against.

Within weeks of receiving the letter from Winston, Cayton had wised up to the damage he had done himself with the champion's wife, and rather than advise her, in effect, not to meddle, he was now saying: "The wife is entitled to be interested in her husband's welfare. Anything she wants to know, she's entitled to know."

But Mr. Bill's olive branch was too little and too late for Givens. She and Roper were not appeased, and in the weeks and months that followed they conjured up a Cayton who was a caricature of evil, one of those Dick Tracy rogues with Beelzebub's own dark heart instructing his every move. For newcomers to boxing, the ladies got right into the swing of things.

Money talked, and in boxing what it said was "more." Or "still more." Tyson vs. Spinks, as the richest bout in boxing history, concentrated the acquisitive tendency of the sport's citizenry—and not just with King, Cayton, Givens, and Roper. Arum, for instance, who was an enemy of both the Tyson and the Spinks camps, did not sit this one out. He phoned Chwasky one day to discuss his getting involved with the closed-circuit and pay-per-view facets of the Tyson-Spinks bout. Chwasky told Arum: "You know, Bob, Bill Cayton and I don't see eye to eye on many things. But there's one item we agree on. And that is that you're a rotten son of a bitch."

Without missing a beat, Arum said, "So whaaaat?"

If any phrase caught the eccentric spirit of the boxing business, Arum's *so whaaaat* was it. But as accustomed as Sly was to behavioral excess in the manly art, the shimmy and shake that accompanied the evolving and excessive power struggle over Tyson would prove a bonanza.

Typical was a wee-hours automobile accident in early May involving Tyson's $180,000 silver Bentley convertible. When Tyson, who was at the wheel of the car, sideswiped a parked vehicle in Lower Manhattan, conflicting reports followed. Was it a cat straying into the path of his Bentley that had caused him to swerve, as one version had it? Or was it, as Tyson told confidants, that Robin had begun to strike him as he navigated traffic after finding condoms in his jacket pocket? Did it really matter? For that was the night Tyson would try to give away his Bentley to two Port Authority police officers who investigated the collision. "I've had nothing but bad luck and accidents with this car," he was quoted as saying at the time.

Tyson now found himself one of those celebrities whose private lives are public entertainment. Every detail—from the BMW he had bought his mother-in-law to the state of his wife's pregnancy (was she or wasn't she?)—was suddenly fit for print. And even if the story didn't involve him directly—as when a suit that Roper brought against the baseball star Dave Winfield, accusing him of giving her a sexually transmitted disease, became page-one tabloid news—it added to the impression that Tyson's world was turning strange.

Tyson himself was changing, his words reflecting a brooding discontent. He spoke of moving to Monaco, a place that was "far away from home and you can go there and be welcomed." He spoke of "people going to sleep dreaming and fantasizing how I'm going to separate you from your money." He spoke of the negative press Givens and Roper were getting: "This drives them crazy because no one never said anything bad to them or anything derogatory about them in a paper . . . they are proud people."

TYSON: But I say, well, she married me and this is going to happen. As long as you are in the spotlight these incidents happen. If you want it to stop, the only thing you have to do is get knocked out, or get beat. It would all stop. You'll stop working and it will never happen again. But that's how the pressure is.

Q: Do you sometimes want to get away from all
                the—?

TYSON: Yes, absolutely. Like a lot of times, I said,
                'God, is it really worth it?' But I mean if it was
                a job to me, I would have been retired prior.
                But I love this. I love fighting. I'm a groupie
                for fighters. I love fighters. Let alone being a
                fighter, I just love fighters. You know what I
                mean? If I was a woman I'd be a super
                groupie only with fighters because I love
                fighters. And it's just hard for me to stay away
                because I just love these athletes.

Meanwhile, the struggle to unseat Cayton continued. Like
Marlene Dietrich in her relentless pursuit of a French Legion-
naire in the film *Morocco*, King followed Tyson from Los Angeles to New York to Catskill, talk, talk, talking as he went.*
After spending four days in mid-May holed up near Catskill,
King departed. But his echo lingered. "I fought in the richest
country in the world in Japan," Tyson told the *New York Post*'s
Mike Marley, "and only got eight point seven million"—in a
sworn affidavit Cayton said it was $6.8 million—"when he
[Cayton] said I'd get ten million. Ali and Foreman went to the
poorest country in the world [Zaire] and got five million each."

King had been one of the promoters of the match between
Foreman and Ali, both of whom were major attractions, as opposed to Tubbs, who was not. To get $6 million to $9 million to
beat on Tubbs was practically white-collar crime, but to Tyson,
who was now set on thinking the worst of Cayton, it looked
otherwise.

For Cayton, it was becoming increasingly clear that what
Tyson thought of him was more and more influenced by Roper
and Givens and that Tyson-Are-Us, as some weisenheimers had
taken to calling the aggregate fighter-wife-and-mother-in-law,
was a problem that was not about to go away.

On May 26, when Tyson turned up at the Manhattan Center in New York to shoot a Diet Pepsi commercial that Cayton
had negotiated for him—part of a $1.25 million Pepsi deal—

---

*King even talked Tyson into signing an agreement while he was up there that would
have given him the right to promote Tyson's next bout after he fought Spinks. The
agreement was never activated.

Roper and Givens were with him, as was the attorney Winston. The production may have been ready to roll, but Tyson wasn't. He withdrew before shooting could begin, insisting that the 33⅓ percent cut to which Cayton was entitled by the terms of his personal services contract with him had to be renegotiated. For the next four hours the shooting stood at a dead halt as Winston and Cayton conferred and hundreds of extras sat about in the spacious auditorium, from whose flanks machines occasionally emitted clouds of ersatz smoke that would be necessary if the scene was ever shot.

It was, finally, when Cayton agreed to cut his share. Sly, eavesdropping on Winston's backstage phone call, heard the attorney say, "We got him down to twenty-five"—25 percent, from the 33⅓ percent.

Cayton understood now what lay ahead. Not long after, he retained Thomas Puccio, the federal prosecutor in the Abscam bribery trials and later the defense attorney for Claus von Bulow, as his counsel.

In the prime of Leon Spinks, that gusto-loving boyo, the editors of *Playboy* magazine had ordered an illustration to go with Sly's profile of the fighter.

The artist had delivered a drawing of Spinks attached to endless strings—some of them broken, some of them intact: a portrait of the champion as a puppet, a Leon lurching to the variegated dreams and schemes of others.

That image came sneaking up on Sly now as he watched Tyson grope for the answers the way Spinks, Jr., had a decade before. Now it was Tyson's turn to muddle his way. As Leon once had, Tyson exclaimed and declaimed with Solomonic certainty and in the next breath changed his mind and made confusion his accomplice.

At dinner in Vegas on that April night, he had said he would lay over for two weeks in Los Angeles; the next night, with Robin pleading the case, he had flown to New York instead. There he had met with Steve Lott, then spoken by phone to Cayton from Bernardsville, a conversation that had cheered Cayton enough for him to report afterward: "Mike is entirely with me."

That was relatively early on in the turmoil that followed Jacobs's death and well before Tyson began talking Kingspeak. So when Cayton rode the commuter rail back to Larchmont that night, his certainty about his future association with Tyson did not seem unreasonable.

In the weeks that followed, the manager would continue to be optimistic, but there was too a bit of clenched-teeth rigor in his words. For the impulse that had made Tyson bolt Vegas for a late-night flight to New York and rapprochement was abating, and the new Tyson more nearly resembled that hippety-hop Leon on the strings—he seemed to be speaking with a voice that was a jabberwocky impersonation of his own.

There was the "Jews in suits" quote of his that raised brows. In the few days in May during which King had parked himself in Albany, near Catskill, Tyson was quoted in the *New York Post* as saying: "I don't need nobody, and that includes Bill Cayton and Don King. But I'm vulnerable because of my wife. If I deal with Don King, they'll slaughter me. I should only deal with Bill and Shelly because they're guys who are Jewish and are good guys because they wear three-piece suits."

In that rambling, fragmented, dyspeptic discourse, he had struck a note that even with the tumults going on about him sounded strange. Not that Sly held any fairy-tale notion that because of his Dickensian tale of ennobling success, Tyson was obliged to be perpetually grateful or beholden to white people, or even to like them. But something was troubling him, as his vague expression of discontent made clear. *Vulnerable . . . wife . . . they'll slaughter me . . . Jewish . . . three-piece suits.* What was he saying? Who were his oppressors? How did smartly dressed Hebrews figure in what ailed him? What Sly made of it was that the fucker was confused, and that in his confusion was parroting the cues of others—force-fed recriminations and allegations and shitstirring innuendos.

The day he read his "Jews in suits" quote, Tyson threw up. The word that filtered down from Catskill to Cayton's office was that he had become very upset seeing his words in print. Over the next few weeks, even as he began training in Atlantic City late in May, he remained agitated, crying one afternoon there while being interviewed by several reporters.

The tears came as he talked about Cus D'Amato. Sly suspected they were tears for the end of innocence. D'Amato was the link to those years of learning and struggle, the years in which Tyson had created himself. Compared to what he was going through now, it had been a simpler time, a happier time, a time that was slipping away from him.

For a while he had been that most American of stories—the bootstrap jack who had raised himself out of the hard times and into the lap of luxury. That was the Tyson the public had found—the kid Cus had wrought. But with success he had changed, into that species of newly rich athlete who gets the hang of Gucci and Giorgio Armani and cars that are priced as high as other men's homes. That life had its complications; it was riskier than the world that began and ended in Catskill, New York.

While there were tears, before crowds of reporters there was also a new surliness. At a satellite-linked news conference in Atlantic City a few weeks before the fight, he responded to questions with snappish answers.

"None of your business," he told a reporter who asked what his relationship was with Bill Cayton.

"None of your business," he told another reporter who wondered how he felt about going into the Spinks match without Jacobs or D'Amato.

Then he zeroed in on press coverage: "I've been reading a lot of negative press. People are coming down. I don't know where they're getting their information from. But in all the bad things they've been saying, anybody I had a good relationship with, that's a writer or something . . . they can throw it away. They've been printing a lot of bullshit."

A heavyweight champion was a potent figure in the pop culture, a paradigm of strength and stability. But the ability to incite crowds with his derring-do and courage did not confer on him the wisdom or the maturity to roll with the punches outside that prize ring.

Tyson loved a woman, and the woman he loved wanted him to cut the ties to his past. If being in love meant having to shitcan those who had helped on the way up, it was love at the extreme. And by now, Tyson was speaking in extremes, about Cayton. Saying Cayton was a bad guy, an egomaniac, paranoid, and all-purpose strange. And this too: "Bill will be dead and gone in ten years but I'll still be with my wife."

Bill Cayton was now viewed as one of the fight game's lead-

ing charmers. There was a coolness there, a touch of top-dog
hauteur of the sort that used to be associated with the management of those dynasty New York Yankee teams of the 1950s.
Like Jacobs, he spoke with black-tie formality that could be dis-
tancing to those who preferred conviviality and lowbrow humor
in their fight guys. Cayton was a suit-and-tie straight man who,
as even his critics would concede, with Jacobs had skillfully
taken Tyson to the top. Whatever faults he had, Cayton had
looked out for Tyson, and he continued to do so—even as his
fighter was turning away from him.

The day after Tyson crashed his Bentley, King had bought
the fighter a white Rolls-Royce Corniche. But the auto dealer
had phoned Cayton afterward to say that the $15,000 insurance
coverage for the car seemed perilously thin. Cayton agreed,
and contacted Tyson to explain his liability and suggest trans-
ferring ownership of the Rolls to C.J.T., Inc., a company in
which Tyson was a principal. That would allow him to increase
his coverage to $6 million—from the mere $50,000 protection
available to him as an individual with violations on his driving
record. Tyson agreed to the change.

Still later, Cayton had to straighten out another problem
involving King. On May 3, King had entered into an agreement
with Tele/900, a California company, on his own; he had arranged for a round-by-round blow-by-blow account of Tyson
vs. Spinks on a 900 telephone number the night of the bout.
King had gone so far as to persuade Tyson to do tapes advertising the telephone arrangement.

Cayton saw the setup as infringing on the rights of closed-
circuit exhibitors; he feared lawsuits that could jeopardize
Tyson. Again he phoned his fighter and explained the potential
problem. At Tyson's request, King sent a letter rescinding the
agreement. When Tele/900 resisted, Cayton retained David
Wood, the Los Angeles attorney who had settled the parking-
lot-kiss caper.

"The matter," said Wood of the 900 number, "was resolved
by their agreeing to back off the blow-by-blow and, in lieu, run
some sort of contest in which callers pick the winner and get a
certificate as a prize if they correctly call the outcome."

Though Cayton's intervention had spared Tyson further
difficulties, the manager seemed to understand that the die was
cast—that while Tyson would gladly benefit from these timely

rescues, William D'Arcy Cayton was on the outs no matter what.

He and the fighter would talk easily from time to time, but on nearly each occasion a new twist would follow that would reinforce the disaffection of Tyson-Are-Us and leave Cayton shaking his head at the influence he felt Givens asserted over the heavyweight champion. "He's obsessed by her," he would lament.

It nagged him that his working relationship with Tyson had been undone. Increasingly he was, like the Ancient Mariner, a man with a tale he felt compelled to tell. That was a narration of the swell job that he and Jacobs had done—from the $250,000 they had spent on Tyson in the years he was an amateur*, without any guarantee of recouping their money, to the moves they had made to secure pro glory in the arena and fiscal security out of it.** Whatever new conflicts might develop, Cayton was quick to cite that managerial record. *As I'm sure you're aware . . .*

At the same time he was cautious about exacerbating hard feelings. When Lott, who was not a favorite of Givens's, was fired by Tyson in Atlantic City, Cayton feared that it could break up the smooth flow of the camp. Over a lunch he discussed it with Roper, and afterward Tyson's aide-de-camp was quietly restored to his job.

As chaotic as the months following Tyson's marriage had been, with the fight upcoming it was a time to simplify matters so Tyson would not be diverted from what he had to do. The conventional wisdom was that a fighter had to be walled off from the civilian world of distractions so that he could draw into himself and prime the beast for one intense night in public. A fighter's commitment to his moment of truth did not begin, after all, when he took his walk to the ring; it began long weeks before. The hard physical workout was only one part of it; unless a fighter came to terms with the emotional demands

---

*From an affidavit of Cayton's: "When he [Tyson] was about fifteen, we hired Larry Holmes's sparring partners (Holmes was then heavyweight champion). At another point Carlos DeLeon, himself a champion, was Mike's sparring partner. When Mike was still an amateur we nevertheless paid on occasion up to $1,000 per week for his sparring partners. I believe at that time Muhammad Ali was paying $1,000 a week for his sparring partners."
**The managers had invested $2 million of Tyson's in single-payment life insurance, to generate approximately $250,000 a year for life before Tyson turned thirty.

of a violent sport, all his training was apt to be wasted. A body that was finely tuned but hadn't a lively malice was like a fancy car with junk under its hood.

The weeks leading to a fight were meant, then, to align body and mind so that the swift and brutish moves on fight night worked as an extension of the boxer's aroused nervous system. While that was not always a natural state, most fighters moved toward it in the solitude of training camp. It was there a fighter began to accept the icy realities of his business and what he meant to do about them. Cayton figured it might be tough to impose the kind of isolation Tyson was going to need before the Spinks fight, but even he had not figured on the mysterious Olga.

Some time ago, the Vice-President of these United States, Spiro Agnew, described the press as "nattering nabobs of negativism."

Tyson called the writers worse. By June, he was telling them they were parasites, dicksuckers, and idiots. "You ruin people's lives," he said to a group of them in Atlantic City one day. "I'm a sucker even to be talking to you guys. I should be ready to rip your heads off."

What troubled Tyson most was the bad press his wife and mother-in-law had gotten. They had been depicted as connivers, eagerly entangling him in a web of sticky complicity designed to leave Tyson sadder and quite a bit poorer somewhere down the line.

In that way the press was to become part of the convoluted Tyson story, as it reported on the backstage maneuvers and shifts in power, and in the tabloids treated the more bizarre turns—the Bentley giveaway, Roper's Dave Winfield problem— as worthy of big headlines and front-page display. It wasn't long before Tyson-Are-Us was accorded the sidelong glance that Spinks, Jr., had gotten a decade before, as newsgathering folks not usually concerned with boxing began picking up on the seriocomic story.

For the most part, the tale was nudged along by the New York scribes—by the *Daily News*'s Mike Katz, a rotund, bearded man who looked as if he belonged in Lenin's political cabinet; by the *Post*'s Michael Marley, who in his rumpled suits and with his heckler's approach was the classic newspaper skeptic; by Sly;

and by *Newsday*'s Wally Matthews, who, it turned out, was handed the baton by Olga.

Matthews, a former amateur boxer, was checking out Tyson and Spinks in Atlantic City on June 13 when he got a message from his office in New York that a caller identifying herself as a friend of Givens/Roper had phoned, wanting to speak to him. Matthews did not get around to dialing the number until the following day, when he did so from a rest stop on the drive back from Atlantic City.

"The woman who answered the phone identified herself as Olga," Matthews said. "No last name. She told me she worked for Ruth Roper as a vice-president in her company."

R. L. Roper Consultants in midtown Manhattan designed or modified computer systems for businesses. Olga Rosario, who had worked for the company for several years now, thought that Roper was miscast as the villain in the troubles of Tyson.

Rosario said that when she had walked out on a bad marriage and come to New York, Roper had helped her, not only giving her a job but encouraging her to reestablish contact with her two sons.

"I had an I-don't-care attitude," said Rosario. "I'd put them out of my life. Ruth kept saying, 'Olga, you can't do that.' I will always be in debt to her, because my sons are my best friends now. My youngest son, Braulio, did not want to go to college. Ruth talked him into going. He's majoring in music. He sings and writes lyrics. He tells me he wants Ruth to manage his career. 'And she can invest my money,' he says."

"Olga," said Matthews, "told me that she was coming forward because she couldn't stand what was happening with the family. She also said some things about Mike Tyson—that he was abusing them, that he hit Robin and spit at her. 'I fear for them,' she said.

"Naturally my curiosity was aroused, and I asked her would she go on record. She said no, she was just concerned. She was worried for Ruth and Robin. They were good people. I told her, 'It's a terrific story. I can't write it unless somebody goes on the record. Because (a) those are strong accusations that could affect the marriage, and (b) I have to protect myself.' Olga said, 'I'll talk to them and get back to you.' On Wednesday, Olga called early in the day and said neither Robin nor

Ruth would go on record. 'But I told them what I told you and they said it'd be okay if you wrote it.'"

Matthews tape-recorded the conversation with Rosario. Later that night, there was a message from her on his home answering machine, asking him to call back at any time, it was "very, very important." At midnight Wednesday Matthews returned Rosario's call.

"She told me," Matthews said, "'If you dial this number, there'll be somebody at the other end that will talk to you about this.' She gives me an overseas number. I said, 'What is this number?' She says: 'It's in Portugal.' 'Who is it?' She says, 'If she wants to identify herself she'll identify herself. She's waiting for your call.'"

The number was of a hotel in Madeira, Portugal. Matthews asked the switchboard operator for the room number Olga had given him and was put through. As Matthews's tape recorder ran, the woman on the other end identified herself as Stephanie Givens, Robin's younger sister. She was to depart Portugal that morning after having competed in a USTA satellite tennis tour.

"Stephanie," said Matthews, "repeated the story Olga told about Tyson hitting Robin and the fear that she and her mother had for Robin's safety. She said it was why Ruth and Robin always traveled together—out of fear for Robin."

Stephanie related to Matthews how Tyson once had hit his wife with a closed fist but had done so without leaving marks on her. Stephanie, who was in an adjoining hotel room at the time, had made Robin come into her room and had then closed both doors. As she told Matthews: "I put the latch on, and the dead bolt. He just kicked the two doors in. I knew he was strong, but I was like amazed. You can be so sweet to him, and you'll never know what will set him off. He's the type of person who feels, he's Mike Tyson, he can do whatever he wants. He loves to damage things in the house, just for no reason. If he feels like kicking in the TV set, he'll do it. If he feels like punching a hole in the wall, he does it. If he feels like hitting you, he does it. Why? I guess he gets bored."

The conversation with Stephanie lasted thirty-some minutes. Afterward, Matthews phoned the hotel again and asked for "Stephanie Givens" to confirm she was in the room to which he had been put through earlier. She was. Hanging up, he thought about what Stephanie had told him, and as he did, it occurred to him that her stories were not only similar to Olga Rosario's, but her word choices were as well.

"Because," said Matthews, "Olga didn't blame Tyson. She said, 'He hasn't been *socialized.' Socialized:* that surprised me. It wasn't a word used to talk about people. Now when I talked to Stephanie, she said, 'Michael can't help it. He hasn't been socialized.' A light went off in my head: two people saying the same thing. I had asked Stephanie how a story like this would affect the family, and she said, 'Robin would welcome it. Michael needs to have his eyes opened.' And Olga: 'The family wants you to write it. The family will be relieved.'"

On Thursday morning, June 16, Rosario phoned at Matthews's Long Island home.

"I have somebody who wants to talk to you," she said.

Ruth Roper came on the line. "I understand you spoke with my baby last night."

"Your baby," said Matthews, "told me quite a story."

"I think you and I ought to speak in person. The press is so against me and my daughter."

Matthews and Roper met at her office on East 42nd Street in Manhattan.

"A small office," said Matthews. "Three or four rooms, darkly lit. Like a witch's coven. The walls were black, or dark purple."

Ruth Roper appeared with her attorney, Michael Winston, the same attorney now representing Tyson. Matthews brought out a tape recorder and asked, "Do you mind the tape recorder?"

Winston minded. So Matthews put the machine away and switched to a hidden vest-pocket recorder. Roper proceeded to relate a tale of an embattled mother wanting the best for her daughter and ending up paying what now seemed a disproportionate price—a mother-daughter reputation as gold diggers, a shock to their dignity. That wasn't all, she said. She alleged that there had been a smear-and-scare campaign orchestrated by Cayton that included death threats, obscene phone calls, and a private investigator running a background check on her.

"Every once in a while, Winston would throw me out to have a talk with her," said Matthews. "He supposedly was reprimanding her. Then Ruth would come back, insisting she 'wanted to set the record clear.' After an hour the door to her office opens and it's Robin. 'Oh, Mom. I didn't know you had company. Oh, and a member of the press. I didn't know the press was here today.' And I said, 'Yeah, why don't you sit down and talk.' She's been reading a manuscript, was in jeans and a sweater, no makeup, looked terrific. Robin continued the tale. Said she had been smeared in the press and so had her mother. Michael didn't stand up strongly enough and they were all angry about it.

"I tell her that I spoke with Stephanie, who said the marriage had problems, that he's hit her a couple of times. She looks down, averting her eyes, and begins crying, shaking her head, yes—he had hit her. It was like Mary Astor in *The Maltese Falcon*. At this point, I say, 'So is this true?' She says, 'You can't quote me. It has to be off the record.' 'I need you to confirm.' At one point, she blurted out an incident that had to do with Steve Lott. She said Lott was in the next room on an occasion when Tyson was hitting her. Lott came in to investigate. Tyson told him to get lost, so Lott just turned and walked out.* The understanding was that I couldn't write any of that from her. But she confirmed the hitting incident. She also gave some hints that Tyson was insecure. He would get drunk and say, 'You don't think I'm man enough?' It was a mood that he'd get into. As though he was obsessed with his own manhood."

Matthews had his story save for one thing: he needed a reaction from Tyson. On Friday, June 17, he began phoning the fighter's aides in Atlantic City. He left word for Rory Holloway, Lott, and José Torres, hinting he had damaging material that it would behoove the champion to answer.

The afternoon lengthened: no Tyson.

At about 4:40 P.M., Matthews was away from his desk when the phone rang. An unidentified woman told the desk clerk who answered, "Tell Wally Matthews to put on *Live at Five*."

---

*The incident had happened before the marriage, at Lott's apartment. Lott had been asleep in his bedroom; Tyson and Givens were on the couch in the living room. At 4:00 A.M., Lott was awakened by a "tremendous crash." He got up to investigate and, in the living room, found Givens screaming, "You hit me, you hit me, how can you hit me?" The intensity of the ruckus led a doorman to knock at Lott's apartment to inquire, discreetly, "Can we get you a car for Miss Givens?"

"Robin was crying," Lott said. "Mike was on the telephone. I told the doorman, 'It's okay.' I looked at Mike, who said, 'Steve, you can go back to sleep.' I turn, go back to sleep. Next day Mike says to me, 'Steve, you have to remember. She's a great actress.'"

Live at Five was a late-afternoon newscast shown on the NBC-TV affiliate in New York. Ten days before the biggest fight of her husband's career, Robin Givens had decided to appear in studio because, as she would tell the interviewer, Sue Simmons, "I'm angry." Angry, she said, at the notion circulating that she and her mother were opportunists meddling in Tyson's career.

GIVENS: First of all I'm Michael's wife. Not only that but we're family. My mother has become Michael's mother. An incident happened and we noticed a discrepancy with Michael's money. That's what sort of opened up everything. I heard a reporter once say that he [Tyson] is sort of a puppet and people are sort of pulling at him. Michael has orchestrated everything. He's clearly learned to enjoy business and he wants to know what he has. And he has every right to know. If Michael has fifty million dollars and he's supposed to have seventy million, that's a problem. And that's what we're finding out.

SIMMONS: The odds on this fight are changing. People are now putting money on Michael Spinks, saying that perhaps the personal problems of Mike Tyson might affect him in this upcoming fight.

GIVENS: No. That's absurd. It might affect Spinks more, actually, because Michael's become so angry. And, really, just hurt. He loves me, and he loves my mother. And he sees the pain that we've both been going through. And we'd kept quiet for so long, while I believe his manager, Bill Cayton, has clearly fed the press. He's hired a private detective that comes to our building and asks the doorman questions about us. He asks questions about Michael. That's ridiculous. We talked to the deputy police commissioner. She said we should get security. My mother's now walking around with security.

SIMMONS: Why security? I don't understand.

GIVENS: Well, there's so much money involved and for some reason they consider us such a threat.

When basically all we are is family. And if
you've got nothing to hide, if nothing's
wrong, then what's the problem? Why go out
and hire Thomas Puccio, who was a lawyer
for Abscam? If there's no problem, then
what's the problem? And I'm angry. I'll tell
you. I'm angry. . . . I can tell you a person
very close to us, he [Cayton] offered him
money, fifty thousand dollars to help us get a
divorce.* He said he'd stop at nothing less
than our getting a divorce. This is something
out of *Dynasty*.

"Half an hour later," said Matthews, "I called Robin and
said, 'I saw you on TV.' She said, 'I couldn't hold it in any
longer. I had to go public.' I told her, 'No problem. My story
goes Sunday. She was happy to hear that. 'Oh, good, I look
forward to seeing it.'"

After that, Matthews set up in a glass-walled office where
he could finish his article without being disturbed. He was eating his dinner there when a clerk tapped on his window and
signaled that there was a phone call for him. Matthews picked
up the receiver to find the heavyweight champion of the world
on the other end.

"What's the problem?" said Tyson. "What's so urgent? Am
I in trouble?"

"Your family's said some pretty damaging statements,"
Matthews told him. "I want your comment."

Matthews proceeded to read the transcripts from his interviews with the Givens sisters and their mother.

"Tyson listened in complete silence," recalled Matthews. "I
asked him several times, 'Did you hit Robin?' The first couple
of times he said, 'She's my wife. We have arguments.' 'Did you
hit her?' He said, 'I'd never bruise my wife. I love her.' I didn't

*A few days later, Don King would identify the person as the Rev. George Clements.
Cayton would deny approaching Clements or hiring a private detective. Cayton would
say that after Jacobs's death he had seen Clements's name on a note pad of Jacobs's and
had phoned him to see whether there was any business that needed to be completed. In
the course of conversation, Cayton said he mentioned the $50,000 he claimed King had
charged for the Tillis exhibition. But Cayton believed that after King had spoken
to Clements, Clements was persuaded to tell a different $50,000 story. Clements:
"I'd rather discuss this with the parties involved. If Bill wants to talk with me, I'd be
happy to."

press him. I asked him a lot of questions. Through those questions I could feel the mood change. He became like ice-cold. Told me, 'I'm a professional. Nothing can hurt me. Nothing can hurt my career. Maybe that comes from Cus. If nothing else, if it makes me a horrible human being, I'm just a professional. When you think about it, it's my whole nature. I'm a product of my environment. My main objective is to win, not so much to make money, but to win.'"

Matthews asked Tyson for his reaction to the family's revelations. "He told me," said Matthews, "'I feel great. I really do. You opened my eyes to a lot of things here. You can't say bad things about a person, call them an asshole, and then say that you love them. What they're saying, basically, is that I'm useless. I can't understand it. Maybe I'm not the man for them. You know what I mean? Maybe I'm not man enough for them. I'll get by somehow. I always find a way to get by.'"

On Saturday, June 18, Tyson finished his workout in Atlantic City and retreated to Bernardsville for the weekend with Givens.

As the Sunday *Newsday* hit the stands with Matthews's story, the articles behind Monday's tabloid headlines repudiating the tale of marital strife were already in the works.

IRON MIKE'S FIGHTING MAD
**My marriage isn't on the ropes,
says the boxing champ**

And now Robin was saying, "They're trying to destroy us. Really, it is hell."

Somehow the wild and woolly accusations and innuendos of the Matthews piece were defused in Bernardsville. It was not Robin, or Ruth, or Stephanie whom Tyson faulted, but rather Cayton. As Tyson told it, Cayton was behind the stories that were creating the impression that the heavyweight champion couldn't control his wife, and that she and her mother were in cahoots as gold diggers. "He's got my mother-in-law giving the shovel to my wife," Tyson said of Cayton.

With each new twist, the two women in the champion's life were forcing the press to shift focus from the usual boxing types to them. But as Givens and Roper drew the kind of look from the press that fighters' wives and mothers-in-law don't often command, questions were raised about what mother and daughter were up to.

Ruth Roper, forty-two, was an attractive woman, soft-spoken and on the demure side when addressing the press. Which wasn't often. As the complications in Tyson's career grew, Roper was selective about when and to whom she would talk.

Because of his consistently anti-Cayton position in print, Matthews of *Newsday* had been the beneficiary of the family's earlier revelations about Tyson's domestic violence. Later, when Matthews began to put the knock on the fighter and his women, only Marley of the *New York Post,* who wrote kindly about Givens and Roper, had the ever-changing Bernardsville phone number. That gave him access to the sayings of chairwoman Ruth and, more important, to Tyson himself, whose calls were now screened so that old friends, reporters, and even Cayton did not get to him so readily.

Of course, what Tyson said tended to be an echo of The Package, as Givens eventually would refer to the double-headed creature—she and her mother—he had, in effect, taken on by marrying. "We come as a package," she would say.

As Cayton's grip on Tyson's business loosened, a new entity, Mike Tyson Enterprises, was set up, and though Tyson was president and sole stockholder of MTE, it was Roper who took over the daily activity. MTE was located at R. L. Roper Consultants: two new phone lines—that was Mike Tyson Enterprises.

Once Roper became the unofficial boss of heavyweight business, the press became increasingly curious about who she was and from where she had come. The facts began to emerge.

She was born Ruth Newby in Lexington, Kentucky. In June 1964, four months pregnant with Robin, she had married Reuben Givens, older brother of the University of Kentucky basketball star Jack (Goose) Givens. While he pursued a minor-league baseball career in Buffalo, she settled into her mother's apartment in the Bronx and raised Robin, who was born November 27, 1964. Stephanie was born two years later, by which time the marriage was floundering. Soon after, Roper and her daughters were on their own, and, save for a short-lived second marriage, Roper would bring up both daughters by herself.

"I've totally sacrificed my life for my children," she said.

"There were times when it was very difficult, but I've struggled to make a good life for them. The girls were raised in Mount Vernon and New Rochelle and educated in private schools."

Roper's struggle took her out into the business world, where she worked as an airlines ticket agent, head of a travel agency, an executive head hunter, and finally as the owner of R. L. Roper Consultants.

Roper decried the stories that made her out to be a collaborator with her daughter in fleecing Tyson. What role she had taken on in his career was, she said, an extension of the logic and organizational sense of the computer-systems person, as well as her mothering instinct.

"Michael is one of my children, and he loves that," she said. "He doesn't trust easily. I think I've earned this trust because he puts you through a lot. When he was dating Robin, I gave him a hard time. I'd give him hell. I'd yell at him. Mostly about staying out late. He'd take it like a son, with respect. He knows the way I feel about the children. In fact, he'd talk about it with me, sometimes negatively. He'd say I was being too protective. But Michael became part of it. He chose a wife who's a wonderful smart girl, and he got a family too. For me, he's one of my children. He feeds a need, because I like mothering. He'll call, for instance, in the middle of the night when he can't sleep, to talk.

"When I first met him, Michael owned a bunch of cars and jewelry. He rented his apartment in New York for a couple thousand dollars a month. People let him invest two hundred and fifty thousand dollars to renovate a rental apartment. Just poor decisions about managing his money. In terms of owning something real, he owned nothing. Now he has a family and a home, and he's very proud of that."

Skeptics saw Roper as being more opportunistic than she let on. Dolores Robinson, mother of a Sarah Lawrence classmate of Givens, quoted Roper as having said, during Robin's undergraduate years, "Now my goal is to find her a rich man."

A businesswoman who feared Roper enough to ask for anonymity in discussing her had told Sly of a dinner she and her boyfriend had had with Roper. Roper, the businesswoman said, had doubts about the fiscal potential of the boyfriend. The day after the dinner she gave her a book entitled *Smart Women/Foolish Choices*.

That notion of "marrying well" was taken seriously by Roper, who was reported to have taught Robin to make daiquiries "because rich people drink daiquiries" and to drink martinis so she could mingle with the swells.

Before she met Tyson, Givens had dated the comedian Eddie Murphy and the basketball player Michael Jordan. The word from ProServ Inc., which represented Jordan, was that Givens had sought the relationship by writing Jordan and enclosing photos of herself. Jordan had lunch with her a couple of times and bailed out, later telling friends, "Those women are crazy."

Roper herself sought to do well by marriage and had hoped that the baseball player Winfield might be persuaded to make her a bride again. But Winfield was said to have told her, "You're not the kind of woman a man would marry."

Later, Roper retained Marvin Mitchelson, the famous Los Angeles palimony attorney, when she sued Winfield for allegedly giving her that sexually transmitted disease. Recalled a source who knew Roper back then: "When I asked her why she was suing, on what grounds, she didn't want to say. She told me, 'He wouldn't want it in the papers. It's free money for me.'"

Then there was Givens. Details from her account of her life, and her marriage, came bouncing back at Sly like slugs down the chute of a cranky pay phone. Creative autobiography was no crime, certainly. But it hardly seemed necessary in the case of this beautiful and intelligent young woman. But taking liberties with the facts was, as it turned out, routine for Robin Givens.

Givens said she had been a Ford Agency model, but the head of the agency, Eileen Ford, couldn't remember her. "She was never with my division. . . . I'll find out if she was with any other division. . . . Hold on, hold on. . . . No, can't find her in the computer. . . . My division? It's high fashion. The other divisions are heavy girls or older girls and God knows she's not either of those. Hang on. Let me check. . . . No, the testing people don't remember her. Let me ask the TV department. Hold on. . . . Well, TV doesn't have anything on her either. Nobody can remember her."

Givens said she had been a Harvard Medical School student, but Barbara Steiner of the school's news office had this disclaimer: "We have no record of Ms. Givens being a student at Harvard."*

At the time she and Tyson traded vows, Givens had said the wedding happened on the spur of the moment. By that account, it was performed by the Rev. George Clements in Chicago and again in a civil ceremony in New York. Yet Sly had heard that that was not a strictly accurate account and had phoned Clements to ask.

Q: Did you marry the Tysons?
CLEMENTS: Yes, I did. It was a religious ceremony.
Q: The kind sanctioned by the state?
CLEMENTS: *(hesitating)* No. It was a blessing on the marriage. They asked if I'd bless the upcoming marriage and I told them I would. It took place in the rectory of the church.

As life's distortions went, this was a small one, really. But it made a reporter curious. Why embellish the facts of a marriage? Well, it turned out there was a reason. Just before the wedding, in a phone call to Jacobs at his East 40th Street office, Roper had said that her daughter was three and a half months pregnant by Tyson. When Jacobs hung up, he rushed up the stairs of the office to tell Cayton: "Ruth wants Mike to marry Robin immediately. They're on the way to Chicago to see Father Clements. Ruth doesn't want them to stay in Chicago. She says they have to come to New York and marry immediately."

Whatever.

In March, Tyson told the press for the first time that Givens was pregnant.

On May 26, when Sly saw Givens at the Diet Pepsi shoot in New York, he noted no sign of pregnancy. By what Roper had told Jacobs, Givens would have been nearly seven and a half months pregnant at the time.

By June, when Givens's publicist, Karen Samfilippo, was quoted in *Sports Illustrated* as saying the pregnancy was "not official yet," a certain sensitivity was developing about the subject.

At a news conference in Atlantic City on June 8, three

---

*Through a spokesman, Dan Klores, Givens declined to comment on these and other contradictions in her history.

weeks before the fight, when a TV talk-show host, Ross Shafer, asked, in seeming innocence, what academic subject Tyson was good enough at to help the child he was expecting, Tyson snapped: "You know. Could I tell you something? You're a wiseass and you shouldn't get personal with me like that."

Not long after, Givens claimed she had had a miscarriage, blaming Cayton for the distress he had caused her.

Whatever.

In the weeks before the Spinks fight, as Givens and Tyson turned up on the covers of *People, Life,* and *Sports Illustrated,* Givens had become what her upbringing meant her to be—a woman of accomplishments and material means. But getting there had not been easy.

Ruth Roper had raised her daughters to be "smart, beautiful, and gutsy—everything that can be intimidating to a man." Robin was responsive enough: she accelerated through school, skipping three grades so that by the time she arrived at Sarah Lawrence, she was only fifteen years old. Fifteen, and geared for success.

"She had lovely clothes, and a sports car," Sue Ritt, a fellow student, said. "She was a very strong girl, very clever, very intelligent. She knew what she wanted and how to get it. She was very ambitious. And I don't mean that in a bad way."

However, many of her classmates were offended by Givens's airs. Susan James, a black student, said, "She had a reputation for being snobby. She was not very friendly. And Robin was vindictive. Most of her relationships ended in conflict."

Kim Alexander, another black classmate, recalled a scene from early in Givens's collegiate life: "I was sitting in the lunchroom. And all of a sudden there was a ruckus, I hear a chair being thrown. I turn around. It's Robin Givens. She's screaming at another girl, a white girl: 'I pay my goddam tuition just like you do.' A lot of black kids thought she was a bitch. It was like, 'What's her problem?'"

Another black student at Sarah Lawrence was Holly Robinson. Robinson's father, Matthew, had played Gordon on *Sesame Street* and later became a coproducer of Bill Cosby's show. Her mother, Dolores, was a California talent manager whose clients had included Martin Sheen, Randy Quaid, Margot Kidder, Lukas Haas, Harry Hamlin, and Nick Mancuso. Holly would go from Sarah Lawrence to a year at the Sorbonne in France, and later into the role of Judy Hoffs in Fox Broadcasting's TV show *21 Jump Street*. But in 1982, Robinson was just a Sarah Lawrence freshman who happened to admire an upperclassman, Robin Givens.

"She thought Robin was the greatest," said Ritt. "They became close, traveling to the city—the New York thing, a lot of openings and stuff that Robin knew about."

Dolores Robinson recalled the first time she heard about Givens from her daughter:

"My daughter went to Malibu Park Junior High and Santa Monica High School, where she was one of just a few black girls. Her experience was almost all-white. So she was excited when she found a peer who was black, smart, and pretty. I remember freshman year she called and begged me to let her bring Robin here for Christmas. We lived in Malibu, and as I opened the front door, my antenna went beep beep: 'Oh, my God, my poor child.' Robin knew I was in show business, and that my daughter and I knew people. And it became clear to me that the only reason she came was because she was so ambitious. While she stayed here, Robin got my daughter to introduce her to one of my clients, who had quite a name, an actor. She made a beeline for this actor, who said to me later: 'What's that girl's story?' It was so clear: she was after all she could get.

"When Robin stayed at my house, she told Holly her family had a house in Hastings-on-Hudson, a big mansion, she said, as well as an apartment in New York. In the meantime, I'm on the phone with Ruth and we're talking. I had been through hard times. I had lost a major client; my son, Matt, was at NYU and Holly was at Sarah Lawrence; I had bought the house in Malibu, I was in way over my head. So I was saying to Ruth, who was living in New York City, 'I just lost a client,' and so on and so on. And Ruth said, 'Yes. We used to have a home a couple years ago out in the suburbs; we were forced to sell.' I thought, so much for Hastings-on-Hudson."

Eventually, Givens and Holly Robinson ceased being friends. Some classmates say that Givens was miffed when Dolores Robinson wouldn't handle her career. Others say that Givens viewed Holly as acting competition.

Soon after Givens and Robinson returned to school from Christmas break, Dolores Robinson said, "Money turned up missing in the dorm. It's an open dorm. Money was missing from a wallet."

According to Sue Ritt, the victim of the robbery was Holly Robinson's roommate.

"People were talking about the theft," said Ritt, "and Robin said, 'Oh, yeah, I think Holly did it.'"

"And," said Dolores Robinson, "Robin told Holly's roommate and everybody else that Holly and her mother stole money from her wallet when she was in California, and that Holly's mother was a slut."

When Holly Robinson heard what Givens had said she punched Givens and then wrestled her to the floor. A dormitory counselor broke up the fight.

"The next day," said Susan James, "Robin's mother sent a car out to protect her from danger."

"And," said Dolores Robinson, "Mrs. Givens said to me, 'You know how Robin can be. She didn't mean it. Let's have lunch, you and your daughter.' I said, 'Wait. Your daughter calls me and my daughter thief and slut, then let's-have-lunch? No thank you.' I never talked to her after that."

Holly Robinson did not easily shrug off the incident. "She was very upset for years after," said Ritt. "She cried a lot. That someone she thought highly of could do that—she felt betrayed."

"And Robin," said Dolores Robinson, "was such a convincing actor that for three or four months she turned people against Holly. People grabbed their wallets when Holly came by. I had to fly back to Sarah Lawrence a couple of times. Her counselors suggested my daughter have therapy because she was so upset. I understand why they turned against her. Robin Givens was so cool, they believed her. Holly was so emotional and upset by it, they said: 'Get therapy.'"*

---

*Ruth Roper declined to hear the particulars of the Sarah Lawrence stories involving her daughter, but of Robin's difficulties with Holly Robinson she said that the tales that circulated were inspired by "jealousy." "Obviously this girl [Robinson] is jealous. Robin is a serious talented actress; she's serious about anything she does. She's serious and very very smart. And also in her own way shy. But she can force herself to be outgoing. Call Sarah Lawrence. They'd say some positive things about Robin. Talk to the president of the school." Sly did call. Curiously, when he asked Sarah Lawrence's public relations department for a Xerox copy of Givens's yearbook page, he was told that it had to be cleared first through Givens's spokesperson. That man, Dan Klores, said Givens declined to comment on her college days.

Robinson said that eventually some students who had accepted Givens's account and had been cool to her daughter apologized as they came into conflict with Robin. Among those she cited was Lauren Holly, an actress who currently appears in the soap opera *All My Children.*

"That's not totally wrong," Lauren Holly said. "I will say Holly [Robinson] and I did become better friends."

Givens graduated in 1984 in a ceremony that was not without incident, as Kim Alexander recalled:

"Graduation took place on Westlands Lawn, a grassy rectangle. It was held in a tent, a huge tent. There were about one hundred and thirty of us graduating. The speaker was Jane Alexander, the actress. After we heard her speech, everybody got a diploma. In alphabetical order. When they said Robin Givens's name, people booed. We booed her. It was terribly conspicuous. . . . No, it was not planned. Nobody said they were going to boo Robin. There was no way to. Everybody was running around, getting ready to graduate.

"When she heard the boos, Robin's mouth pursed in disdain, and I think she was a little hurt. There was disdain and an I'm-not-going-to-let-you-get-to-me look."

In February, the month she married Tyson, Robin told Sly that in her second year at Harvard Medical School, she had taken her Christmas vacation in Los Angeles so she could audition for a role in a made-for-TV movie called *Beverly Hills Madam,* starring Faye Dunaway. Not only did she land the part of a high-class call girl, but the six weeks of shooting, she said, gave her the "perfect reason" to quit medical school, which she said she had been wanting to do for some time.

Q: Why did you need a pretext? Why didn't you just leave?

GIVENS: I'm not like that. I'd invested time. And my mother invested money. We'd planned since the third grade.

That was what she said before Harvard Medical School announced that Robin Givens had never matriculated there. It turned out that well before *Beverly Hills Madam* she was auditioning for and getting small parts in television. Agents from a

New York talent agency, Frontier Booking International, sent her up for a made-for-HBO series based on Raymond Chandler's Philip Marlowe character, and Givens had won a bit role in one hour-long show.

Then Givens was submitted for a guest shot on Bill Cosby's show, playing the college girlfriend of Cosby's daughter. Givens got the job and, eventually, the attention of Cosby, by telling him she was in Harvard Medical School. Cosby, who has a Ph.D. from the University of Massachusetts in education, was impressed. Givens said he suggested she try acting for a year; if it didn't work out, he would pay for her medical education. In Roper's office on 42nd Street, the mother and daughter later were heard making fun of Cosby, calling him a "megalomaniac."

In the fall of '86, Givens and Roper landed in Los Angeles and were whisked by Cosby's limousine to his place in Pacific Palisades. "She stayed at Cosby's until she got settled," said Barbara Stark, Frontier Booking's West Coast agent. "That wasn't very long. Her mother picked out her apartment in the Valley. The Oakwood Apartments."

Soon after *Beverly Hills Madam*, Givens read for and got her role in *Head of the Class*. Frontier Booking agents claim *they* submitted Givens for the TV sit-com and that Givens/Roper elected to give the booking to the more high-powered William Morris Agency. But Steve Glick of William Morris said that it was he who made the moves that got Givens the parts in *Beverly Hills Madam* and *Head of the Class*, and that he had done so after Cosby had recommended her to the New York office.

However it happened, Givens was now a regularly featured TV actress, one whom Tyson, flipping the TV dial, would eventually discover. With his two gold teeth and his name crudely tattooed on his right arm, Tyson hardly seemed the Prince Charming for a well-brought-up young woman from New Rochelle, Mount Vernon, and West End Avenue—and a Sarah Lawrence graduate. He was the Brownsville street tough who two years before he married had told a reporter from *The Ring* magazine: "Every day of my life I look in the mirror and I know I'm not Mr. Black America. I don't have the most charming personality in the world."

What he did have was an inordinate craving for affection. Sly had seen that side as far back as his first visit to Catskill, in

November 1985. As he interviewed Camille Ewald for the Tyson story, the fighter suddenly entered the room. He settled onto the arm of an easy chair, leaned over, hugged Miss Ewald in a childlike open way, and joked: "Is Mr. Berger interrogating you, Camille?"

Ewald told how Tyson slept on couches rather than a bed so he could hug the oversized pillows. The scribes who had seen the films of Tyson sobbing at fifteen to Teddy Atlas about losing the love of those who held him in esteem, if he was defeated, who had caught him lowering his head onto Jacobs's shoulder when boredom overcame him at news conferences, had a sense of the fighter's emotional neediness.

Yet poised against that was a ghetto kid's hard attitude toward women—a mentality rooted in manipulating them and treating them as objects. Stepping out of a party after he had won the heavyweight title from Berbick, Tyson had spotted an attractive woman talking on a payphone in the Las Vegas Hilton. He had thrown her over his shoulder and, with the woman good-naturedly protesting, had proceeded on his way.

Sometime later, Tyson was back in the same hotel, this time as a spectator for a boxing card. At two that morning, hours after the arena had emptied, Tyson got a call from Jimmy Hilton, whose brother Matthew, the IBF junior middleweight champion, had fought that night. Jimmy told Tyson to hurry over to his room: "There's two broads here."

A few minutes later, Tyson knocked at the door of Matthew Hilton's cornerman, Mario Costa. Though he was awakened by the knock, Costa knew Tyson so he opened the door. Tyson was breathing hard, as if he had run to the room. There was alcohol on Tyson's breath. "Where's the broads?" Tyson demanded. Costa tried to explain that Tyson had the wrong room, that Jimmy's was one door down. But Tyson, touching himself on the outside of his trousers, didn't want to hear it. He saw a patch of sandy brown hair above the covers in one of the beds and started toward the object of his affection.

"Mike. Wait," Costa said.

But Tyson would not listen. The sleeping figure felt the giant shadow of an intruder and, as Tyson neared, awoke with a start. Tyson recoiled. "That's no broad," he said.

"That's what I was trying to tell you," said Costa. "You want Jimmy's room."

Tyson hurried out of Costa's room and toward his wee-hour assignation.

Torres said that before Tyson had married, Iron Mike had revealed he liked "hurting" women when he had sex with them and that he did not much trust them for what they might want of him.

Olga Rosario, who had handled Tyson's personal affairs and managed his house from the time he moved to the Bernardsville estate, had experienced his brutish side.

"Once I started working for him I was spending three, four days a week there, then back to the office," said Rosario. "It was a part-time live-in situation. He had awful mood swings. He can be nice. The next minute, he'd be telling you off. A foul mouth. Names that amazed me. 'Fuck you, bitch. Fuck you, whore.' Or he'd talk sexually. 'Did you get enough last night from your boyfriend? How long is he going to hold you?' I'd say, 'Michael. Please.' And I'd walk away. I'd never tell Robin because I didn't want to hurt her. Sometimes he'd touch my neck, play with my neck, and try to drag me and hold me. 'Why don't you let me hug you? Are you afraid?' Because I'd pull away.

"Women were always calling the house. Always calling the office. Once a woman called and asked, 'Is Mike there?' We told her no. She called back: 'I know Mike is there.' Told her, 'Tell you what. You can speak to Robin if you want.' She hung up. Six times we changed the number at the house, and they still got the number."

In the February satellite press conference for the Tyson-Tubbs fight, a questioner in Tokyo had asked Tyson: "Miss Robin Gibson [sic!]—which part of her do you like most?"

Tyson said, "Everything. Especially a set of legs that's awesome."

The same question went to Givens about her husband.

Givens said, "I love his mind. His sensitivity. He has a great heart, whether anybody knows it or not. He's lovable. And very special."

The TV that stood in the vestibule of Givens's Los Angeles home was rather unique too. In a fit of temper, Tyson had kicked the screen in, Givens told people. Yet she chose not to remove the wreckage. The TV stood there like some modern-art irony, an objet de Tyson. Regular visitors to the house on Briar Summit Drive would wonder why Givens insisted on keeping the thing around. Once in a while someone might even ask her. Givens had no answer.

Nor was marital violence restricted to inanimate objects. Those close to the couple—Stephanie Givens, Rosario, and Givens's press liaison, Phyllis Polaner—had seen Tyson shake and shove his wife. Sometimes he even threw things at her.

A strange marriage. On occasion he would disappear for days with his pal Holloway and, when finally Roper located him, she would lecture him the way a mother does an errant son: "You're a married man. How does it look to be seen in such places, acting that way?"

For their part, Roper and Givens were constantly trying to reign Tyson in. Roper would say, "Keep him busy and he'll stay out of trouble." Yet the way they monitored him struck some as being a species of mind control, not unlike what religious cults used. Let Tyson slip away by himself to Catskill for a few days, and urgent phone calls would follow, as Givens and Roper summoned him back for some reason or other.

Rosario was often used to make the case for whatever it was that mother and daughter wanted Tyson to do, a role that did not endear her to the heavyweight champion. Yet more often than not Tyson would accede to his wife's wishes.

There was even an instance of Roper trying to track Tyson's daily travels, as Jay Bright, who like Tyson had grown up in the Catskill house, attested. "Normally," said Bright, "when you rent a limousine, there's a slip and it says time and destination. Ruth wanted a slip listing every single time the driver stopped the car for Mike. The lady from the limo company called me. She said Ruth wouldn't pay unless she got every single stop on the slip."

No matter that he called her alma mater "St. Lawrence." He had, it was clear, a devotion to her that had made him responsive to her cues. That was his pattern. From Bobby Stewart at the Tryon School to D'Amato to Jacobs, he had always taken direction. While many in the press thought of Givens as manipulative—there were stories of her haranguing Tyson, hitting him, even throwing wine at him—Roper would say that reporters mistook familial closeness for Tyson's slavishness.

"We're a family," she said. "And Michael is really. . . . I

don't want to minimize Camille, but Camille never had children, and Michael saw me with the children, and friends of the children.

"Let me tell you a little story. I have an apartment in the West 80s, and the kids spend as much time there as New Jersey. Michael sleeps over a lot. One time we were having the floors done, so we were all in the back room. I slept on a futon. Anyway, we tried a game. You start a story and the next person has to keep it going. I said, 'There once was a little boy named Bob . . .' And Michael continued: '. . . who ran away from home. To the circus. Where he became a juggler, and made bags and bags of money. And the family was proud.' To me it showed Michael's need for family. It was a deliberate choice."

When Givens had appeared on the *Live at Five* newscast and insisted Tyson took pleasure in "orchestrating" his business affairs, Sly studied the screen, waiting for her nose to grow long. The Tyson whom Sly knew was not the kind of guy who sat up late worrying about the dollars and cents of closed-circuit revenues and foreign sales and subsidiary bout incomes, unless he was being perpetually prodded on these matters.

Tyson's agenda hewed instead to the pleasures and gratifications of drink and—married or not—womanizing, his release from the hard wages of boxing. When he did speak about money matters, he was a transparent echo of King, and/or Roper and Givens. Not that educating a fighter was a wayward act. There was simply a question as to whose end was being pursued when Tyson expressed himself on business. A practiced ear caught in his attitudinal shifts inflections that, like new shoes, were not quite so comfortable as they might have been. The strings were being pulled.

Was it the persuasion of the moon that set up a blood season in which that other fighter Sly had seen put through changes would materialize, at the moment that Tyson was having his difficulties? A nice twist that L. Spinks should surface now, at age thirty-four, strictly as an opponent.

His record, of late:

1987

January 17	— José Ribalta, Coconut Grove, Fla.	TKO by 1
April 28	— Jeff Jordan, Nagoya, Japan	W 12
May 22	— Angelo Musone, Jesi, Italy	KO by 7
August 30	— Jim Ashard, Eugene, Ore.	D 10
October 20	— Terry Mims, Cleveland, Ohio	L 10
December 20	— Ladislao Mijangos, San Antonio, Tex.	L 10

1988
March 1   — Randall (Tex) Cobb, Nashville,
                   Tenn.   L 10

For $12,500, Leon was to box a Canadian named Tony
Morrison in an eight-hundred-seat hotel ballroom in Trumbull,
Connecticut. Sly felt duty-bound to connect the final dots on a
story to which he had once been as close as any working journalist. So up the turnpike to Trumbull he went in a rental car.

That afternoon he sat in the hotel bar with Spinks's manager, Marvin Haupt, a pudgy pale-complected man whose De-
troit-based company manufactured plastic parts for the auto
industry. Haupt said he had been managing Spinks since February 1985 and had seen his fighter through bankruptcy and a
foreclosure on Spinks's Colonial home in Michigan.

"The bank foreclosed for fifty-six thousand," said Haupt.
"That's what they got at a sheriff's sale. Fifty-six thousand dollars.
I offered to pay the fifty-six and the accrued interest, which would
have been a total of sixty-five thousand. There was no reason not
to accept my offer. I found out later, [world champion] Thomas
Hearns wanted the home for one of his relatives and, being a
major depositor in the bank, the bank sold it to him."

Spinks was now settled in a three-bedroom bungalow,
Haupt said ("It's modest by comparison"), and was preparing
for life beyond the ring by taking a six-month restaurant management course. "He wants to obtain a restaurant with a liquor
license," said Haupt.

For a scarcely educated soul like Spinks, Jr., that sort of
business venture sounded a tad risky. But Haupt insisted it was no
problem: he would fix Leon up with a sound business manager
and with his six-month course Leon would be cheatproof. If it
seemed to Sly a bit like giving a bank teller's job to a kleptomaniac,
that was Leon's problem—and someday, perhaps, a lawyer's.

Even as Sly was conjuring with the notion of Leon sam-
pling the Hollandaise sauce, here was that little round man,
Haupt, with another notion sure to steal the breath of a rational
man. Never mind that L. Spinks won about as often these days
as monsoon season in Arizona, Haupt was possessed of a plan
as improbable and multijointed as a Rube Goldberg construct, a
plan that would return Leon, in his *éminence grise* phase, to past
glory. A victory that night against the Canadian, and another

one later in the summer against another pug, Phil Brown, would, as Haupt saw it, empower him to match Leon against top-ten opponents. Then:

". . . if Michael succeeds in winning the title," pronounced Haupt, "I think he'd be willing to vacate one of the titles so that Leon . . ."

That night, with the first barrage of punches that the other man dealt him, Spinks fell sideways to the canvas, rising on creaking legs at the count of eight, a glazed look in his eyes. The referee stopped it right there—thirty-three seconds of the first round—and Spinks, who had dressed for the bout in his hotel room, was hurried to an elevator and back upstairs.

Sly went looking for Leon, but until he ran into a woman friend of Spinks's, he couldn't locate him. She had his room number, 423, but gave it with the admonition that Spinks was not seeing the press. As soon as the woman went around the corner, though, Sly was rapping at the door to 423 and was, with another reporter, let in.

Spinks was in jockey shorts. He did not recognize his old pal Sly. As he explained what had happened in the fight—I got caught, there's nothing I can say—he was professionally attentive. His disappointment sounded more like resignation; chronic losing did that.

Sly and the other man were posing the usual postfight questions—What'd he catch you with? Did the ref stop it too soon? Is this curtains for bubba Spinks?—when Leon's woman friend reappeared. And as a decade before, here in Trumbull the puppet act began again.

"You don't have to answer these questions," she reminded Spinks.

"Baby, go down and do what you have to," Spinks said.

"I don't like the fact they ignored me."

"Baby. Stop."

"I told them no," she said. "So it's like *fuck me*."

"They came to talk to me, baby. Please."

On March 30, under the chandeliers and vaulted ceiling of a ballroom at the Plaza Hotel in New York, the other Spinks had considered the prospect of fighting Mike Tyson and promptly thrown a fit.

"I don't want to go on!" Michael ranted. "I don't want to! I don't want to go in!"

For the briefest moment the audience was taken aback. Then Spinks collapsed into robust, convulsive laughter, laughter that saw him roll forward from his waist, toward the microphone into which he had been speaking conversationally an instant before.

"I know you all thought I was cracking up," he told the audience that had gathered that afternoon for the press conference at which the Tyson-Spinks match was formally announced.

It was an odd yet beguiling moment, and entirely in character for the thirty-one-year-old man who sprang it on the crowd. Michael Spinks had made a career, and a small fortune, doing the unexpected in prize rings across the United States.

If the likelihood of his confounding Tyson was largely discounted by the fight crowd, that was okay with Spinks. He was used to being taken for granted. In April, on the very day Spinks began his workouts in Kiamesha Lake, New York, he showed that however fearsome a figure Tyson might seem, Michael Spinks would try to treat him as just another opponent.

As his handlers toweled him dry that day, Spinks, wearing a T-shirt with the words YOU CAN DO IT across its front, said to no one in particular, "Gonna have fun all the way through. Ain't anybody gonna tell me I've got to be sad."

That night there would be no long faces at the dinner table. Anytime an attractive woman passed, Spinks or other members of his camp—sparring partners and aides—would utter, "Test, test," meaning the very sight of a woman was to be construed as a challenge to their purposefulness as fighters. "Test, test" became a comic buzzword, with nobody enjoying it more than Spinks, who smiled broadly.

Later, when a sparring partner of his, Bernard (Bull) Benton, posed, for effect, with and without his dental work, Spinks cracked up again.

Soon after, most of his mealtime companions were gone and Spinks sat at the dinner table, staring off into space. He stared awhile before he began repeating the same words over and over: "Won't be easy, won't be easy, won't be easy."

A full week before the fight, the world press began descending on Atlantic City. What a strange place was this A.C. On its six-and-a-half-mile boardwalk were soaring casinos with interiors full of baroque excess. But just beyond those gaming halls, out where the Monopoly-board streets of Atlantic and Pacific and Baltic lay was a city sagging and creaking from neglect, streets sunk in doom and poverty. The comedian Jackie Gayle would quip later in the week: "The hotels here are worth millions of dollars. You look out, it looks like downtown Beirut."

Even where tourists loitered—the A.C. of white rolling chairs and saltwater taffy—the boardwalk could seem a pitiful stop. Every day old folks on coupon deals were bused in, and the sight of them nickel-and-diming at the slot machines—all those old-timers in fogy clothes, belts hitched up to their pectorals—lent a pathos to the glittery scene. For Sly, A.C. was the low-rent version of Vegas. To the public, Tyson-Spinks was a big event, the chance to see a fighter who might reasonably be expected to test Tyson as he had not been tested before. To Atlantic City, the fight was a lure, attracting increased numbers of civilians who were, by the laws of casino mathematics, obliged to make the house wealthier. To the scribes, the fight was an article a day, more when necessary.

With the potential for abrupt turns that the Tyson end of the story held, a reporter spent his prefight week checking and rechecking sources to make sure no seismic fibrillation went undetected, permitting the competition to advance the story a stride ahead of his own newspaper.

But the week leading to Tyson vs. Spinks was in most respects much like that of other big fights—an agenda of boxers' workouts and mob interviews. Tyson's training at Trump Plaza was mostly open to the press, a concession to the magnitude of the event. Tyson, the man, was not available. After the troubles of the past months he was keeping his distance from newspaper guys, and, save for an impromptu session he convened late in the week with the British press, which he regarded as a comparatively civil breed ("Lucky for us," quipped Colin Hart, "he doesn't read our stuff"), he was not in a talky mood.

By contrast, Spinks's sessions at a gym in nearby Pleasantville, New Jersey, were not accessible—the windows of the gym were papered over when Spinks toiled—but at the end of his daily training he was available to the press.

Happily for the scribes, that world-class filibuster Don King was on hand, and when he got going, blank newspaper column inches disappeared. King, who would punctuate his speed-rapping ring-a-ding-dong speechifying with his signature cry, "Only in America," was everywhere during the week, doing what he does best: selling Don King while scalding his enemies, in this case a single target, Mr. W. D. Cayton of Larchmont, New York.

When he worked himself up, King was a rhetorical robot, indifferent to objections, quibbles, even insults. He just talked his way past any and all obstacles. By King's account, Cayton was an inveterate liar, a power zealot, Satan in disguise. "He wants you to be a sycophant," King said. "'Yes, massa.' Mr. Cayton rules with an iron hand. 'Mr. Cayton. Yassah.'"

King went so far as to depict Cayton as a B-movie evil manager, phoning Tyson in his dressing room and warning him that unless he did as Cayton said it would be curtains for the lovely Robin. It was funny stuff, and on a slow news day it got King the headlines he knew it would.

It also got him brownie points with Tyson-Are-Us. King

was a master of positioning himself amid the infighting so common to boxing. But in this instance, he didn't realize that he
was about to become odd man out. Givens and Roper already
were looking elsewhere for guidance. Namely, to Donald
Trump, who, surprise surprise, singled out Givens as a "class
act" at the final press conference for Tyson-Spinks.

But the real story came on June 27, fight night.
Spinks had Dressing Room 104 in the Convention Center,
a room that featured a hole in its left wall, near the padded
rubbing table. There was a tale about that hole.
On the night Tyson fought Holmes in January, he had
been warming up in 104, punching the hand pads Rooney always put on five minutes before it was time to head to the ring.
Wearing his boxing gloves, Tyson would whack those pads, and
maybe the fourth or fifth time he struck, one of the pads would
go flying and Tyson would swing his forearm into Rooney, a
violation of the rules but Tyson's way of letting his camp know
he was in fighting trim.
On this night, after his fighter had assaulted the pads for a
minute or so, Rooney told him: "You're ready." So Tyson set up
before a mirror and shadowboxed. Then, as he had for pre-
vious fights, he drove a left-right combination into the plaster-
board wall. The left was uneventful, but the right brought light
to Room 104: it drove directly through the three-quarter-inch
wall.
"Holy mackerel," was the comment of a state inspector
monitoring the dressing room.
A billboard across the street—6 HOURS/PARK FREE/ATLAN-
TIS/CASINO HOTEL—was now clearly visible through a ten-by-
twelve-inch aperture.
"When that fist went through," recalled Lott, "Mike turned
to the inspectors and looked like a kid who's been caught dip-
ping into the cookie jar. 'I didn't mean it, I didn't mean it,' he
said."
Quite a legacy for Mr. Pitiful.
Then again, Pitiful was only the civilian persona of the
fighter. Through thirty-one professional fights, the Spinks who
had stepped forward when the bell sounded had always figured
what to do, even against sometimes bigger and supposedly better men.

To the cognoscenti, however, who saw his combination of quickness and brute power as unprecedented, Tyson seemed a special case. His arsenal was wedded to a temperament that was foul and nasty, perfect for what a prizefighting man had to do.

A few opponents—Tucker, for instance, and Tillis—had been able to stymie Tyson for a portion of their bouts, but finesse had gone only so far. Rage superseded the slick and power made it surrender, according to the law of Tyson.

Yet Spinks had a genius for disrupting and a disposition like that of a raggedy prophet. With him, one plus one was three.

The hole in the form sheet for civilians and working press alike was, what had all that prefight shoo-bop-de-doo done to Tyson's mind? Were those tears he had shed in front of reporters a sign of a nervous system that would unravel at Pitiful's deft provocations? Or was he the stone pro who, in his violent world, could stand resistant to any and all distractions?

Now as the clock swept toward midnight in the Convention Center, as the last prelim was fought and factored into the ring-side computers transmitting north, east, south, and west, as Cayton (served with a lawsuit from his fighter even as he occupied his ringside seat) pondered a litigious future,* as Ali, summoned to the ring amid that loving chant of *Ah-lee Ah-lee, Ah-lee,* conjured with a sweeter past, as Givens was booed when introduced to the crowd, as visions of a record pit drop of $11,549,000 cheered Trump, the answers were imminent. The fighters moved out from their dressing quarters.

In a white robe with black trim, Spinks came first. To the sound of Kenny Loggins's "This Is It," he moved briskly down the aisle, his phalanx of aides and Trump strongarms shielding him from the crowd. Spinks raised up one glove, then the other, to acknowledge the encouragement of the fans. At one point he even said aloud: "I'll do my best." He looked uneasy, which was par for the course, as he climbed into the ring with knee wraps on both legs.

Then came Tyson, stepping to a synthesized, ominous sound created by a Baltimorean named Tom Alonzo—a sky-rumble of computerized drum plus a digital sample of a Coke

---

*By an out-of-court settlement a few weeks after the fight, Cayton would agree to reduce his managerial share from 33⅓ to 20 percent.

bottle being blown into. Eerie. A snatch of that tense musical phrasing, then silence. The thunder notes, then silence. Again and again it played as Tyson advanced in his usual skin-primitive look, without robe, without socks, just the hulk on a half shell.

"And now," bellowed the ring announcer, Michael Buffer, "let's get ready to rumble. Twelve rounds for the undisputed heavyweight championship of the world."

And like that, it was over.

A minute into the fight, Spinks went down for the first time in his career, as Tyson hit him with a left uppercut to the jaw and then drove a twisting right hook that caught him just below the heart. Spinks fell to one knee, was up by the count of two, and took the mandatory eight from the referee, Frank Cappuccino.

As Tyson came forward, Spinks tried to ambush him with a right-hand lead at the very instant Tyson was firing a left hook. Neither punch landed, but Spinks's miss was more costly: it sent him lurching forward, into Tyson's next punch, a short right thrown waist-high that landed on Spinks's jaw with the impact of a hammer against a light bulb.

Down went Spinks, his head bouncing twice against the canvas as he fell straight back. Spinks's eyes rolled inward. With his right knee as a pivot, he tried to roll himself off his back and onto his feet. But he hadn't the clear senses yet to accomplish that, and he instead pitched forward to the canvas, his butt canting north, his head nuzzling against the bottom ring rope. He was in that fetal heap as Cappuccino's count reached ten.

By then, Tyson was heading for his corner. His face was expressionless as he held his gloves in front of him, palms up—a conqueror's easy gesture. Twenty million dollars in ninety-one seconds and a reaction as emotional as sherbert. In this world of studied violence what he had done was, for him, a practical matter, like hanging a picture on the wall. The prize ring was his domain; he was the master of the cruel ballet.

Yet if the night was now frozen in the public record, the warrior who had created it was not: he was obliged to step beyond this ring and, as all of us do, confront himself at every bend in the road. That would turn out to be harder than any intricacy of the fight game.

Where once Tyson's yearning for respect and love had driven him to become a great boxer, now success brought its own trick freight and pressure that twisted joy out of shape.

On July 10, Spike Lee, the filmmaker, was riding his bicycle to his new shooting location in Brooklyn when he encountered Tyson.

"Mike was driving a white Rolls-Royce," said Lee. "On one set for the film I'd had a big mural painted on the side of the building, a mural of 'Brooklyn's Own Mike Tyson.'"

Tyson followed him to the set to see the artwork, and afterward, Lee said, they rode around Brooklyn in Tyson's vehicle. "A week before, I had bought one of those small Super-8 movie cameras, and I had it with me," said Lee. "So for two hours, Mike just talked into the camera, talked about himself. On the condition that it was for my eyes and ears only.

"He's a complex young man. I think he has the weight of the world on his shoulders. I got that much from the conversation. One thing I'll tell you, and I hope I don't betray his confidence. He said to me, 'Spike, I don't know if I'll ever be happy.'"

As brother Lee found the champion out of whack, so did Sly, who could not help but feel that Tyson was a candidate for serious turmoil. Tyson seemed lost in the universe, moving about with his compass impaired. The champion had always been moody, restless, needy, and romantic to a flaw about violence. That was a volatile mix for any man—never mind one with the millions of dollars and the wide public acceptance Tyson had. Added in now was a paranoiac edge—an us-against-them perspective that pervaded Tyson's outlook. That summer he would order a custom-made $850 white leather jacket with black-and-gold trim and the words DON'T BELIEVE THE HYPE written across the back. That phrase, it turned out, was the title of a rap song which seemed appropriate at the time:

The minute they see me, fear me
I'm the epitome—a public enemy

Used, abused, without clues
I refused to blow a fuse,
They even had it on the news,
Don't believe the hype. . . .
They claim that I'm a criminal,
By now I wonder how
Some people never know,
The enemy could be their friend [or] guardian,
I said I was a time bomb. . . .
Some media is the whack. . . .
Suckers, liars, get me a shovel
Some writers I know are damn devils,
Their pens and pads I'll snatch.
'Cause I've had it,
Don't believe the hype. . . .

There was an ominous hint in those words that Sly thought reflected the roiling soul of the fighter. A premonition crept upon Sly, and wouldn't let go, that this was another Joplin or Hendrix—live fast and die. Dead or arrested before his time— that was the creepy intuition that played in his mind, and when he told that to Katz, of the *Daily News,* as the two of them flew cross-country on assignment July 4, the Wolfman, as he was known, nodded matter-of-factly, as though the same bad news had inhabited his dreams.

What set Tyson off? Was it Roper and Givens, or did he just detonate on his own? That was a question that would occupy fight people and civilians alike. Was Mike Tyson a bad guy—trouble-prone, or perhaps seriously disturbed—or just reacting, finally, to being so pussywhipped that the violence in him was trip-wired by his own blooming intuition that he had been ill served by his marriage?

Whatever.

Bad things began to happen.

On August 23, nearly two months after he had whupped Spinks for $20 million,* he popped Mitch Green for nothing. On a street in Harlem, in the wee hours of the A.M., Green, the Little Richard of heavyweights, got in Tyson's face, yipping and yapping about the money King owed. Maybe as he harangued

---

*According to a statement filed by the accountants Kaufman, Greenhut, Lebowitz & Forman, Tyson's gross purse as of December 31, 1988, was $19, 298,230.

he pushed Tyson, maybe he didn't. The accounts were conflicting. About what Tyson did, there was no doubt. He laid a bare-knuckled shot on Green and the right hand that sent "Blood" to the emergency room for five stitches sent Tyson for X-rays and the diagnosis of a hairline fracture.

Green, who swore out a complaint, eventually would drop his charges, but that was beside the point. The point was what Tyson told a friend of his, which was: "I guess I could have avoided it."

A week or so later, as Olga Rosario drove Tyson to the office of Dr. David Chiu to have his injured hand examined, she said Tyson put his finger in her ear and said, "Suck it, suck it. Show me how you suck it."

"Then he grabbed me by the hair, so hard that tears came into my eyes," said Rosario.

Later, on September 3, on a street in Albany, Tyson saw a man eat from a trash can. Tyson, who was with his friend Holloway at the time, said to the man, "Come here," then handed him a $100 bill, saying, "Go buy something to eat."

The next day, September 4, Tyson drove a BMW into a tree on the Ewald property, a collision that one published report claimed occurred after Tyson had phoned Robin from Catskill to say, "I'm going to go out and kill myself. I'm going to crash my car."

Hospitalized at Columbia-Presbyterian Medical Center in Manhattan, registered under the name Cisco Esteban, Tyson would meet with Dr. Henry L. McCurtis, the director of psychiatry at Harlem Hospital. Cayton heard about it for the first time that Tuesday, September 6. "Ruth told me Henry McCurtis was a stress expert and asked me how I felt about Mike seeing him. I told her: 'I don't know if he needs it. If you feel he should I have no reservations.'"

As Sly would write:

> Another source said Roper conferred with McCurtis about Tyson even before the accident took place. "She told McCurtis," said the source, "there's problems and he needs help and guidance. What problems? Well, Tyson is very moody. He can be charming and childish one minute, at other times he's angry and exhibits it."

Early in Tyson's hospitalization, Givens was standing watch in his room, a forlorn expression on her face.

Dan Klores, who was acting as a spokesman for Tyson, tried to lighten the mood by telling her: "Just think. It could have been worse."

"How do you mean?" Givens said.

"Well, you could have married Mitch Green."

Lowdown though she felt, Givens laughed.

Out of the hospital on September 7, Tyson flew the next day with her to Moscow, where she was shooting two episodes of *Head of the Class.*

In the Soviet Union, in public view, the couple were all smiles and kisses. But in the hours before the Tysons flew from New York, a source close to the couple *and* to Roper would tell Sly: "The doctors believe he shouldn't travel, but there is concern how he will be without her for the two weeks Robin's supposed to be in Russia. Because what happens when they're apart is he builds up a lot of things in his head. 'She doesn't love me.' 'What's she doing?' If she's in L.A. or New York, he just picks up the phone. Ruth and Robin are aware of how he is. They worry that if he does become upset, he might be prone to get in trouble."

Tyson was complication-free his first days in Moscow. In Gorky Park, he watched his wife shoot sequences for her TV show; he visited Lenin's Tomb, shot pool, and caught adventure films with Marines assigned to the U.S. Embassy; he did some window shopping, listened to street musicians perform, and flirted with Russian women.

It was toward the end of the trip that Tyson began to experience mood swings. During that time, he had difficulty sleeping and kept Givens, Roper, and their press liaison, Phyllis Polaner, up with him through the nights. From Moscow, Givens and Roper phoned McCurtis frequently for advice. "By the weekend," a closely placed source would tell Sly, "Michael was starting to get out of control."

By now Givens was so fearful of her husband, she insisted on sleeping either in the same room with Roper and Polaner, or by herself. Tyson complained to Polaner: "My own wife won't even sleep with me."

On Monday, September 18, the day before the Tyson party was to leave Moscow, Tyson made trouble. As Givens later would state in court papers: "At the peak of his manic state, Michael went down to the bar and started drinking vodka, glass after glass, like it was water. He then returned to our room, grabbed a handful of lithium, and locked himself in the bathroom, saying he was going to kill himself."

When he emerged he started in on Givens. According to sources, Tyson's abuse of Givens, only verbal at first, turned physical, and led to her screaming. By now it was early Tuesday morning, and Givens, Roper, and Polaner, all in their pajamas, bolted their seventh-floor room at the Hotel Mezhdunarodnaya to get away from Tyson. Tyson chased them to the hotel lobby.

"Michael was out of control," said a source. "He was grabbing for Robin and tossing her around. He made no sense. He was almost, like, growling. He was threatening Russian militiamen in the lobby and the guards at the door. 'What are you looking at? What are you looking at?' He was looking for an altercation."

At one point, as Tyson chased the women through the hotel, he kicked Polaner in her backside. For a while, he reportedly held the women in a hotel elevator and rode up and down with them. Later, he hung for ten minutes from the seventh-floor double railing, overlooking an atrium. Givens said he threatened to kill himself.

"On each floor of the hotel," said a source, "was a woman, an employee of the hotel, who gave you room keys. On the seventh floor this poor Russian woman was standing in the back hallway. You could see her shaking. She was holding her hand over her heart and pointing to Michael."

On the flight from Moscow, Givens charged, "Michael swore at me, called me a 'whore' and a 'slut' and said he was going to kill me, that he had guns at home. He told me, 'The world will forgive me because I have succeeded in making everyone think you are the bad one.'"

Headlines followed his return—*Iron Mike admits he suffers from manic depression*—and, according to Olga Rosario, so did more domestic turbulence.

While Tyson slept in Bernardsville, Roper, Givens, and Rosario made their way to New York and to Roper's Upper West Side apartment.

"Ruth was upstairs," said Rosario. "Robin and I were going out to buy pizza when Michael drove up. He saw Robin and shouted: 'You fucking bitch. You left me alone.' Then to me: 'You bitch, I'm gonna get you.' He threw a punch at my face. I pulled back, it missed. But I was very shaken.

"He goes in and comes back down and tells the doorman, 'Ruth is up there, you asshole. I'm gonna get you. I'm gonna get you.' Robin takes him upstairs. He's screaming and cursing. Someone calls the police. The police come to the door. We tell them everything's okay. No complaint is filed. Michael says, 'You called the cops on me.' Ruth says, 'I didn't call. The neighbors must have.' He goes out to the hallway and sits on the floor of the hallway. Ruth follows him out. 'What are you doing? You can't sit like this.' He says, 'Ma, you know I love you.' Ruth says, 'Why do you do these things? You almost hit Olga.' 'I did? Sometimes I have memory lapses.' He comes back in the apartment and says to me, 'I'm sorry. Do you forgive me?' He hugs and kisses me. Same for Robin. And says: 'I don't know why I do these things.' "

Roper and Givens had an explanation for his behavior. Manic depression, they insisted. But those who had known Tyson for years—Ewald, Cayton, Torres—didn't buy that diagnosis, and when Roper was resistant to a second opinion, they suspected she preferred to stick Tyson with that designation for her own reasons. Wasn't a manic-depressive an easier mark in a divorce proceeding than a merely moody spouse?

By now, Madame Ruth had ascended to a position of supreme control in Tyson's career. She had anointed Trump as the champion's adviser, a story that Sly had broken in July. Trump, bless him, had wanted it to be BigGoddamnNews. He had tried to negotiate for the story's appearance on the front page of the high-circulation Sunday issue of the *Times*. The story ended up in the sports section on Saturday.

Trump was miffed and, insisting he had an understanding the story would be published on Sunday, said he would get even in the sequel to his best-selling autobiography, *The Art of the Deal*.

Anyway, through the summer Roper's hand was seen in various Tyson moves—from the addition of Trump,* to the

---

*Trump's ascent meant King was no longer in favor with Tyson's women. So in August, King signed Jose Ribalta to a contract to fight Tyson, a rematch Tyson began talking up. But alerted by Cayton, two weeks later Roper and Winston reined Tyson in and had him sign to fight Frank Bruno of England, checkmating King for the moment.

fighter's signing with Norman Brokaw, an agent who was to represent him in subsidiary income areas, to his letter to Warner Books saying he wanted no part of an authorized biography if it was written by Jose Torres, the former chairman of the New York State Athletic Commission, who had signed to write it.

Brokaw, who had represented Loretta Young, Marilyn Monroe, former President Gerald R. Ford, Alexander Haig, and Bill Cosby, was co-chairman of the William Morris Agency, which represented Givens.

Torres came into conflict with Roper in July. At that time, Torres told Katz of the *Daily News* that Roper suggested that if he shaped his testimony in the anticipated trial to break Cayton's contract, a position for him might materialize on the board of Mike Tyson Enterprises. Torres was quoted as saying, "I've never lied in my life and that includes for Mike Tyson."

Even Camille Ewald, eighty-three years old now, began having problems with Roper, whom she accused of trying to force her to make Tyson the heir to her property.

Ewald said that Roper, through her role in Mike Tyson Enterprises, did this by withholding the money Tyson had been contributing to the upkeep of Ewald's home.

At one point during the summer, Ewald said that Rooney had to give her money when she faced the possibility of having her phone service disrupted.

"Once Mike Tyson Enterprises was set up," said Ewald, "I sent the bills—phone, electricity, repairs—there, and they were supposed to pay them. When I'd ask why the bills were not paid, they'd always give me an excuse."

By late September, Roper was phoning Ewald to say: "I don't think we should pay the bills unless Mike'll be inheriting the property."

"I got angry," said Ewald. "Ruth said, 'Why is Mike paying and not Jose Torres and Floyd Patterson?' I told her that Jose and Floyd did not live in the house, and the arrangement for Mike to pay was made through Jim Jacobs."

Ewald would tell Sly that Givens and Roper were both angry with her for advising Tyson to seek other medical opinions on Tyson's mental state.

"Ruth and Robin wanted me to make an appointment with them and Mike and Dr. McCurtis," Ewald said. "I told them it was okay, providing I could bring my own doctors to examine Mike. Ruth said, 'We'll talk.' That was the last I heard of it.'"

Time and again, Roper and Givens had proclaimed how much Tyson cared for them. *Michael loves me. Michael loves my mother.* The frequency with which they uttered that—and the presumptuous tone their words had—offended Sly. In their mouths, Michael-loves-me had less to do with affection than with the power that one-sided love, or obsession, could muster. When Givens said "Michael loves me," she had a frosty delight in her eyes, the pleasure of the lion tamer over his beast, but propping it up, it turned out, was dumb arrogance.

How else to account for the matter-of-fact dissection she did of Tyson's mental state on ABC-TV's *20/20*? As he sat by passively, his wife said: "Michael is a manic-depressive. He is. That's just a fact." In blunt terms, she described a husband who was "scary" and who "gets out of control, throwing, screaming."

"He shakes," said Givens. "He pushes. He swings . . . and just recently, I've become afraid. I mean, very, very, much afraid."

GIVENS: But if we left Michael . . . and I do come with a package . . . that's how I am . . . he would be . . .

WALTERS: "We" is you and . . . ?

GIVENS: My mom, my sister. He would be alone. He would undoubtedly be alone. And I don't want that to happen. He would have gotten so, so bad that I think maybe one day he would have been more deliberate and killed himself or hurt somebody else. That undoubtedly, unquestionably, would have happened.

Two days later, Tyson reacted. It was Sunday morning in Bernardsville.

"I woke up at eight A.M.," said Olga Rosario. "Michael was on his way upstairs. 'How are you?' I said. 'Fuck you, bitch.' I go downstairs. Into the den, and find two empty champagne bottles. I go into the kitchen, where Ruth was. 'What's wrong?' I ask her. Ruth says, 'He's been drinking.' Michael comes back. I ask him, 'Why are you drinking? Let me fix you a breakfast.' He goes into the refrigerator and takes out an open bottle of white wine and starts drinking. Ruth takes away the bottle and tells him, 'Have some breakfast.' He goes upstairs, as I make grits and eggs and orange juice. Robin comes downstairs: 'Michael is hitting me. Over the head. What is wrong?' By now Michael was up on the roof of the house, on the ledge. It's three or four stories up there. I walked out and shouted for him to come down and have breakfast. He shouts: 'Fuck you, fuck you, fuck you.'"

Soon after, Tyson was back in the kitchen. As Givens sat reading a newspaper, he picked up a glass, Rosario said, and threw it at his wife.

"It missed her by a little," Rosario said, "and shattered, scratching her forearm. He started throwing other glasses and dishes. She was stunned."

The Bernardsville police version: "This is a domestic violence incident not unlike many others, except for the fact that it involves a public figure."

Rosario: "I said, 'Why are you doing this?' Michael said, 'You fucking bitch. Get out of my house. Get out of my house.' He threw a wine bottle at me. I went out the back door. He was alone, tearing up everything. Throwing things. Glasses, dishes, a chair from the kitchen."

The Bernardsville police version: "Mr. Tyson felt the police presence was unwarranted."

Rosario: "When the police came, he screamed, 'Fuck you, fuck you. It's my house. I can fuck it up if I want to. No one tells me what I can do in my home.' The police tell him, 'Maybe you should leave.' They don't want to do nothing to him. He gets into his car and drives off."

Five days later, in Los Angeles, Robin Givens filed for divorce. When Sly phoned Trump that afternoon for comment, he said, "Boy, she sure played some tricks on Mike, didn't she?"

By the weekend, Tyson was hanging out with Don King at the promoter's Orwell, Ohio, farm. If he was not certifiably crazy anymore—a second doctor had declared he was no manic-depressive—he was certainly a sucker for complications.

Trouble, it suddenly seemed, was an attraction for him, a crazy roulette that pulled him away from a pittypat regular life. In a world that had marked Mike Tyson a hero, he was leaving the distinct impression that maybe he wasn't.

He was twenty-two and a master of intricate violence, taking pleasure in the formal eloquence of move-countermove in a prize ring. Away from his sport, confusion occupied him as dark clouds did the horizon.

And soon, come what may, he would step out into an uncertain world, shake his ass, and find out who next season's Tyson meant to be.

Whatever: Somebody with a note pad would for damn sure be watching.

Epilogue

Not long after he was knocked out by Tyson, Michael Spinks retired from boxing. At a press conference in New York, he said, "I can't thank you and kiss you enough for all the wonderful things you've said about me. It makes me feel very deep inside."

At that point, Spinks paused and looked down while he struggled with his emotions. He spoke a few more words, sniffled, and wiped away tears.

These days, Spinks keeps fit riding his stationary bicycle at his home in Greenville, Delaware. Not long ago, at a theater in Wilmington, he made a one-night appearance in the play *The Mystery of Edwin Drood,* in the role of the town crier. In December, after three days of shooting a film, *One for the Money,* in Los Angeles, he traveled to Norway to appear on a television show hosted by Steffen Tangstad, his opponent back in September 1986.

A year after Spinks had sent him into retirement, Gerry Cooney was back in Atlantic City as a fight promoter, in collaboration with his former comanager Dennis Rappaport and an attorney named Mike Perlman.

"I'm happy I fought," he told Sly a few days before the Spinks-Tyson fight. "But I'm glad it's over. There were some fond moments and some not-so-fond moments."

After the loss to Spinks, Cooney struggled through a period in which, he said, he drank too much. "Anytime you lose, it's a terrible pain you go through," he said. "Accepting defeat is kind of difficult for anybody." Cooney said he stopped drinking, and through weekly sessions with a psychologist, was trying to come to terms with his life. "I've found some peace in talking to her," he said. "The whole ten years I was fighting it was scary, all the things put on my shoulders."

By the end of the year, Cooney was suing both his former managers, Rappaport and Jones, claiming they had diverted millions of dollars that should have gone to him.

After he knocked out Spinks, Mike Tyson was scheduled to fight a Britisher, Frank Bruno. But before 1988 ended, the bout had been postponed several times because of complications in Tyson's life.

In October, Tyson signed a four-year-exclusive promotional contract with Don King that Cayton called "onerous." When Cayton refused to sign the deal, on November 23 Tyson sued him to break his managerial contract. Again.*

As Tyson grew closer to King, he put on weight and was reportedly drinking hard.

In public, he now tended to be boisterous in the John L. Sullivan manner. In a restaurant in Chicago, where he dined with King and others, he proclaimed, loudly enough for strangers to hear: "I'm a one-hundred-million-dollar nigger and I don't need no white people to take orders from!"

In November, Tyson was baptized in Cleveland.

A week or so later, after Kevin Rooney suggested on TV that Tyson might date Robin Givens again, Tyson fired his trainer, claiming Rooney didn't know when to butt out of a fighter's personal life.

---

*In a deposition given little more than a month later, Tyson continued attacking Cayton, tactlessly alluding to the manager's blind and retarded adult daughter, Merrie: "I let Bill Cayton live the rest of his life with his wife and his child he takes care of and stop being so concerned with me."

* * *

After she filed for divorce, Robin Givens moved through her days with Israeli bodyguards, supposedly hired because of threats made against her life by anonymous fans of the heavyweight champion.

Givens publicly announced she did not want any money from Tyson to effect a divorce; then, when he spoke badly about Roper and her to the press ("These two are the slime of the slime."), she sued him for libel, asking $125 million.

By December, Tyson was phoning her regularly, and they began to see each other. On Christmas Eve, they caught a film—*Hellbound Hellraiser II*—together in Studio City, California.

By New Year's Eve, 1988, the lawsuits were on hold.*

In Bingham Farms, Michigan, Leon Spinks, retired from boxing, was tending bar.

---

*On February 14, 1989, as this book was in production, Tyson's divorce from Givens was finalized.

INDEX